The Evolving Pension System

THE EVOLVING PENSION SYSTEM

Trends, Effects, and Proposals for Reform

WILLIAM G. GALE
JOHN B. SHOVEN
MARK J. WARSHAWSKY

Editors

BROOKINGS INSTITUTION PRESS
Washington, D.C.

Copyright © 2005
THE BROOKINGS INSTITUTION
1775 Massachusetts Avenue, N.W., Washington, D.C. 20036
www.brookings.edu

Library of Congress Cataloging-in-Publication data

The evolving pension system : trends, effects, and proposals for reform /
William G. Gale, John B. Shoven, Mark J. Warshawsky, editors.
    p.   cm.
  ISBN-13: 978-0-8157-3118-4 (hardcover : alk. paper)
  ISBN-10: 0-8157-3118-3 (hardcover : alk. paper)
  ISBN-13: 978-0-8157-3117-7 (papercover : alk. paper)
  ISBN-10: 0-8157-3117-5 (papercover : alk. paper)
  1. Pensions—United States. I. Gale, William G. II. Shoven, John B.
III. Warshawsky, Mark. IV. Title.
  HD7125.E96 2005
  331.25'20973—dc22   2005032577

9 8 7 6 5 4 3 2 1

The paper used in this publication meets minimum requirements of the
American National Standard for Information Sciences—Permanence of Paper
for Printed Library Materials: ANSI Z39.48-1992.

Typeset in Adobe Garamond

Composition by Cynthia Stock
Silver Spring, Maryland

Printed by R. R. Donnelley
Harrisonburg, Virginia

Contents

8 *From Fiduciary to Facilitator: Employers
and Defined Contribution Plans*
PAMELA PERUN AND C. EUGENE STEUERLE

Foreword

Private pensions play a crucial role in today's economy. They provide a valuable second tier of retirement income for many retirees, supplementing the basic support provided by Social Security and Medicare, which were never intended to provide for all retirement needs. Private pensions help employers shape orderly personnel and turnover policies. They provide massive amounts of much-needed patient capital to finance long-term investments.

Despite these impressive credentials, the private pension system faces numerous problems. Coverage has stagnated at about 50 percent of the labor force for the last thirty years. Employees with low wages and those who work for small businesses have extremely low rates of coverage. Pension rules and regulations have become enormously complex and quite possibly counterproductive. The collapse of Enron showed the dangers of allowing workers to over-invest their retirement funds in their employers' stocks. Likewise, the drop in the stock market values between 2000 and 2003, coupled with declines in interest rates over the same period, put extreme pressure on pension funding formulas and led to many underfunded plans.

The legislation governing all of this activity, the Employee Retirement Income Security Act (ERISA) of 1974, was signed into law in a world that is quite different from today's. The last thirty years have seen a massive shift away from traditional defined benefit plans, where workers are automatically enrolled, face no direct investment risk, and automatically receive payments based on wages and years of service for the rest of their lives after retirement. Defined contribution plans have arisen in place of traditional defined benefit plans. In defined contribution plans—like the ever-popular 401(k)—workers literally own a financial account that builds in value over time. Although defined contribution plans offer portable and easy-to-understand benefits, they also raise concerns about workers' ability to make appropriate choices regarding participation, contribution levels, investment allocations, and withdrawals.

A related issue is that Social Security and Medicare, the primary government programs for the elderly, face significant financial shortfalls that may well require that benefits in those programs be cut back in the future. If this occurs, it would heighten the role of private pensions in providing for the income and financial well-being of future retirees.

For all of these reasons, improving the private pension system should be a top public policy priority. This book is one of two concurrent volumes that take a hard look at pension realities and reform. The contributions in this volume provide a framework for understanding the broad role of pensions in the American economy and paradigms for reform. The first chapters describe trends in the pension system and their causes. Later chapters look at how pensions influence labor markets and wealth accumulation. The last chapters examine options for broad-based reform. The companion volume, *Private Pensions and Public Policy*, examines more of the "nuts and bolts" of pension reform issues.

This project was funded in part by the TIAA-CREF Institute and by Stanford University and its Institute for Economic Policy Research, as well as the American Council of Life Insurance. Brookings thanks them for their generous support.

STROBE TALBOTT
President

Washington, D.C.
December 2005

The Evolving Pension System

1

Introduction

WILLIAM G. GALE, JOHN B. SHOVEN,
AND MARK J. WARSHAWSKY

At least since World War II, retirement income in the United States has relied on the so-called three-legged stool: Social Security, employer-based pensions, and private saving. Along many dimensions, this system has generated remarkable success. The incidence of poverty among the elderly has fallen dramatically over the last several decades, even as people retired at younger ages and lived to older ages. Millions of Americans enjoy well-funded retirements fueled by a combination of public and private retirement income. The ability of the private and public sectors to provide well-financed, lengthy retirement periods at the end of working lives is a historic achievement.

But substantial problems have also emerged. Policymakers' responses to the looming shortfall in Social Security finances, longer life spans, diminishing family networks, and low levels of personal saving will combine to challenge the adequacy of resources in meeting future retirement needs. Labor mobility has also increased, and the participation of many in the labor force has become more sporadic, increasing the difficulty of long-range retirement planning. For these and other reasons, ensuring adequate retirement income will be one of the most pressing public policy issues of the next several decades.

The looming insolvency of Social Security has been the focus of a huge number of studies and of public attention in recent years, while the role of private pensions in meeting future retirement needs has received less attention. Nevertheless, the private pension system already carries a large load: it accounts for

1

significant portions of the retirement income of the elderly and total net financial worth in the United States and for nearly all of the net personal saving since the mid-1980s.

The principal legislation regulating pensions today is the Employee Retirement Income Security Act (ERISA), which was passed in 1974 in a pension world that was far different from today's. In 1974 defined benefit plans dominated the pension landscape. In traditional defined benefit plans, participation is automatic, plan sponsors bear the risk, and workers receive benefits in the form of annual income payments—annuities—from the time they retire until they die. Benefits are not portable across jobs, though, and every worker in the plan receives the same structure of benefits.

Since the mid-1980s almost all of the growth in pensions has occurred through defined contribution plans, which is now the primary type of plan for the majority of pension participants. In defined contribution plans, the onus of participation, investment risk, and form of payout is placed on the worker. Benefits are easily portable across job changes, and workers have more choice about investment and distribution options. At the same time, however, the advent of defined contribution plans raises concerns about workers' ability to make appropriate decisions regarding participation, contribution levels, portfolio allocation, and withdrawals.

Some of the growth in defined contribution plans is attributable to ERISA's regulatory structure, which placed relatively heavier burdens on defined benefit plans. But defined contributions plans also grew as the result of shifts in the composition of industry and the labor force. Increases in job mobility also made the defined benefit plan, with its back-loaded structure, less appealing. And the superior performance of asset markets in the 1980s and 1990s made investing in defined contribution plans especially attractive.

While ERISA and subsequent legislation may have accomplished the goal of securing and perhaps even broadening the accrued benefit rights of participants in defined benefit plans, the pension system still contains weak spots. Pension coverage has stagnated since the early 1980s. Many low-wage workers are not covered. Most small employers do not offer pension plans.

Regardless of the relative merits of ERISA to date, the overarching point is that the features and problems of the pension world today are very different from those of the one in which ERISA was legislated. The papers in this volume are intended to address broad issues in the evolving pension system. The original versions of the papers were presented at a conference in the fall of 1999 and have since been revised. Since the conference, numerous additional factors have combined to influence pension outcomes. These include the substantial decline in asset prices since 2000, which reduced defined contribution balances and, in conjunction with falling interest rates, decimated the finances of defined benefit plans; the collapse of companies like Enron; continuing evidence that many households approaching retirement are not preparing adequately, even given the existing Social Security and Medicare programs; and the likelihood that the latter programs will be downsized over time relative to currently scheduled benefits. Despite these recent events, the central issues facing pension policy remain the same: can the federal pension rules be reformed to expand employer interest in sponsoring—and employee interest in using—plans that generate adequate retirement income without jeopardizing protection for participants or the public fiscal position.

This book is part of a broader project intended to analyze these issues. This volume provides a framework for understanding the broad role of the pension system in the American economy and options for reform. A companion volume, *Private Pensions and Public Polices*, also edited by us and published by Brookings, delves into more of the "nuts and bolts" of pension reform issues.

The papers in this volume are divided into three sections. Papers in the first section explore the goals, features, and effects of legislation, as well as the causes and effects of the secular shift from defined benefit plans to defined contribution plans and, more recently, the shift among defined benefit plans from traditional plans to cash balance plans. Papers in the second section explore the role of pensions in the economy, in particular their influence on labor markets and on savings behavior and wealth accumulation. Papers in the third section present three proposals for broad-based pension reform, one emphasizing a substantial loosening of government regulations, one emphasizing a tightening of regulations, and one emphasizing the need to free employers of unnecessary legal and administrative burdens.

The Development of the Modern Pension System

Sylvester Schieber provides a historical, economic, and political overview of the development of pensions and, especially, public policy toward pensions. Schieber divides the 125 years of pensions in the United States into four periods: early development (1875–1920), spread of coverage (1921–64), pension policy concerns leading to the passage and implementation of ERISA (1965–81), and tax policy concerns leading to limitations on deductible contributions and other legislative and regulatory changes (1982–present). Overall, pensions have arisen and grown to address important employer and worker needs and have been alternatively encouraged and constrained by various manifestations of public policy.

According to Schieber, the first historical period established the essential form of pensions, reflecting the motivations of employers in sponsoring plans: the need to manage labor relations and productivity (especially by allowing and encouraging the dignified retirement of older workers) and to remedy the lack of life-cycle savings among rank-and-file workers.

The second historical period saw the development of some essential public policy features for pensions: tax-favored status, required nondiscriminatory treatment of workers, disclosure of information, assignment of exclusive benefit of pension assets to workers, and integration with Social Security. Schieber views this last feature as key to the spread of pension coverage in this period because the pay-as-you-go nature of Social Security and the generous, unfunded benefits given in the early years of the system provided a large subsidy to employers with integrated defined benefit pensions trying to encourage their older workers to retire. This time period, however, also saw the development of problems: benefit rights that workers misunderstood or perceived to be unfair (particularly arising out of long vesting schedules) and a lack of benefit security (arising out of lack of adequate funding for defined benefit plans). ERISA was implemented largely to address these concerns and led to improved plan funding and fairer rights to benefits.

The most recent historical period followed the development of the concept and estimation of tax expenditures as part of the federal budget process and coincided with large budget deficits arising from tax cuts. These intellectual and political developments focused increased attention on the significant tax benefits available to participants in pension plans and resulted, according to Schieber, in a tougher policy environment. In particular, pensions now face reduced permitted funding and lower allowable benefits for defined benefit plans, lower contribution limits for defined contribution plans, tighter nondiscrimination and integration rules, and lower maximum compensation levels in the calculation of benefits and contributions. Schieber claims that these changes have led to stagnant pension coverage, fewer defined benefit plans, less secure benefits, and benefit cuts for older workers (manifested most recently in the advent of cash balance plans). Schieber concludes that all the efforts to enhance retirement security could actually end up reducing the retirement security of the baby boom generation.

William Gale, Leslie Papke, and Jack VanDerhei focus on the substantial secular shift toward defined contribution plans. They document the magnitude of the change and of subsidiary shifts within defined contribution plans to 401(k) plans and within defined benefit plans to cash balance plans. They examine the implications for pension coverage as well as the possible causes and impacts on workers and employers. Gale, Papke, and VanDerhei show that the absolute number of defined benefit plans has declined dramatically. Because most of the defined benefit plans that were terminated were small, however, the impact on the number of active workers covered has been comparatively modest. As a share of the work force covered, defined benefit plans have declined significantly, because most new pension plans are defined contribution plans in general, and 401(k) plans in particular. More recently, many traditional defined benefit plans have been converted to cash balance plans.

From 1975 through 1985, the growth in defined contribution plans represented both replacement of and supplements to defined benefit plans. Since then, defined contribution growth has come almost entirely at the expense of defined benefit plans, according to statistics and formal studies cited by Gale, Papke, and VanDerhei.

The authors cite several types of evidence in examining the causes of the shift. Changes in the composition of the labor force and industrial make-up of the economy seem to be able to explain a significant portion of the decline in defined benefit plans, as unionized manufacturers and utilities, which naturally favor such plans, have experienced declines, in relative terms, in the economy. The increasing cost of complex and ever-changing regulations has also burdened defined benefit plans (and small plans of all types) more than large defined contribution plans. Finally, the flexibility of defined contribution plans seems to be increasingly important in a more competitive and faster changing business environment.

The impact on workers and employers of the shift from defined benefit to defined contribution plans is complex and uncertain, according to Gale, Papke, and VanDerhei. Issues for workers include the effects on the level and variability of retirement income, the liquidity of pension assets, job mobility, and the opaqueness of benefits. Issues for employers include matching worker preferences, the efficiency of work and retirement incentives arising from plan design, and administrative costs. The empirical evidence on many of these issues is mixed, and a summary measure of the "aggregate impact" of the shift from defined benefit to defined contribution plans considering all the issues taken together is not feasible. Gale, Papke, and VanDerhei conclude with a full description and analysis of cash balance plans, explaining why these plans are preferable for younger, more mobile workers, while an abrupt transition from a traditional defined benefit plan can adversely affect older workers.

Pensions and the Economy

Robert Clark and Joseph Quinn focus on the impact of pensions on labor productivity and job mobility during employees' working years and on the timing and nature of retirement at the end of the work cycle. After describing the different rates of benefit accrual over the work cycle in defined benefit and defined contribution plans and explaining how these accrual patterns might differentially affect productivity, mobility, and retirement behavior, they examine previous evidence on the nature and size of the effects. Economic theory suggests that there should be a trade-off between wages and benefits, as the employer should peg total compensation to the marginal productivity of workers. The empirical evidence, however, ranges from mixed to negative on this hypothesis. This empirical finding, in turn, may suggest that pensions have a positive effect on worker productivity, allowing the employer to raise total compensation when it sponsors a pension plan. Other evidence is somewhat supportive of this view, as pensions, especially defined benefit plans, reduce worker turnover and presumably enable the employer to conduct on-the-job training and still recapture its investment in its workers.

Clark and Quinn find even stronger evidence of the impact of pensions on retirement behavior. Defined benefit plans in particular provide large financial incentives for workers to retire at specific ages, and workers respond strongly to these incentives. Clark and Quinn conclude, however, by noting the increasingly fuzzy notion of retirement, as more and more workers leave their career employer and take on a part-time or full-time bridge job with the same or another employer.

William Gale provides a critical review of the large theoretical and empirical literature on the impact of pensions, including 401(k) plans, on household wealth accumulation. This is an important public policy issue because it relates to the key questions of whether and how pensions can contribute to raising national saving and improving retirement preparedness. In this regard, information on heterogeneity across households in the response of savings to pensions is particularly pertinent to pension policy questions; participation and nondiscrimination requirements are in large part meant to encourage saving by and ensure retirement preparedness of low-income workers.

In the simplest theoretical model of life-cycle saving, workers save only for retirement. Increases in pension wealth would therefore be offset completely by reductions in other wealth. Other factors complicate the theoretical analysis considerably. Empirical studies generally find that pensions have little or no offsetting effect on savings, a somewhat surprising set of results given the basic theoretical model. Stated another way, savings are raised about a dollar for every dollar invested in a pension, according to these studies. Gale points out, however, that several biases lurk in these studies, including controlling for cash earnings rather than total compensation, omitting retirement age as an independent variable, assuming that pensions are exogenous with respect to saving behavior, and reporting pension wealth gross-of-taxes. Correcting for these biases would, according to Gale, produce a larger estimate of the offset of pensions on savings.

Gale also summarizes results indicating that groups that are more likely to have high demands for precautionary saving, to be borrowing constrained, to be economically literate, or to have low tastes for saving show less offset of pensions on other saving. This implies, according to Gale, that expanding pension coverage in the current environment may be an effective way to raise national saving because most households currently not covered by pensions may be in the groups that exhibit little offset between pensions and other wealth.

Comprehensive Pension Reform Proposals

The final section of the book contains three proposals for large-scale reform of the private pension system. The basis of the first two proposals is an agreement that it is unreasonable to expect that the private pension system would or should provide universal coverage. Both sets of authors (Theodore Groom and John Shoven, and Daniel Halperin and Alicia Munnell) advocate instead the creation of a government-sponsored system of individual accounts for all workers, although they disagree strongly on the methods of funding these accounts and any connection to reform of the Social Security system. They also disagree on the extent of actual penetration of pension coverage into the lower tail of the wealth distribution, and therefore the extent of the "failure" of the current pension system. For the most part, however, their differing approaches to pension reform do not reflect different facts, but rather differing philosophies of the role of government in the retirement income system.

The central policy argument advanced by Groom and Shoven is that pensions should not be viewed as a tax subsidy; rather the tax treatment of assets in qualified pension accounts should be considered as consistent with a consumption tax. Groom and Shoven prefer this approach to the classic income tax approach because in their view the latter taxes savings too much, promoting current consumption. They would theoretically prefer a complete conversion to a consumption tax (such as a national sales tax or a value-added tax), but they recognize that political and practical considerations make this change impossible. Therefore, as a second best alternative, Groom and Shoven favor the elimination of most of the current detailed tax requirements governing pensions, thereby expanding and liberalizing their use in the direction of consumption taxation. They note that the complex nondiscrimination rules and contribution limitations that currently apply to pensions largely do not burden the other main area of economic activity for households currently using consumption tax principles—homeownership.

More specifically, Groom and Shoven believe the diversity of limits and restrictions across different types of plans makes no sense; they think that the only sensible distinction is between broad-based employer-sponsored plans and individual plans. Groom and Shoven would eliminate the current complex and mechanical nondiscrimination requirements in favor of a simple requirement that each feature of a plan be currently or effectively available to all workers. They would significantly liberalize limits on employer contributions and plan benefits and would somewhat liberalize limits on employee contributions. Groom and Shoven would eliminate the minimum distribution requirements. While they believe that pension coverage and benefit provision currently extend quite deeply into the lower end of the wealth distribution, they recognize the importance of Social Security to this segment of workers and are concerned about the future solvency of the system. Groom and Shoven would therefore create a system of personal security accounts funded by an additional payroll tax.

Groom and Shoven would also make changes in the nontax regulations governing pensions. They advocate the elimination of the Pension Benefit Guaranty Corporation (PBGC), or at least they would require that market annuities be purchased for all terminated defined benefit plans, and they would restrict the PBGC's ability to intervene in arm's length business transactions. Consistent with their belief in the importance of participant education, Groom and Shoven would limit the liability of plan sponsors who select providers of investment advice by use of a good faith, rather than a fiduciary, standard.

Halperin and Munnell take as given the premise of existing tax law that qualified plan treatment is an exception to the norm and is warranted only to the extent necessary to provide adequate retirement income to rank-and-file workers. They believe that pensions already have generous tax incentives and are not currently giving much retirement income to lower-income workers. Hence, they generally would tend to decrease these tax incentives or strengthen restrictions. Halperin and Munnell would agree to increase incentives only as part of the political give-and-take needed to achieve a comprehensive reform of the system.

Halperin and Munnell advocate a number of changes meant to increase participation and benefits for those who work for employers that already offer pension plans. More specifically, they advocate shortening the vesting period and substantially strengthening the nondiscrimination requirements by mandating that a plan sponsor provide uniform coverage and benefits to all full-time employees and more part-time employees. They would require equal benefits or contributions at all income levels without regard to Social Security (effectively eliminating integration). They would also require sponsors of elective plans—such as 401(k)s—to make a substantial contribution for all participants. In general, Halperin and Munnell prefer defined benefit plans; in acknowledgement of the mobility problem these plans represent for many workers, they favor career average and cash balance plans as well as inflation adjustment of accrued benefits in final average plans. They also generally dislike the cashing out of retirement assets and favor incentives for annuitization and the requirement that plans offer an inflation-indexed annuity distribution option.

Halperin and Munnell would agree to the increase of current contribution and benefit limitations only as part of comprehensive reform package. This package would include most of the changes mentioned above as well as the creation of a government-sponsored system of universal retirement accounts, a type of national 401(k) plan. The accounts would be financed largely through the imposition of a 5 percent tax on the investment earnings of private and government pension plans. In acknowledgement of the likely sufficiency of Social Security and these accounts for providing retirement income to lower-income workers, Halperin and Munnell would agree that workers earning less than $20,000 annually could be excluded from employer-sponsored pension plans.

While the Groom-Shoven and Halperin-Munnell proposals focus on contrasting approaches to the role of government in ensuring outcomes, a third proposal, by Pamela Perun and Eugene Steuerle, focuses on changing the role of the employer. Currently, employers are expected or required to perform many roles, from the simplest facilitation of saving—through payroll deductions and wiring the funds to an account, for example—to extremely complicated regulatory tests involving funding rules, contribution limits, nondiscrimination standards, and the maintenance of fiduciary standards. There appears to be no logical reason why employers should be saddled with such responsibility under defined contribution plans, especially since such plans are similar to other products offered by the financial services industry that do not face such rules. In addition, pension rules on all of these concerns in general, and fiduciary standards in particular, are inconsistent across types of plans.

Perun and Steuerle would encourage firms to do more—that is, increase coverage and contributions—by requiring them to do less—that is, relieve them of fiduciary responsibilities. In particular, they would maintain and emphasize the role of the employer in facilitating saving behavior by workers. This includes providing payroll deductions, simplified enrollment, periodic reports, investment education, and matching contributions, and serving as an intermediary between their employees and the financial services industry. But employers would also move the defined contribution system toward a system of individual accounts that are held, managed, and administered by the financial services industry. Under this approach, tax law would continue to encourage employers to offer plans and make contributions, but employers would do what they do best, and the financial services industry would provide the other services, which represent its comparative advantage. Overall, the plan would take the pension system back to a pre-1974 standard and away from the standards and practices that have developed since the passage of ERISA in 1974.

Conclusion

The papers in this volume provide a sound basis for developing a broad, bird's-eye view of the pension system's features, trends, strengths, and weaknesses and of alternative paradigms for reform. Although new proposals and concerns will inevitably arise over time, we suspect that the issues, evidence, and conclusions addressed in the volume will continue to play a key role in providing a framework for analysis of pension policy alternatives.

2

The Evolution and Implications of Federal Pension Regulation

SYLVESTER J. SCHIEBER

$\mathbf{P}$assage of the federal Employee Retirement Income Security Act (ERISA) in 1974 was a landmark event in the evolution of employer-sponsored pensions, marking the shift from a period of laissez-faire regulation of retirement plans to a period of much more active government regulation. Although federal pension regulation was relatively lenient during the first three quarters of the twentieth century, the broader public policy environment that prevailed at least from the signing of the Social Security Act in 1935 until the passage of ERISA tended to encourage the creation of employer-sponsored pension plans and the proliferation of pension coverage. Nearly half of all workers were covered under such plans by the mid-1970s. At the same time, however, there were also widespread concerns, such as whether the existing pensions were broadly available to most employees or whether they instead served mainly as additional compensation for top executives. And there were occasional horror stories; some retirees discovered, for example, that their employers had not set aside the resources to pay the promised pensions.

Developed in response to these concerns, ERISA imposed a range of new regulations on the pension system, but its initial provisions also encouraged the creation and maintenance of plans. During ERISA's first decade the private pension

The author thanks Kyle Brown, William Gale, Gordon Goodfellow, Richard Joss, Alexander Miller, Tim Taylor, and Mark Warshawsky for helpful comments on earlier drafts.

system continued to expand and flourish. Since the early 1980s, however, the regulatory environment for employer-provided pensions has become significantly more restrictive, primarily because of efforts to change pension regulation in an attempt to increase federal tax collections, at least in the short term.

This more restrictive environment for employer-provided pensions, combined with certain ways in which pensions interact with a mature Social Security system, has significantly changed the economics of retirement plan financing in the last fifteen years or so. One result has been a substantial curtailment of traditional defined benefit plans, in which the employer promises a certain level of benefits after retirement, and a corresponding shift toward defined contribution plans, in which the employer promises that a certain level of contributions will be made on behalf of an employee to a pension plan before retirement. In many cases, the funding patterns behind the remaining defined benefit plans have also been changed in a way that portends lower retirement benefits than in the past. This continuing evolution of the pension system has significant implications for the retirement prospects of the baby boom generation.

A Brief History of Pensions

In the United States employer-sponsored retirement plans first arose in the rail industry in the 1870s, out of industry concern about the continued employment of superannuated workers. The railroads initially reassigned older workers to positions as night watchmen or other jobs that minimized their risk to the companies' rolling capital and the public's safety. Often such reassignments were coupled with a reduction in pay to represent the reduced responsibilities of the new position. As the railroad industry matured and the average age of the work force increased, the industry became less able to create jobs that could absorb the flow of superannuated workers.[1] The initial plans were created to satisfy three specific needs of the sponsors: to maintain an efficient work force, to encourage labor peace within a restive work force, and to retire older workers no longer able to perform their duties.

The Grand Trunk Railway of Canada set up the first private retirement plan in North America in 1874 as a mechanism to attract, retain, and retire workers in the interest of running an efficient bureaucratic organization. American Express set up the first private retirement plan in the United States in 1875, but it was a loosely defined plan that was essentially a bookkeeping convenience for an existing ad hoc plan that provided assistance to employees injured or "worn out" on the job. In 1880 the Baltimore & Ohio (B&O) Railroad set up a more fully specified plan as part of a wider worker welfare initiative. This package was an attempt to improve relations with labor after a violent clash in the late 1870s.

---

1. Graebner (1980, p. 14).

B&O management thought that providing a comprehensive welfare package would wean workers away from their participation in secret societies, brotherhoods, and similar organizations that were believed to be the breeding ground of worker discontent. On January 1, 1900, the Pennsylvania Railroad established a plan that was motivated purely by the need to remove older workers unable to do their jobs. "As large, government-regulated corporations, railroads were sensitive to employee and public opinion. So they avoided summary dismissals," one historian wrote.[2] The creation of pension systems thus allowed the railroads to meet their business needs without causing unnecessary disruptions.

By the turn of the century, private pension plans began to appear in higher education. Cornell, Harvard, the University of California, and Yale all established pension plans to retire faculty members no longer able to fulfill their duties. In 1905 Andrew Carnegie established a free pension system for college professors that he endowed with $10 million. Carnegie had become concerned about the low level of wages that persisted among faculty members in higher education and that he felt kept many of them from providing for their own old age. By 1906 fifty-two institutions had been accepted under the umbrella of the system. The system ultimately proved to be underfunded and was closed to new entrants, but not before ninety-six institutions allowed faculty to retire under this system when they met its eligibility criteria. Although the system did not survive, it served as a precursor to the Teachers Insurance and Annuity Association (TIAA) of America, created in 1918.[3]

Public utilities also began to establish retirement plans around the turn of the century. Many public utilities at the time were local streetcar systems, which may explain the timing of the introduction of pension plans in this sector. The issues they faced were not significantly different from those of the long-haul rail firms. Of eleven plans set up in the utilities industry by 1911, seven were sponsored by street rail employers. The plans in the street rail industry tended to be structured like those in the larger railroad firms.[4]

During the second decade of the twentieth century, retirement benefits began to spread to other industries, including banking and insurance. As the plans spread, they began to be structured with the intent of discouraging worker turnover in firms that required organization-specific "human capital," according to Leslie Hannah. He also noted a growing appreciation that retirement plans could be structured to encourage desirable behavior on the job. Writing about the evolution of pensions in England, Hannah pointed out that banks used pensions as a substitute for fidelity bonds that had been common for workers handling cash. The pension, paid only to workers who had successfully completed a

2. Sass (1997, pp. 18–30).
3. Greenough (1990, pp. 5–16).
4. Latimer (1932, pp. 35–36).

career, provided a capital lever that employers could use to encourage desirable behavior in lieu of a fidelity bond.[5] Sass writes that pensions in the U.S. banking sector took their shape because of the "great discretion over cash and credit that banks *by necessity* delegated to their staffs."[6]

For the insurance companies, pensions were a business opportunity. Many of the plans that were adopted early on required employee contributions. Between the middle of the 1910s and the end of the 1920s, Murray Webb Latimer wrote, "insurance companies were largely or wholly responsible for all the contributory schemes adopted by textile, iron and steel, paper and printing, insurance, and merchandising companies."[7] Working with these plans surely made the management and workers in these companies sensitive to the potential benefits that could be provided through a pension. By 1920 fourteen insurance companies had set up plans for their own employees.

The initial development of the employer-based pension system in the United States was largely driven by a host of market considerations that larger employers were facing with the shift from a craft and agricultural economy to an urban industrial one. The evolution of employer-sponsored pensions from the 1910s until the passage of ERISA was strongly influenced by three key factors: the tax code, regulations involving the pension system, and the implementation of Social Security.

Tax Preferences

Reasonable employer pension payments to retirees or contributions to trust funds have been tax-deductible expenses for plan sponsors since the start of the federal income tax in 1913—even before explicit provisions concerning pensions were included in the tax code. The 1921 Revenue Act eliminated taxation of corporate income contributed to employer-based stock bonuses or profit-sharing plans established for "some or all" of a firm's workers. The 1926 Revenue Act permitted reasonable deductions in excess of currently accruing liabilities, so that firms could provide pensions based on years of employment before the pension system was in place. Pension trusts also were accorded preferential tax treatment by administrative ruling.

This favorable tax treatment of private pensions has continued up to the present day. Under the current Internal Revenue Code, a range of deferred income arrangements is granted tax-deferred status. An employer's contributions to a qualified pension plan can be deducted as a business expense in the year in which it is made for determining business income taxes. The contribution is made to a plan trust that is itself tax exempt; that is, neither contributions to the

5. Hannah (1986, p. 24).
6. Sass (1997, p. 50).
7. Latimer (1932, pp. 49, 51).

trust nor interest accruals are taxable. The benefits accumulated in this fashion are taxed only when they are dispersed. These tax provisions have been highly controversial during the last two decades, however, and as government has tinkered with these provisions in an attempt to raise short-term revenue, it has contributed to waves of change throughout the pension system.

Evolving Regulatory Structures

The lack of funding requirements for employer-sponsored pensions during the early decades of the twentieth century meant that employers could set up plans without immediately bearing the cost of the long-term commitments in them. Many plans were funded on a pay-as-you-go basis or in ways that were significantly less stringent than funding in accordance with the rate of liability accrual. Benefits were thus susceptible to the risk that the plan sponsor might not be willing or able to pay them over the long term. Moreover, the early proliferation of plans and employer support for them was probably attributable in part to the relatively low costs of initially setting up and operating a plan. In a seminal study of the industrial pension system in the early 1930s, Latimer wrote:

> The rate of growth of pension payments, rapid as it is, requires some time to become burdensome. In those companies where the expense factor has been determinant in forcing abandonment of the system, whether so stated or not, its operation probably requires a long time before its significance appears. The relatively short experience of most pension schemes, the rapid growth in the number of employees of most companies until recent years, and possibly the relatively low age distribution of the employees as compared with what it may be after another generation, explain why the expenditures for pensions have not yet mounted sufficiently to compel the abandonment of many plans.[8]

Latimer went on to report that between July 1, 1929, and April 30, 1932, the height of the Great Depression, plans were discontinued at unprecedented levels, largely because of the financial conditions of the companies involved.[9]

Until 1938 trusts set up by employers to hold and manage retirement funds for employees were revocable. Plan sponsors could thus set up such trusts during profitable periods and revoke them during unprofitable ones. The 1938 Revenue Act modified the revocability provisions to require that retirement trusts be for the exclusive benefit of employees covered under the plans until all obligations were met. The pension regulatory environment that evolved during this period allowed plan sponsors to extend pension benefits selectively among their

8. Latimer (1932, pp. 635–36).
9. Latimer (1932, pp. 846–47).

workers. The 1942 Revenue Act, along with certain amendments to it in the 1954 Internal Revenue Code, changed the tax code to preclude plan sponsors from discriminating in favor of the sponsoring firm's owners and officers.[10]

In 1958 the Federal Welfare and Pension Plans Disclosure Act required that plans file annual statements of operations with the Department of Labor and make plan documents available at plan participants' request, but it did not allow the department to prescribe forms for the plans to report such information. This omission was changed in 1962, when the secretary of labor was given new powers. In addition, embezzlement, bribery, kickbacks, and the like involving a pension plan were made criminal offenses. Thus, as the pension regulatory structure was evolving through the early 1960s, its focus was on protection of plan assets rather than on protection of the rights of individual plan participants.[11]

In the decade before the passage of ERISA in 1974, federal regulation of employer-sponsored retirement plans focused on preventing discrimination in favor of officers, managers, or the highly compensated employees of sponsoring organizations and on limiting the loss of federal revenues through excessive deductions associated with the plans. Until 1974 no federal law or regulation dealt with the actuarial soundness of plans. Although the tax code prevented plans from discriminating in favor of select individuals, there were no requirements for vesting or preservation of benefits for workers who terminated their employment before they were eligible for retirement. There were no regulations requiring reporting of benefit accruals or enforcing benefit rights for participants. Beyond general trust law and the criminal code, little in the law protected plan participants against mismanagement of plan assets.

Adoption of Social Security

A third major development that helped spur creation of employer-sponsored pensions was the implementation of Social Security. In large part the adoption of Social Security was the result of the same problematic symptoms of industrialization as employer-sponsored pensions were addressing. Three historians who have written about the evolution of the retirement movement in America—Andrew Achenbaum, William Graebner, and Steven Sass—all point to the period of the late 1800s and early 1900s as one of changing attitudes toward older people.[12] Industrializing America came to the conclusion during this period that older workers interfered with organizational efficiency. They had to be gotten out of the way. Simply throwing them out at the end of a long period of service was either unseemly, for socially conscious capitalists, or a threat to an already tenuous relationship with labor that early industrialists were facing.

10. McGill (1979, pp. 23–28).
11. McGill (1979, p. 30–32).
12. Achenbaum (1978); Graebner (1980); and Sass (1997).

Hannah observes that the life-cycle model provides a reasonable description of the way the business and professional classes funded their own retirement during the late nineteenth century. In essence, workers saved part of their earnings during their robust working years in anticipation of retirement needs during the latter portion of their lives. Of course, the process of accumulating savings during their working years required that workers trade current consumption while working in favor of consumption later in life. The willingness of workers to make such trade-offs depended on the nature of their time horizons, the returns they could expect on their savings, and the extent to which they favored the immediate gratification of current consumption over the potential gratification of deferred consumption. Regrettably, the other needs that many low-income workers experienced during their working years in the late 1800s and early 1900s led them to discount the value of future consumption to the point that little retirement provision resulted. As Hannah points out, "the savings ethos of the mass of the population remained quite sharply differentiated from the patterns established by the Victorian bourgeoisie, and this severely constrained their retirement options."[13] This environment, in combination with employers' desire to retire superannuated workers, begot the development of organized retirement plans. The inability of older members of society to find gainful employment became so overwhelmingly apparent during the Great Depression that policymakers were moved to adopt the Social Security Act in 1935, long after many other countries around the world had adopted similar measures.

From the outset employer-sponsored retirement plans have relied on earnings replacement targets in setting benefit levels. The need to retire workers meant that they had to be provided sufficient income during retirement to meet some perceived level of living. If workers could not or would not save on their own to meet their retirement needs, the pension plan would have to do so. In the early literature on pensions, the goal of how much income should be replaced by a pension was often quite specific. For example, the Committee on Economic Security that developed the Social Security Act for Franklin Roosevelt's administration in 1934 said that "payment of benefits at a rate . . . approximating 50 percent of previous average earnings is socially desirable."[14] Although the committee did not explain how it reached that particular threshold, it is consistent with the level that Dan McGill laid out in 1955 in the first edition of his classic pension textbook, *The Fundamentals of Private Pensions*. There he wrote that "pension technicians have generally regarded as adequate a plan which will replace, inclusive of OASI [Old Age and Survivors' Insurance] benefits, one-third to one-half of the employee's average earnings during the five or ten years preceding retirement."[15]

13. Hannah (1986, p. 5).
14. Committee on Economic Security (1937, p. 202).
15. McGill (1955, p. 35).

Figure 2-1. *Coverage under Social Security, 1940–80*

Percent

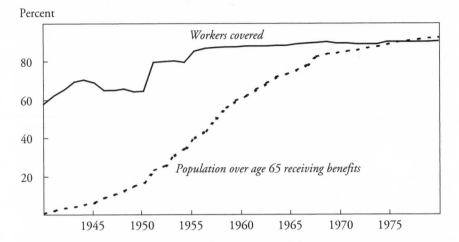

Source: Coverage data for 1940 to 1970 are from U.S. Census Bureau (1975, p. 348); for 1971 to 1979, from U.S. Census Bureau (1980, p. 331); and for 1980, from U.S. Census Bureau (1982, p. 326). Beneficiary data for 1940 to 1969 are from U.S. Census Bureau (1975, p. 357); for 1970, from Social Security Administration (1981, p. 73); for 1971 to 1974, from Social Security Administration (1978, p. 75); for 1975 to 1979, and from Social Security Administration (1982, p. 66).

By the time the Social Security Act was adopted in 1935, many large employers had been running their pension plans for as long as twenty years. The original Social Security Act covered wage and salaried workers in private commerce and industry, which amounted to roughly 60 percent of all workers in the economy. Tax collections began in 1937, and the first benefits were paid to retirees reaching age sixty-five in 1940. The overwhelming majority of people age sixty-five or older in 1940 who were retired never qualified for benefits because they had not paid into the system in the preceding three years. By 1950 only 17 percent of the elderly were getting benefits, as reflected in figure 2-1. By 1960 the rate was up to nearly 60 percent, and by 1970 to 86 percent. It was not until 1975, forty years after passage of the Social Security Act, that the percentage of elderly receiving benefits equaled the percentage of workers paying into the system. But virtually all of the workers who were already covered by a private employer pension when the Social Security Act passed in 1935 were immediately brought into the system as though they had participated in it most of their working lives. For employers sponsoring a pension plan or thinking about it, the cost of providing a private pension to raise workers to a certain earnings replacement level diminished at the point Social Security was introduced.

The implementation of Social Security encouraged the proliferation of employer-sponsored pensions by even more than one might have predicted on pure actuarial grounds because the federal retirement system was largely being run on a pay-as-you-go basis.[16] Because relatively few retirees were receiving benefits compared with the number of workers paying into the system during the implementation phase, policymakers could pay benefits that were much larger for a given cost rate than the system would be able to provide over the long term. The heavily subsidized provision of Social Security benefits lowered the overall costs that employers faced in setting up retirement plans that would be effective in getting superannuated workers to retire.

John Shoven and I have developed an analysis of the effect of early Social Security windfalls on the cost of providing retirement benefits. We looked at hypothetical workers who were being paid the average wages of nonsupervisory production workers on the payrolls of a manufacturing firms and considered the situation of such workers retiring at age sixty-five in 1950, 1955, 1960, and 1965. For 1950 we assumed that the combination of Social Security and the employer-sponsored retirement plan was designed to provide an annual benefit to a long-career worker equal to 45 percent of the retiree's final salary before retirement. We assumed the benefit would be paid over the remainder of a normal life expectancy for someone retiring at age sixty-five in each year for which estimates were developed. For 1955 we assumed the plan was designed to pay a benefit equal to 50 percent of final earnings in combination with Social Security. For 1960 we assumed the combined plans would pay 55 percent, and finally for 1965 we assumed the combined benefits would be equal to 60 percent of final earnings.[17]

The assumption that the share of income replaced by the combination of public and private pensions would rise over time was made for several reasons. During this period many employers enhanced the generosity of their pension benefits, and unions often negotiated for benefit enhancements once they were covered under a plan. In addition, professionals involved in the design of pension plans generally agreed that the level of benefits required for workers to maintain pre-retirement standards of living was rising over the period. By 1980 the broad consensus was that retirement income would have to be around 70 percent of final earnings for average-wage workers to maintain their pre-retirement standard of living.[18]

The results of our analysis are presented in figure 2-2. Each of the bars in the figure is composed of three parts. The bottom part shows the portion of total

16. Technically, the original Social Security Act called for Social Security to be largely funded. During its early years, however, Congress repeatedly held back scheduled payroll tax increases, resulting in the system migrating toward pay-as-you-go financing by the mid-1950s. For a full discussion of the early financing of Social Security and its implications, see Schieber and Shoven (1999, ch. 7).

17. Schieber and Shoven (1999, p. 131).

18. McGill and others (1996, p. 382).

Figure 2-2. *Purchasing Retirement Benefits under Social Security and Pension Programs during the Phase-in of Social Security*[a]

Value of single life annuity at age 65 (dollars)

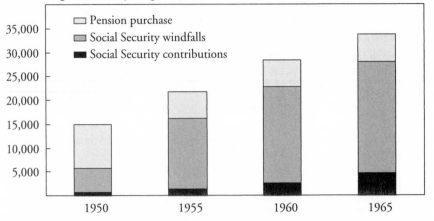

Source: Schieber and Shoven (1999, p. 132).

a. The relative magnitude of the Social Security windfall benefit provided in 1955 is so much larger than in 1950 because the 1950 amendments to the Social Security Act increased future benefits by nearly 80 percent but did not affect benefits paid that year.

benefits financed by the combined employer and employee contributions to Social Security plus interest accrued at the rate of return on the Social Security trust funds during the period the workers were covered under the system. The middle part of the bar represents the Social Security windfalls for the particular workers, or the benefits that were paid over and above the actuarial value of the contributions paid on the workers' behalf plus the accrued interest. The top part shows the value of the private pension that would have to be added on top of Social Security to achieve the target benefit levels set out above. If employers needed to provide a certain level of pension benefits to persuade their older workers to retire, the provision of highly subsidized Social Security benefits significantly reduced the cost of getting the job done. It also likely reduced the burden that unions faced in getting employers to consider offering an adequate retirement package.

In October 1951 the U.S. Chamber of Commerce, which had reservations about Social Security from the start, ran an article in its membership magazine expounding the tremendous benefits that were accruing under the system. "If you got a letter in this morning's mail telling you that you had suddenly inherited $41,000 free of income and estate taxes, how would you feel?" the article asked. It went on to explain that under recently enacted amendments, a worker could "be entitled to $20,000 worth of pensions by paying as little as $81 in social security tax."[19] The windfall gains being provided by Social Security do not appear to have been a tightly held secret from the business community!

Some businesses, however, saw how the free money available from the expansions of Social Security could serve their interests. Originally coverage under Social Security was restricted to wage and salaried workers in private firms. Marion Folsom, a Kodak executive who served on several Social Security advisory councils and who ultimately was appointed secretary of the Health, Education, and Welfare Department, spoke directly to the issue. He told about the situation Kodak faced after the company had been operating for about forty years. "Some of the older people had passed their peak of productiveness. The management was becoming quite concerned about what they were going to do with them. They looked into it and found that some of them couldn't get along very well if retired. The company didn't have a pension plan." After a while, Kodak founder George Eastman was persuaded to set up one of the first funded plans in industrial America. Folsom indicated that many business "people were worried about what effect the government plan would have on existing pension plans" when the original Social Security Act was under consideration. He told his business counterparts that "as far as Kodak was concerned, we simply would make a reduction in our plan. Part of it would be from Social Security, part of it from the company plan."[20] The part coming from Social Security would be provided on a heavily subsidized basis that made the program an extremely good deal for Kodak and other employers in similar situations.

In practical terms the key question was how the tax treatment and government regulation of pensions would interact with the growing Social Security program. Although the 1942 Revenue Act prohibited retirement plans from discriminating in favor of officers, shareholders, and supervisory or highly compensated employees, it also recognized that employer-sponsored plans supplemented Social Security and indicated that judgements about discrimination would be based on total benefits from pensions and Social Security. In July 1943 the IRS permitted employers to reduce their normal retirement benefit by up to 150 percent of an employee's primary insurance amount from Social Security. The reduction of more than 100 percent assumed that the worker would not only be receiving a Social Security benefit, but would have a spouse receiving a spousal benefit as well. In addition, this rule let the employer take full credit for the Social Security benefit, including the windfall benefits as well as the parts financed by the employer and employee contributions.

The 1950 Social Security Act Amendments raised both contribution rates for taxpayers and benefits for retirees. In 1951 the IRS reduced the amount of

19. J. K. Lasser and Walter Roos, "You Are Richer Than You Think," *Nation's Business,* October 1951, pp. 25, 84.

20. Folsom (1970, pp. 45, 50–51).

Social Security benefits attributable to employer contributions and set the allowable offset percentage at 140 percent of the primary insurance amount. Further enhancements in Social Security benefits reduced the offset percentage to 117 percent of the primary insurance amount in 1961, and then to 85 percent in 1967, and 75 percent in 1969. In 1971 new regulations recognized the inclusion of disability benefits and allowed plans to offset normal retirement benefits by up to 83.3 percent of the primary insurance amount.[21]

Not all private pension plans took full advantage of the extent to which IRS regulations allowed them to consider Social Security benefits in the determination of their residual obligations. But the surplus value provided through Social Security's start-up provided tremendous subsidies that had to have made employer-sponsored plans much more attractive to both sponsors and their employees than they would have been otherwise.

Policy Concerns Arising from Growth of Pensions

During the first half of the 1940s, as the country fought World War II, the high demand for workers combined with the impact of tax legislation, the regulated economy, and the beginnings of Social Security to give private pensions a considerable boost. Some employers began to offer retirement plans during this period because the wartime restrictions on pay increases did not apply to benefit programs. High marginal tax rates also made the tax treatment of pensions much more valuable than it had been in the early days of the federal income tax. By 1945 the employer-based pension system covered 6.5 million workers.[22] Organized labor won the right to negotiate over pensions toward the end of the 1940s, and retirement plans became a central element of union bargaining efforts thereafter. By 1950 roughly one-quarter of the private work force was participating in a pension plan. After the war labor demand slackened, and once again older workers became a surplus commodity for many employers, who sought to use pensions as a tool for encouraging targeted retirement. The share of the private work force participating in plans roughly doubled during the next twenty-five years, from 25 percent in 1950 to 46.5 percent in 1974.[23] But not everyone was sanguine about the evolving world of pensions.

By the early 1960s questions were being raised about the evolution and operation of the pension industry. One issue concerned the way assets in pension trusts were handled—or mishandled. One of the more notorious cases involved Teamsters president Jimmy Hoffa, who initially invested the assets of the union's Central and Southern States Pension Fund through hometown banks of the plan's trustees. Later, he promoted loans from the fund for friends, associates,

21. Schulz and Leavitt (1983, pp. 21–23).
22. Sass (1997, p. 118).
23. Schieber and George (1981, p. 54).

and influential people outside his immediate circle. Special interest rates were charged on these loans, and Hoffa and his friends got a piece of the action as loan intermediaries or brokers. By early 1962 loans representing one-quarter of the assets were in trouble.[24]

A more important problem, at least in the public's mind, was the insecurity of benefits in cases where plan sponsors went out of business. The headline case in this instance was the financial collapse of Studebaker in 1964. When it closed its plant in South Bend, Indiana, on November 1, 1964, it had inadequate funds to pay off accrued benefits. In the liquidation of the plan, Studebaker paid full benefits to the 3,600 people already retired and those at least age sixty with ten years of service who were eligible to retire under the plan. These benefits were covered by annuities purchased through Aetna at a cost of $21.5 million of the pension fund's total $24 million in assets. The next group to receive benefits included 4,080 participants over age forty with at least ten years of service. Their average age was fifty-two, and average service with the firm was twenty-three years. This group received benefits equal to about 15 percent of their vested accrued benefits paid out in the form of lump sums. The amounts ranged from $200 to $1,600, with an average of $600. The remaining group of 2,900 participants received nothing.[25] The public clamor after the Studebaker shutdown set off alarm bells in the halls of the U.S. Congress that could not be ignored.

Another set of concerns on policymakers' minds at this time related to the nature of the pension promise. Employers structured their plans to bond their workers to them in long-tenured relationships. The plans' structure and the way they were often explained gave workers the impression of an implied contract on the part of the employers to stand by the benefits. But employers often drafted their plans with protective language that allowed them to modify the benefits at will or in some extreme cases to sidestep paying benefits altogether, raising questions about the soundness of the implied contract.

These questions were enough in the public eye to cause President John Kennedy to appoint a President's Committee on Corporate Pension Funds in 1962, a committee that sowed the seeds of the ERISA legislation. For more than a decade, ERISA's development was as deliberate and inclusive of interested parties as any major piece of legislation ever considered in the U.S. Congress. Developing the legislation was further complicated by the relative roles of the Senate Finance Committee, the Senate Committee on Labor and Public Welfare, the House Ways and Means Committee, the House Committee on Education and Public Welfare, and the Joint Committee on Internal Revenue Taxation.[26]

24. James and James (1965, ch. 15–18).
25. Sass (1997, pp. 183–84).
26. McGill and others (1996). Sass (1997, ch. 8) provides a reasonably brief history of the development of ERISA. He cites a number of references for anyone interested in probing the matter further.

The Regulatory Structure under ERISA

The Employee Retirement Income Security Act and the associated regulations are one of the most massive and complex sets of requirements in the panoply of federal rules controlling business activities.[27] The mass is attributable to the scope of issues covered and the specific detail with which Congress articulated its intent in enacting the law. The complexity is related partly to the technical nature of the subject matter, as well as to the multiplicity of legislative committees involved in the development of the legislation and to the continuing jurisdictional authority of those committees over its various elements. The law comprises four titles and in itself has created some complexity.

Title I deals with the protection of employee benefit rights. It addresses matters related to reporting and disclosure by plan sponsors, participation and vesting standards for workers covered by plans, funding of plans, and the fiduciary responsibilities of various interested parties. The reporting and disclosure provisions replaced and expanded earlier law. The participation and vesting standards and funding requirements were new to federal law under ERISA. The Department of Labor was assigned primary jurisdiction and enforcement in matters pertaining to reporting, disclosure, and fiduciary regulation of plans. The Treasury Department was assigned primary jurisdiction and enforcement over matters pertaining to participation, vesting, and funding. The Labor Department is entitled to intervene in any matters that materially affect the rights of participants, even in cases under Treasury's formal jurisdiction.

Title II was an amendment to the Internal Revenue Code of 1954 and is primarily concerned with tax matters. It contains essentially the same participation, vesting, and funding standards that are included in Title I but specifies the conditions that a plan must satisfy to meet tax-qualification status. Without such status, contributions to and earnings by plan trusts do not receive the preferential tax treatment accorded these plans. Title II also specifies the minimum standards for funding of pension plans, provides excise tax penalties of 10 percent on the extent of underfunding for failure to comply, and gives the IRS responsibility for enforcing the actuarial soundness of the tax-qualified plans that fall under its jurisdiction. Title II also liberalized the provisions covering pensions for self-employed individuals (Keogh plans) and created individual retirement accounts. It changed the tax provisions on lump-sum distributions and set limits on tax-deferred annuities provided under section 403(b) of the tax code.

Title III directed the secretaries of labor and the Treasury to establish a Joint Board for the Enrollment of Actuaries who would be qualified to certify the periodic valuations of pension obligations and assets required under the law.

---

27. The following brief description of the legislative content of ERISA draws on McGill and others (1996, pp. 35–37).

This board was to set the standards and qualifications for performing actuarial services for plans. An "enrolled" actuary who has met the board's qualification standards must sign the periodic actuarial reports specified in the law. In signing the report the actuary certifies that the actuarial assumptions and methods used to determine the costs and funding requirements of the plan are reasonable in the aggregate and reflect the actuary's best estimate of anticipated experience under the plan.

Title IV created the Pension Benefit Guaranty Corporation (PBGC) to provide a program of pension benefit insurance that had not existed previously. The PBGC was set up within the Labor Department with the secretary of labor as the chairman of its board. Other board members include the secretaries of the Treasury and commerce. The PBGC guarantees all basic benefits, up to a limit, that are nonforfeitable under a pension plan in cases where the plan sponsor terminates the plan. A pension plan can be terminated for a variety of reasons, but termination insurance issues almost always come into play when a plan is being terminated because of business necessity. When a plan with sufficient funds to meet benefit obligations is terminated, typically the plan administrator liquidates the plan assets and either makes a lump-sum distribution to the eligible participants or buys single premium annuities for each eligible participant from a life insurance company. When a terminating plan has insufficient assets and the plan sponsor is unable or unwilling to contribute enough to cover liabilities, the plan is brought under the PBGC's control. In virtually all such cases, the PBGC itself becomes the plan trustee and assumes the administration of the plan.

Pension Operations under ERISA's Initial Regulatory Structure

The business community greeted ERISA less than enthusiastically. This cold reception was partly just the natural reaction of any group to new governmental regulation. Partly it was a reaction to new costs and administrative complications associated with the law. Participation and vesting standards increased plan costs where employers had not voluntarily implemented such provisions themselves. Funding requirements meant many plan sponsors had to increase their contributions to plans within a relatively short time span. Disclosure requirements meant some plan sponsors would have to undertake actuarial review of their plans with more frequency than they had in the past. The PBGC premiums generally were perceived as a head tax that bore no resemblance to the actual risk of default that any particular plan sponsor posed to the system.

Although businesses voiced concern about government regulation as ERISA was implemented, the early years under the new regulatory environment marked a boom period for retirement plans. Table 2-1 shows the changes in the number of plans and participation in them during the first thirteen years after

Table 2-1. *Number of Private Pension Plans by Type, Active Participants, and Plan Contributions and Benefits, 1975–87*

Plan year	Defined benefit plans	Defined contribution plans	Total plans	Active participants (thousands)	Total contributions ($ millions)	Total benefits paid ($ millions)
1975	103,346	207,748	311,094	68,104	37,061	19,065
1976	113,970	246,010	359,980	71,117	42,780	20,980
1977	121,655	280,972	402,627	73,254	47,061	22,950
1978	128,407	314,591	442,998	75,939	55,943	26,516
1979	139,489	331,432	470,921	78,058	61,279	28,680
1980	148,096	340,805	488,901	78,349	66,157	35,280
1981	167,293	378,318	545,611	80,282	75,374	44,753
1982	174,998	419,458	594,456	82,318	79,502	55,307
1983	175,143	427,705	602,848	84,410	82,447	65,333
1984	168,015	436,419	604,434	86,732	90,625	79,086
1985	170,172	461,963	632,135	88,293	95,188	101,898
1986	172,642	544,985	717,627	90,267	91,503	130,483
1987	163,065	569,964	733,029	91,559	92,070	122,254

Source: U.S. Department of Labor (1999, pp. 64, 67, 77, 80).

the passage of the new law. The total number of plans almost doubled during the first decade, as shown in the third column. When considering the effects of ERISA, it is useful to divide pension plans into two types. The traditional pension plan provides a defined benefit, where the pension sponsor specifies the level of benefit that will be provided to the worker after retirement. Typically the benefit in these plans is based on service under the plan and a worker's covered salary level. The alternative is a defined contribution plan, where the plan sponsor commits to making a contribution to an employee's account in the plan. The benefits ultimately provided depend on the accumulated contributions and interest in the worker's account.

Both types of plans grew significantly after passage of ERISA, but certain provisions of the law helped defined contribution plans to expand more rapidly. One set of provisions actually encouraged the creation of supplemental plans. For all practical purposes, before ERISA was enacted no upper limits had been placed on the level of benefits that could be paid to an individual from a defined benefit plan or on the amount of contribution that could be made to a defined contribution plan.[28] ERISA amended the Internal Revenue Code to add Section 415, which capped the annual benefits that could be funded for a worker from a

28. The amount that a plan sponsor could deduct for contributions to these plans was limited to a maximum annual deduction of 15 percent of covered pay for a profit-sharing plan and 25 percent of pay for all plans.

Table 2-2. *Accrued Benefit Security Ratios in Private Pensions, 1978–87*

Survey year	Percent of plans with ratios 1.0 or greater
1978	25
1979	25
1980	31
1981	45
1982	55
1983	64
1984	73
1985	78
1986	79
1987	84

Source: Watson Wyatt Worldwide (1983, p. 15; 1986, p. 4; 1991, p. 4).

defined benefit plan at $75,000. This same section limited the annual contribution to a defined contribution plan to $25,000 for a worker. But a special provision in section 415 allowed a sponsor with combined plans to contribute the full limit to the primary plan and still contribute an additional 25 percent of the full limit to the other type of plan. For any plan sponsor with significant numbers of workers affected by the limits, the ability to sponsor supplemental plans offered the opportunity for greater benefits under the tax preference given to qualified plans. The Department of Labor estimates that the percentage of workers covered by supplemental defined contribution plans doubled from 9 to 18 percent between 1975 and 1984.[29]

Not only were there more plans providing coverage to more workers, there were strong indications that benefit security in plans improved significantly in the years immediately after the passage of ERISA. Table 2-2 shows the percentage of large private pension plans with "accrued benefit security ratios" equal to 1.00 or more in the early years after ERISA's initial implementation. An accrued benefit security ratio of 1.00 means that the actuarial value of a plan's assets is at least as great as the value of the plan's current liabilities; that is, the pension trust has at least enough money to pay benefits that have been earned to date under the plan. The percentage of large plans with accrued benefit security ratios of 1.00 rose from 25 percent in 1978 to 84 percent by 1987. In other words, ERISA was very successful in its early years in encouraging employers to fund pension obligations.

The one sour note in this tune is that the private pension participation rate between 1975 and 1984 did not improve. In 1975, 39 percent of private sector workers were participating in a defined benefit plan and another 6 percent were

29. U.S. Department of Labor (1999, p. 67).

in defined contribution plans. By 1984 these participation rates had changed to 34 and 11 percent respectively. The stable participation rates, however, masked the significant improvement in the pension prospects of workers in plans. The percentage of workers in plans with more than 100 participants who were at least partially vested during this period climbed from 38 percent in 1975 to 67 percent in 1984.[30]

Table 2-1 also illustrates that the general financial status of pensions improved through the late 1970s and into the early 1980s, when contributions to private retirement plans regularly exceeded benefit disbursements. These data are mildly imperfect for various technical reasons—for example, the benefits include both amounts paid to beneficiaries and amounts paid to insurance companies—but the overall positive trend is unmistakable. In fact, the financial status of pensions was even healthier than these numbers might suggest, because the contributions and benefits do not include the earnings accruing to the assets in the system. Total assets in the pension system grew from $260 billion in 1975 to $1.4 trillion by 1987.[31] In inflation-adjusted terms, assets in the plans were 2.6 times larger in 1987 than they were in 1975. The rapid expansion of the assets in the private pension system triggered a public policy response to enhanced pension funding that few anticipated when ERISA had been voted into law.

The Effect of Tax Expenditures on Pension Regulation

From many perspectives greater sums of money flowing into and residing in pension funds would seem a virtuous result of ERISA. But not everyone considered that to be the case. For many years before adoption of ERISA, some policy analysts had been concerned about the implications of tax preferences in the federal income tax code. For example, Walter J. Blum, a law professor at the University of Chicago, told the Joint Economic Committee in 1955 that if it were

> decided to subsidize a certain activity, we should be hesitant about administering the subsidy by way of a tax preference. Subsidies in this form vary directly in amount with the tax brackets of the recipients; they are invariably hidden in the technicalities of the tax law; they do not show up in the budget; their cost frequently is difficult to calculate; and their accomplishments are even more difficult to assess.[32]

By the mid- to late 1960s, Blum's concern about the use of tax preferences took on a more concrete form under the rubric "tax expenditures." These were

30. U.S. Department of Labor (1999, pp. 67, 83).
31. U.S. Department of Labor (1999, p. 74).
32. Blum (1955, p. 252).

the estimated fiscal costs of preferred treatment of certain kinds of income and expenditures in the income tax code.[33]

In 1974, the same year that ERISA passed, the Congressional Budget Act formalized the concept of "tax expenditures" as a required element of the budget document that the president submits to Congress each year. Tax expenditures are defined in the act as "revenue losses attributable to provisions of the federal tax laws which allow special exclusion, exemption, or deduction from gross income or which provide a special credit, a preferential tax rate, or a deferral of tax liability."[34] The notion is that tax breaks cost the government revenue, just as a spending program costs the government revenue, and so "tax expenditures" from tax breaks should be calculated along with actual spending.

By the early 1980s the tax expenditure estimates helped to create a growing concern about the tax treatment of employee benefit programs in general and employer-sponsored retirement plans in particular. Fringe benefits had risen from 5.4 percent of total compensation in 1951 to 16.3 percent in 1981, and Social Security's actuaries projected that they would rise to 38.3 percent by 2056.[35] Most fringe benefits consisted of employer-sponsored pensions and health benefits, both of which were treated as expenses for business, but pensions were not treated as income to individuals until after benefits were received, and health insurance is never treated as income. The fiscal 1981 budget estimated the tax expenditure for individuals associated with employer-sponsored pensions at $14.7 billion, with another $2.5 billion attributed to retirement savings plans for the self-employed and others. The tax expenditure attributed to pensions was among the largest of such items in the budget, although several others were in the same league. For example, the tax expenditures attributed to the tax deductibility of mortgage interest on owner-occupied homes, to capital gains on business assets other than natural resources, and to employer-provided health insurance were each estimated at about $15 billion as well. The tax expenditure from deductibility of nonbusiness state and local taxes was estimated to be slightly higher, at $17.3 billion.[36]

In the fiscal year 1982 budget, the first budget prepared by the Reagan administration, tax expenditures associated with retirement plans were estimated to be even higher, at $30.2 billion, as shown in table 2-3. By comparison the estimated tax expenditure associated with the home mortgage interest deduction in fiscal year 1982 was $25.3 billion. The overall magnitude of the tax expenditures associated with employee benefits was a concern to policymakers and analysts, as was the distribution of these tax benefits.

33. For a fuller discussion of the evolution of this concept, see Schieber (1984).
34. U.S. Office of Management and Budget (1980, p. 183).
35. Wilkin, Gresch, and Glanz (1982, p. 3).
36. U.S. Congress, Joint Committee on Taxation (1980, p. 12); U.S. Office of Management and Budget (1980, pp. 231–33).

Table 2-3. *Estimated Federal Tax Expenditures for Selected Tax Preferences,*
as Reported in Fiscal Year Budgets, 1981–89
Millions of current dollars, except as noted

Fiscal year budget	Home mortgage interest deduction	Net exclusion of retirement plan con- tributions and earnings	Ratio of pension to mortgage preference
1981	14,760	17,260	1.2
1982	25,295	30,210	1.2
1983	25,490	31,260	1.2
1984	27,945	60,790	2.2
1985	25,130	67,710	2.7
1986	27,300	70,205	2.6
1987	29,560	77,445	2.6
1988	33,675[a]	53,945	1.6
1989	32,185	54,745	1.7

Source: U.S. Office of Management and Budget (various years).

a. The tax expenditure associated with the home mortgage interest deduction for fiscal 1988 was taken from the fiscal 1989 budget, because the value reported in the fiscal 1988 budget did not bear a reasonable relationship to either the previous or the subsequent budgets.

These concerns about the costs of pensions became entangled in the politics of the federal budget in the 1980s. Budget deficits swelled in the early 1980s, climbing from $79 billion in fiscal 1981 to $128 billion in fiscal 1982 and to $208 billion in fiscal 1983.[37] There was a bipartisan sense that something had to be done to bring the government budget into balance. But the 1980 election campaign had focused on tax rate reductions, and the tax cuts included in the Economic Recovery Tax Act of 1981 had been supported across both parties. Few politicians favored raising tax rates again as a means to balance the budget. In the aftermath of the Soviet invasion of Afghanistan in 1979, moreover, politicians in both parties supported increases in the defense budget. Although the Reagan administration was willing to propose some reductions in Social Security benefits, an overwhelming bipartisan majority in Congress opposed such a step.[38] Thus, the budget debates in the early 1980s tended to focus on proposed cutbacks to other social programs and on the possibility of raising revenue without changing tax rates by reducing the size of tax expenditures.

In response to President Reagan's proposals to cut Social Security spending, Representative Charles Rangel (D-NY) introduced a bill to cut tax expenditures for employer-sponsored pensions by reducing the amount of benefits that could be funded under ERISA. In introducing his legislation, he said that if the government needed to cut back on retirement benefits to help in rebalancing

37. U.S. Office of Management and Budget (1999, p. 20).
38. Schieber and Shoven (1999, p. 188).

the budget, it would be much fairer to reduce tax expenditures associated with retirement benefits going to the well-off than to cut the benefits needed to sustain the basic needs of the less privileged. Rangel's legislation ultimately evolved into the Tax Equity and Fiscal Responsibility Act of 1982 (TEFRA).

Not everyone was pleased with the original development and passage of ERISA in 1974, but its deliberate development allowed representatives from all interested parties to have input regarding its particulars. TEFRA's development was totally different in character. It was intended to raise revenue, and little consideration was given to the long-term implications of its provisions. TEFRA made many changes across the tax code, but in the particular area of pensions, its focus was to curtail the tax expenditures associated with large pensions for the highly compensated. It reduced and froze, for a period of time, the funding and benefit limits for defined benefit plans and the contribution limits for defined contribution plans. It also created a new set of "top heavy" rules limiting the extent to which employer plans could be targeted toward workers at higher earnings levels. To convey a sense of how TEFRA was cobbled together, it is worth noting that the House and Senate committees with jurisdiction over the legislation never considered the top-heavy provisions; these provisions were introduced only when the differences in the House's and Senate's respective bills were being reconciled in the conference committee convened for that purpose.

After the passage of TEFRA, the tax expenditure associated with retirement plans steadied, rising from $30.2 billion in fiscal 1982 to $31.3 billion in fiscal 1983, as shown in table 2-3. But the estimated pension tax expenditure then started rising, to $60.8 billion in fiscal 1984, $67.7 billion in fiscal 1985, and $70.2 billion in fiscal 1986. For comparison, the estimated tax expenditure for the home mortgage interest deduction in 1986 was $27.3 billion. In 1981 the estimated tax expenditure for retirement plans had been 1.2 times that of the home mortgage interest deduction. By the mid-1980s the retirement tax preference was more than 2.5 times that of the mortgage deduction. The largest increase in the tax expenditures attributed to retirement plans occurred between 1983 and 1984, with no explanation in the budget to account for it. In fact, what drove the increase was the initial inclusion in the 1984 budget of federal civilian, state, and local government employee pensions in the estimates. The inclusion of public workers' pensions made the tax expenditure estimates for pensions the largest of all tax expenditures. The singular magnitude of this particular set of tax expenditure estimates captured policymakers' attention, but the legislative attention that resulted tended to focus primarily on private pension policy changes as the mechanism to raise additional federal revenues.

As the federal budget deficits remained high into the mid-1980s and the size of the tax expenditures related to retirement plans grew, several major budget and tax acts during the remainder of the 1980s and the early 1990s included additional revisions of pension regulations. Much of this evolving body of law and the accompanying regulations followed the lead of TEFRA in curtailing the tax preferences accorded employer-sponsored pensions, especially those related to private plans. The law and regulations also attempted to spread the availability of pensions to workers at lower levels of earnings by limiting the targeting of benefits toward those at higher earnings levels.

In 1984 the Deficit Reduction Act extended the freezes on the funding and contribution limits for pensions that had been adopted in 1982. That same year the Retirement Equity Act (REACT) implemented a series of provisions meant to increase the delivery of pension benefits to workers covered by employer-sponsored plans and their dependents. It changed the requirement in ERISA that plans cover workers over age twenty-five with more than one year of service by reducing the age to twenty-one. REACT also required a spousal signature before a worker could waive survivor benefits; that is, pension benefits would always be available to a spouse unless explicit consent was obtained from the spouse.

The federal income tax system was overhauled with the passage of the Tax Reform Act of 1986. This reform law led to more limitations on benefits that could be funded on a tax-preferred basis and to a rebalancing of the limits for defined benefit and defined contribution plans.[39] It reduced the service requirements under tax-qualified plans that employers could set for workers to vest in their accruing benefits. It was heavily endowed with provisions to limit plan sponsors' ability to discriminate in favor of highly paid workers, including, among other things, fundamentally changing the rules for integrating employer plan benefits with Social Security. The greatest effect of the integration rule changes was for "offset plans," where employers reduced the pension benefit based on the worker's lifetime Social Security benefit. The tax reform law limited the offsets by specifying that they could not accrue more rapidly than benefits in the pension and limiting them to 50 percent of the Social Security benefit rather than 83.3 percent.

Even after the passage of tax reform, pension tax expenditures for fiscal year 1987 were estimated at $77.4 billion. In the Omnibus Budget Reconciliation Act of 1987, Congress reduced the full funding limits for private defined benefit plans from 100 percent of ongoing plan liability to the lesser of that value or 150 percent of benefits accrued at the time of each annual valuation. When the funding limit was based solely on the ongoing plan liability, plan sponsors could take into consideration expected pay increases for plan participants between the time of the annual valuation and their expected date of retirement. In basing the

39. When ERISA was originally passed, section 415 limits allowed the funding of a maximum defined benefit of $75,000 a year or the maximum contribution of $25,000 a year to a defined contribution plan. With the consumer price indexing of these limits, they had grown in lock step at the three-to-one ratio. Under the Tax Reform Act of 1986, the limit on defined contribution plans was to be frozen until the ratio between the two reached a four-to-one level, at which point the indexing was to again move in lock step.

funding limit on benefits that already had been accrued, anticipated pay increases could no longer be considered. True, employers were allowed to fund up to 150 percent of the accrued benefit for each worker, but for most younger workers, 150 percent of the accrued benefit was less than 100 percent of the projected benefit. In effect, this meant that firms were not allowed to put aside as much money in the present to fund the younger workers' eventual retirement benefits in defined benefit plans but instead were required to put aside more money in future years.

By the time the fiscal 1988 budget was released, the combined effects of lower marginal tax rates that had flowed out of the Tax Reform Act of 1986 and the reduced contributions to plans that resulted from the Omnibus Budget Reconciliation Act of 1987 were taking effect. Estimates for that fiscal year put pension tax expenditures at $53.9 billion. Despite the repeated legislative measures to curtail the pension tax preferences, this was the first reduction in the estimated cost of these preferences during the decade. Still, the estimated cost for fiscal 1988 was more than three times the estimated cost for fiscal 1981.

The Omnibus Budget Reconciliation Act of 1993 made certain changes that had the effect of forcing employer pension plans to put aside a smaller share of the cost of a given pension early in a career and a greater share of the cost later in a career. The specific provision reduced the limit on compensation that could be taken into account in funding employer-sponsored retirement plans from $235,840 to $150,000. For defined benefit plans, the limitation delayed the funding of benefits for workers whose projected final salaries toward the end of their careers fell between the two amounts. For example, a thirty-five year old currently earning $35,000 but expected to receive nominal pay increases of 5.5 percent a year until retiring at age sixty-five would have a projected final salary of $165,344. This final salary would exceed the new compensation limit by $15,344, and the benefits that would be attributable to that portion of salary could not be funded. The rules required working backwards. In this case, for example, 9.3 percent of the worker's final salary—that is, $15,344 divided by $165,344—could not be considered in funding the pension benefit. In practical terms this means that 9.3 percent of the worker's current salary—that is, roughly $3,250 of earnings at age thirty-five—cannot be considered in funding the portion of this worker's benefit that is earned this year. The forgone funding while the worker is thirty-five years of age will have to be made up later in the career if the plan sponsor is to deliver the benefits that are implied by the current benefit formula in the pension plan. This provision has a substantial impact on the amount of money set aside for younger workers.[40]

For participants in defined contribution plans, the reduced compensation limits might have had their most significant effects on workers at upper-middle

40. Schieber (1993).

earnings levels. This is because 401(k) and similar plans face a "discrimination test," in which the contribution rates that can be made to the plan by "highly compensated" workers are limited by the actual contribution rates by "non-highly compensated" workers. For highly compensated workers earning from $75,000 up to about $150,000, however, the reduced compensation limits would effectively reduce the amounts they could contribute to their defined contribution plans.

Regulating the Use of Pension Assets

At about the same time as federal law began to restrict the funding of private retirement plans, the phenomenon of employers terminating pension plans to gain access to excess assets in those funds for purposes other than providing retirement benefits received a great deal of publicity. During the later part of the 1980s, the rising stock market helped to push up the asset values of pension plans, and high interest rates made it look relatively easier (in terms of present discounted value) to fund future benefits. Thus, many pension funds appeared to have excess assets. Rather than borrowing at the prevailing high interest rates to finance business investments or other activities, some corporate executives chose to terminate their pension trusts to recover the excess assets in those trusts, even though the corporation had to pay income tax on the reversion.

In the late 1980s the only way to obtain funds from a pension plan that was overfunded was to terminate the plan. Employers who did not want to end their plans found ways to continue to have retirement plans and still recover the excess assets. Some split their plan in two, spinning off the excess assets into a plan for retirees, and leaving the plan for active employees with the minimum funding needed for an ongoing plan. The companies then bought annuities for the retirees and terminated those plans, recapturing the excess assets that had been spun off into the retiree plan. Other companies terminated their pension plans, recovered excess assets, and then started up new plans.

This practice raised at least a couple of concerns from the perspective of federal regulation. First, when these terminations occurred, the tax-preferred mechanism for saving for retirement was being used for general corporate financing purposes. Second, the extraction of assets from a pension system that was overfunded in a high stock return, high interest rate environment could result in the underfunding of a plan fairly quickly when the important underlying economics changed. Plans that became underfunded after a termination created the very real threat of increasing liabilities for the Pension Benefit Guaranty Corporation and reducing benefits for annuitants and workers whose benefits exceeded the PBGC's guaranteed levels. In addition, the attraction of excess pension assets to financiers who had no long-term interests in the successful operation of businesses from which these assets could be extracted created a robber baron environment that many policymakers found unseemly.

The IRS established guidelines in 1983 that regulated termination and reversions. The agency required the purchase of annuities for all plan benefits to protect employees against market fluctuations and confirmed that employers could reestablish plans after a reversion had taken place. The Tax Reform Act of 1986 applied a 10 percent excise tax to the reversions. Later the tax rose to 15 percent, and the Omnibus Budget Reconciliation Act of 1990 pushed it to as much as 50 percent, in addition to corporate income taxes.[41] This punitive tax virtually ended the practice of terminating plans to gain access to surplus funds, although the lower interest rates prevailing in much of the 1990s would have made such terminations less attractive anyway. Although these new rules largely stanched the flow of funds from tax-qualified plans for purposes other than providing retirement income to plan participants, the regulations locked up employer contributions to their pension plans more tightly than ever before.

A Shift in Accounting Rules

One other element of the story regarding pension regulation arose outside the boundaries established by federal law and relates to the financial accounting of pension benefits and obligations by plan sponsors. In 1980 nearly two-thirds of defined benefit plans that based benefits on salaries of covered workers—that is, either final or career average plans—funded the benefit on the basis of the *entry age normal cost method*.[42] Using this method and assuming the actuarial assumptions were met, an employer would contribute a steady percentage of a worker's pay over the worker's career, with the goal of accumulating sufficient resources at retirement to pay expected retirement benefits.

In the early 1980s the Financial Accounting Standards Board (FASB) began to look at the actuarial methods used for calculating pension obligations and expenses that were reported on plan sponsors' financial statements. The FASB was interested in the alignment and reporting of assets and liabilities in pension plans. In this regard, the pattern of funding a pension obligation and the accrual of that obligation were important. Although a pension can be financed with a constant percentage of a worker's pay over his or her career, the obligation faced by the plan sponsor accrues at a varying rate over the worker's career. During the early part of the worker's career, the benefit earned will be much less than the flat amount contributed using the entry age normal cost method of funding, and the assets in the plan during the early part of a worker's career will significantly exceed the sponsor's obligation if the plan were to be shut down. The

41. The excise tax is reduced to 20 percent under any one of the following three conditions: bankruptcy, in which case the plan sponsor is under chapter 7 or chapter 11 bankruptcy proceedings; transfer to a replacement plan, in which case the plan must cover at least 95 percent of the participants in the original plan; or a pro rata increase, in which case the employer provides a pro rata increase to participants of at least 20 percent of the reversion amount.

42. Watson Wyatt Worldwide (1980). The survey covers plans with more than 1,000 covered lives.

FASB believed that a plan funded in the entry age normal method should report a surplus "asset" in the pension fund that significantly exceeded the value of the obligation for a young worker.

The FASB ultimately promulgated accounting rules that required the use of the *projected unit credit actuarial cost method* to account for accruing pension benefits. The differences between the two methods are shown in figure 2-3. Changing from the entry age normal cost method to the projected unit credit method results in lower costs early in a worker's career and higher costs later in the worker's career. The FASB rules on pension accounting have encouraged many plan sponsors to move to a projected unit credit funding method.

In 1983, 10 percent of defined benefit plans (in which the benefits were related to final pay) were funded on a projected unit credit basis; by the mid-1990s nearly two-thirds of them were being funded that way.[43] The baby boomers were in their twenties and thirties as the FASB rules were discussed and ultimately issued. Shifting from an entry age normal cost method to a projected unit credit cost method when such a large cohort of workers was so young slowed the funding of their retirement benefits. The net effect of this shift has delayed the funding of a portion of the baby boomers' retirement benefits from the first half of their careers to the second half.

Implications of the Regulatory Control of Pensions

The legislative and regulatory measures adopted since the early 1980s have clearly diminished the level of retirement benefits that can be funded on a tax-preferred basis and delayed the funding of defined benefit plans until later in workers' careers. These measures have generally been adopted with the stated intent of limiting the extent of tax-preferred retirement saving allowed workers at high earnings levels and making sure tax-qualified retirement benefits are broadly distributed. The net result has not always comported with the stated intent.

ERISA originally set the maximum defined benefit that could be funded for a worker retiring at age sixty-two at $75,000 in 1975 and provided for its indexation by the Consumer Price Index (CPI) into the future. Had it been fully indexed, the maximum fundable defined benefit would have been $227,230 in 1999. Instead, after years of revisions and tinkering, the maximum fundable benefit was $130,000 at a worker's normal Social Security retirement age, with the maximum benefit fundable at earlier retirement ages actuarially reduced. ERISA originally set the maximum defined contribution benefit that could be funded for a worker at $25,000 in 1975 and indexed the limit by the CPI. Had

43. Watson Wyatt Worldwide (1983, p. 23; 1996, p. 4).

Figure 2-3. *Alternative Pension Cost Perspectives for a 25-Year-Old Worker Over a 40-Year Career under Alternative Actuarial Cost Methods*

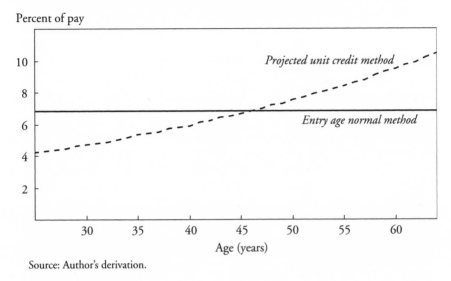

Percent of pay

Projected unit credit method

Entry age normal method

Age (years)

Source: Author's derivation.

this limit been fully indexed since 1975, it would have been $75,743 in 1999. Instead, it was $30,000. The TEFRA legislation in 1982 set limits on the amount of compensation that could be considered in funding a retirement plan for top-heavy plans. The Tax Reform Act of 1986 extended these limits to all plans, set them at $200,000 in 1987, and called for their indexation by the CPI. Had the limits been fully indexed, in 1999 the compensation limit for pension funding would have been $271,580. Instead, it was $160,000.

In many cases, the most important of the limits that affect pension funding is the limit on covered compensation first established with TEFRA. This is so for at least two reasons. The first is that the reduction in compensation limits over time has restricted the retirement benefits that are provided to senior executives in many firms through tax-qualified retirement plans. In many large companies today, these benefits are a relatively trivial part of the total retirement package for senior executives; instead, top executives receive their retirement benefits in other forms, such as unfunded supplemental executive retirement plans. Taking the senior executives out of the tax-qualified retirement pool has the natural, albeit regrettable, human tendency of reducing their personal interest in that pool.

The second reason that the reduction in the compensation limits is so important is that, as noted earlier, this limit applies to future pay levels as well as current pay—even though most ongoing pension benefits will be based on future

Table 2-4. *Percentage of Workers in Selected Pension Plans Affected by Pension Funding Limits, by Age and Median Pay Level in 1998*

	Workers with projected pay above $16,000 limit	
Age of workers	Percent	Median pay (dollars)
Less than 20	17.5	20,280.00
20 to 24.9	47.2	27,831.50
25 to 29.9	59.7	36,614.09
30 to 34.9	57.4	44,875.01
35 to 39.9	45.5	53,982.00
40 to 44.9	30.5	66,573.07
45 to 49.9	17.9	90,100.00
50 to 59.9	12.0	128,893.29
60 to 64.9	6.5	179,301.06

Source: Watson Wyatt Worldwide, unpublished data.

pay rates. In 1999 the limit of compensation that could be considered for funding a pension was $160,000. The average wage growth assumption used in valuing the final-pay pension plans included in Watson Wyatt's Actuarial Assumption Survey for the 1998 plan year was 5.2 percent a year in nominal terms.[44] Using this assumption, a worker who is thirty-five years old today and earning $35,000 would have a final salary of more than $168,000 in the last year before reaching the normal Social Security retirement age of sixty-seven. The plan sponsor would not be able to fund the pension for the $35,000 employee on the proportion of expected final earnings that exceeds the $160,000 limit, which amounts to the top $1,762 of the employee's earnings this year. An employer sponsoring a pension for this worker would have to reduce the funding of the pension below that allowed by current law in any year in which projected final earnings exceed the compensation limits.

To explore the implications of this phenomenon, I have combined data on fifteen large companies that are actuarial clients of Watson Wyatt. These include plan sponsors in the private and nonprofit sectors, manufacturers and service companies, companies with generous benefits and those with not-so-generous benefits. The plans had 165,000 active employees covered under their combined defined benefit plans. Workers whose reported earnings were under $5,000 were not included because these workers were part-time, or data were available for only part of the year, or there was some other explanation for their extraordinarily low pay. The results of the analysis, presented in table 2-4, suggest that the compensation limits in current law are slowing pension accruals for significant numbers

44. Watson Wyatt Worldwide (1999, p. 3).

Figure 2-4. *Alternative Pension Funding Perspectives for a 25-Year-Old Worker Over a 40-Year Career under Alternative Actuarial Cost Methods*

Multiple of salary

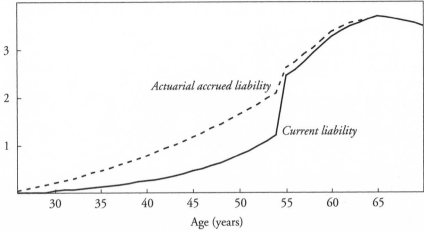

Source: Author's derivation.

of workers and that the pay levels for those being affected are hardly exorbitant, especially for middle-aged and younger workers. The average pay level of those workers between the ages of twenty-five and thirty who were affected was only slightly above $36,600 in 1998.

The implications of the compensation limits on the funding pattern of defined benefit plans are reflected in figure 2-4. The line labeled "actuarial accrued liability" shows the level of funding as a multiple of a hypothetical worker's salary that would be required to fund that worker's benefit at retirement under the projected unit credit funding method. The other line in the figure shows the funding level that would be required to cover the benefits for the worker as they accrue during each year of the worker's career. The Omnibus Budget Reconciliation Act of 1987 changed the amount of funding that a pension plan could have and still allow the plan sponsor to make tax-deductible contributions to it. Before passage of that act, plans could fund at rates up to the upper line in figure 2-4 because contributions to a plan were deductible as long as the asset level in the plan did not exceed 100 percent of the actuarial accrued liability. After adoption of the 1987 act, the maximum funding limit was the lesser of 100 percent of the actuarial accrued liability or 150 percent of the current liability.

A pension plan's total liability is simply the sum of the liabilities for each of the participants in the plan. Thus, the current liability of the plan is the aggregation of the liability for the current benefit shown in the figure for all of the participants in the plan. Similarly, the actuarial accrued liability is the sum of the

Table 2-5. *Alternative Liability Measures and Funding Limit Liabilities as a Function of Plan Maturity*

Participants and liabilities	Case study 1	Case study 2	Case study 3	Case study 4	Case study 5
Active workers					
1. Number	100	100	100	100	100
2. Average age	39.5	43.2	43.2	43.2	43.2
3. Average service	11.0	14.4	14.4	14.4	14.4
4. Average pay	35,495	35,495	35,495	35,495	35,495
5. Current liability	690,659	1,109,138	1,109,138	1,109,138	1,109,038
6. Actuarial accrued liability	2,128,465	2,925,290	2,925,290	2,925,290	2,925,290
Retirees					
7. Number	0	0	11	25	100
8. Current liability and actuarial accrued liability	0	0	513,355	1,134,891	3,913,164
Total					
9. Participants	100	100	111	125	200
10. Percent of participants retired	0	0	10	20	50
11. Current liability	690,659	1,109,138	1,622,493	2,244,029	5,022,202
12. 150 percent of current liability	1,035,989	1,663,707	2,433,740	3,366,044	7,533,303
13. Actuarial accrued liability	2,128,465	2,925,290	3,438,645	4,060,181	6,838,454
14. Full funding limit liability	1,035,989	1,663,707	2,433,740	3,366,044	6,838,454
15. Full funding limit liability as a percent of actuarial accrued liability	49	57	71	83	100

Source: Schieber and Kulash (1995, p. 28).

liability for projected benefits for all participants in the plan. The substantial variation in the relative values of current and projected benefits during various stages in a worker's career takes on major significance in considering adequate pension funding levels because the age structure of the work force and retirees can vary a great deal from plan to plan.

To understand how the maturing of a population covered by a pension affects the relative measures of its various obligations, consider table 2-5, which shows calculations for various liability measures and measures of the plan sponsor's ability to fund the plan for various hypothetical populations. In all five cases shown, the firm has 100 active workers. Case studies one and two show two relatively immature pension plans. Neither of them has any retirees (as shown in the seventh row), but the plan in case study two is somewhat more mature than the plan in the first case study, as reflected in the comparative average age and service distributions in the two cases (second and third rows). In case studies two through five, the age and experience of the 100 active workers is the same, but the number of retirees varies. None of the participants are retired in case two, 10 percent are retired in case three, 20 percent in case four, and 50 percent in case five (reflected in row ten).

Current liability for the active workers, presented in the fifth row, is less in case one than in the other four because of the lower average age of participants and their fewer years of service in the first case. Actuarial accrued liability for active workers, which is the sum of the liability for projected benefits, is presented in line six. Again, it is lower for case one than for the other four, for the reasons just stated.

The eighth row shows current liability and actuarial accrued liability for retirees. The current liability and the actuarial accrued liability for retirees are equivalent because there are no more anticipated pay increases that would affect benefits. In fact, the plan sponsor might provide periodic cost-of-living benefit increases for retirees that would increase the actuarial accrued liability, but those are not legally required and thus are not recognized until they actually occur.

The eleventh row shows the total current liability, which is the sum of the current liability for both active and retired workers. Notice that plans with a higher proportion of retired workers have higher current liabilities as well. Row twelve presents 150 percent of current liability for the basis of a comparison that is used in determining the funding limit for the various plans, as will be explained in a moment. Row thirteen shows total actuarial accrued liability, which is calculated by adding the actuarial accrued liability for the active and the retired workers.

The rationale for going through these calculations becomes apparent in the last two rows of the table. Under the contribution limits, a plan is allowed to fund either 150 percent of current liability or total actuarial accrued liability, whichever is less. The full funding limit liability for the five cases is given in row fourteen. Row fifteen shows how much the firm is allowed to fund, as a percent of the firm's total actuarial accrued liability. Notice that only the most mature of the plans, case five, is actually allowed to fund its full actuarial accrued liability. Thus current law discriminates among plans by allowing sponsors with more mature populations to fund their plans more fully than can sponsors with less mature plans.

When the Omnibus Budget Reconciliation Act of 1987 was signed into law, the baby boom generation ranged in age from twenty-three to forty-one. Using

Table 2-6. *Funding Status of Defined Benefit Plans, 1987–97*

Plan year	All private plans: median funding ratio	All plans: median funding ratio	Watson Wyatt actuarial assumption survey plans			
			Overfunded plans		Underfunded plans	
			Percent	Median funding ratio	Percent	Median funding ratio
1987		1.45	83	1.57	17	0.82
1988		1.44	82	1.56	18	0.83
1989		1.40	85	1.50	15	0.86
1990	1.35	1.36	85	1.45	15	0.83
1991	1.30	1.38	85	1.45	15	0.88
1992	1.30	1.33	85	1.41	15	0.89
1993	1.24	1.27	82	1.35	18	0.88
1994	1.18	1.18	76	1.27	24	0.87
1995	1.13	1.15	70	1.25	30	0.88
1996	1.15	1.20	81	1.27	19	0.91
1997		1.23	84	1.30	16	0.93

Sources and notes: The column labeled "All private plans" is based on unpublished tabulations developed by the Labor Department's Office of Pension and Welfare Benefits from Form 5500 reports that employers must file on the funded status of their pension plans. The other columns are based on plans that have been included in Watson Wyatt's annual surveys of actuarial assumptions and funding. These are included because the time span is greater than for the Form 5500 data and because the plans with assets over or under the liabilities in the plan can be separated more easily from year to year. The national data are included to show the general correspondence in funding levels for the Watson Wyatt sample with the universe of plans.

Watson Wyatt's 1988 Survey of Actuarial Assumptions and Funding of pension plans, Schieber and Graig estimated that 47 percent of the large plans in the United States would be affected by the funding limits of the 1987 law.[45] Many of the employers that had been contributing to their plans under alternative funding methods suddenly found after the 1987 law that their plans now held excess funding. This basically meant that they could stop contributions to their plans until the accruing liabilities caught up with the assets that they had put into the plan under the earlier rules. Many of these employers thus enjoyed contribution holidays, where their plans required no funding at all for some years. But as these plans have matured, their funding status has fallen.

Table 2-6 shows the funding status of private defined benefit plans for years following adoption of the 1987 law. The funding ratios reflect the net value of assets in the plans divided by the current liability reported by the plans. The story that flows out of this table is relatively straightforward. The funding level

45. Schieber and Graig (1994, p. 29). The survey is restricted to plans with more than 1,000 covered lives.

of the typical plan has declined since the 1987 law was adopted. Specifically, plans holding assets in excess of their current liabilities account for this general decline in the funded status of plans. Indeed, the funding status of underfunded plans has continued to improve during the period.

The declines in the funding of pensions cannot be attributed solely to the funding holidays for plans that were at the full funding limit imposed under Omnibus Budget Reconciliation Act of 1987. Funding of pension plans has declined generally, even among employers whose plans were not at the full funding limit. One plausible explanation for this pattern is that when the rules were put in place to make it extremely difficult for employers to gain access to any excess assets, employers reduced contributions to their plans to avoid situations where excess assets are tied up in their plans. Indeed, one can argue that the managers of corporate plan sponsors might simply be carrying out their fiduciary responsibilities to stockholders by not tying up assets in their plans beyond certain levels above the minimal requirements to do so.

The New Economics of Retirement Finance

The institutional context for employer-sponsored pension plans has shifted dramatically in the last sixty years or so. Early generations of participants in the Social Security system received tremendous windfall benefits as it evolved into a pay-as-you-go system. In turn, Social Security benefits made it cheaper for employers to provide pensions, because the plans could, in effect, top off the rising Social Security benefits. But the windfall benefits provided to the early generations of participants in Social Security have now dried up. Looking to the future, the target population for employer-sponsored pensions is generally going to receive rates of return from participating in Social Security that are less than it would have received from investing payroll taxes in government bonds.[46] Moreover, because of changes in contribution limits, the delay in the funding of defined benefit plans has back-loaded the costs of these plans on the latter part of workers' careers. The costs of the plans relative to cash wages will increase significantly if benefits promised under current plan designs are to be met.

Regulatory changes in the quarter century since ERISA was enacted have also had a significant impact on employer-sponsored pensions. Participation rates have remained virtually constant, and the rapid increase in vesting levels achieved during the law's first decade slowed during the next decade. But probably the most important result of the changing regulatory environment was a shift in the nature of the pension promise.

In the latter half of the 1980s the number of private defined benefit plans began to fall off significantly, as shown in table 2-7. By 1995 the number of

46. Schieber and Shoven (1999).

Table 2-7. *Number of Private Pension Plans by Type and Active Participants, 1980–95*

	Defined benefit plans		Defined contribution plans	
Plan year	Number	Participants (thousands)	Number	Participants (thousands)
1980	148,096	30,133	340,805	18,893
1981	167,293	30,082	378,318	20,743
1982	174,998	29,756	419,458	23,448
1983	175,143	29,964	427,705	27,844
1984	168,015	30,172	436,419	30,603
1985	170,172	29,024	461,963	33,244
1986	172,642	28,670	544,985	34,620
1987	163,065	28,432	569,964	34,959
1988	145,952	28,081	583,971	34,062
1989	132,467	27,304	598,889	33,990
1990	113,062	26,344	599,245	35,488
1991	101,752	25,747	597,542	35,771
1992	88,621	25,362	619,714	38,868
1993	83,596	25,127	618,501	39,619
1994	74,422	24,615	615,922	40,357
1995	69,492	23,531	623,912	42,662

Source: U.S. Department of Labor (1999, pp. 64, 71).

remaining plans was only 40 percent of the number of plans that had existed at the high-water mark in 1983, as the legislative onslaught was beginning. The number of active participants in defined benefit plans also declined, although the relative magnitude was much smaller. Clearly, the elimination of defined benefit plans occurred among smaller plan sponsors to a greater extent than it did among larger ones. As the defined benefit world was shrinking, the defined contribution world continued to grow (although the rate of plan growth slowed significantly in the early 1990s relative to the 1980s). The number of defined contribution plans increased by roughly 120,000 during the first half of the 1980s, by 140,000 in the second half of the 1980s, and by only about 25,000 in the first half of the 1990s. The number of active participants in these plans continued to grow significantly during the 1990s. The effect of pension policy on the relative choice between defined benefit and defined contribution plans has been the subject of various analyses, and several explanations have been proposed.

A first explanation shows that structural changes in the economy may have caused a shift in the choice of pension plans. The shift from manufacturing jobs toward a greater prevalence of service jobs had some effect on the nature of pension coverage that workers received. The traditional defined benefit pension had arisen in the heavy manufacturing industries, and it still is the predominant retirement plan in many firms in this sector of the economy. The service sector, arriving at the table later and with a different set of employment issues, had always depended somewhat more heavily on defined contribution plans. As jobs have shifted across sectors of the economy, the characteristics of plan coverage have followed. Various studies have attributed from 15 percent to 50 percent of the decline in defined benefit funds to this structural shift in the economy.

A second set of explanations holds that the change in choice of pension plans was caused by some combination of public policies that tended to make defined benefit plans less attractive or defined contribution plans more attractive. For example, one argument is that the administrative burdens imposed by the regulatory environment have fallen disproportionately on defined benefit plans. Between 1981 and 1996 administrative costs of small defined benefit plans increased by 218 percent, whereas those of comparable defined contribution plans went up only 109 percent. For large plans, the comparable increases were 193 percent and 91 percent, respectively. The administrative costs associated with a defined benefit plan with fifteen participants in 1996 were estimated to be more than twice as expensive as for a comparable defined contribution plan. For plans with 10,000 participants, the differential was 39 percent.[47]

In addition to the indirect costs associated with administering defined benefit plans, the evolution of the Pension Benefit Guaranty Corporation has also created some significant direct costs for sponsors not borne by defined contribution plans. When ERISA originally established the PBGC, it set the "premiums" to support the insurance program at $1 for each participant in a plan. By the mid-1980s that premium had risen to $8.50. Then, the termination of three large pension plans in the steel industry and another large plan in the farm implement industry confirmed the need for a higher premium rate overall and demonstrated the desirability of a variable premium rate because of the variability in the risks posed by different plans. The Omnibus Budget Reconciliation Act of 1987 increased the minimum premium to $16 per participant and created a variable rate premium based on the level of funding in the plan, but capped the variable premium at $34. In 1990 the base premium was raised to $19 per participant and the variable premium was capped at $53. In 1994 the cap on the variable premium was removed. The insurance program today costs significantly more than originally envisaged. Since defined contribution plans have no need for insurance against not receiving the promised benefits, the premiums are a cost borne only by defined benefit plans, which further tilts the playing field toward defined contribution sponsorship.

Different tax treatment of the two kinds of plans has also encouraged the shift toward defined contribution plans. In defined contribution plans, benefits

47. Hustead (1998, p. 171).

can be fully funded on a tax-preferred basis as they accrue. As the earlier discussion showed, however, the funding limits clearly do not permit the funding of the full benefit obligations accruing for younger workers under ongoing defined benefit plans.[48] The delay in funding of defined benefit obligations denies plan sponsors some of the tax benefits they can realize with defined contribution plans.

A final concern revolves around the effect of the contribution holidays that many firms enjoyed during the late 1980s and into the 1990s because of the changing regulatory environment and the booming stock markets. These contribution holidays may ultimately prove to be a "narcotic" that will be the death knell for some defined benefit plans.[49] It is one thing for a company to see its annual contributions to its pension program rising by a couple of percentage points from a starting contribution level of 5 or 6 percent of payroll over a decade as its work force ages. It is quite another to have the contribution rate jump from nothing for several years to 7 or 8 percent of payroll. That is the impact that the contribution holidays will have on many plans. With such precipitous changes in plan funding requirements, some sponsors simply will not continue to support their plans at their current levels of generosity.

The overall effect of the various changes in the regulatory environment affecting pensions was predictable. In 1989 I said that the legislative changes and the resulting "deferral of funding will result in benefit reductions for future retirees."[50] In a similar vein I observed in 1990:

> As we move through the 1990s and into the next century, the delays in pension funding are going to have to be made up if the benefit promises now implied by the benefit formulas are to be met. The important question that will remain unanswered is whether or not employers will be able to play catch-up to the extent the current law implies. The alternative will be that employers will have to reduce their future benefit promises, which they can do in a number of ways, many of them subtle.[51]

In a paper first presented in fall 1993, John Shoven and I pointed out that "benefit reductions to bring plans back into balance in relation to current funding rates could occur relatively late in workers' careers, when the heaviest accrual of benefits under defined-benefit plans occurs." We showed that it was not uncommon in typical defined benefit plans that as much as 40 percent of benefits could be earned during the last quarter, or even less, of a worker's career. It was possible, we said, that "many plan sponsors could readily achieve the savings needed to bring benefit promises into balance with current funding rates by curtailing their defined-benefit plans when the baby boomers were within a decade

48. Ippolito (1997, pp. 159–64).
49. For example, see Schieber and Graig (1994, p. 29).
50. Schieber (1989, p. 32).
51. Schieber (1990, p. 24).

of their anticipated retirement dates."[52] They could do so by substituting lower-cost defined benefit or defined contribution plans.

These predictions seem to be coming true. A recent spate of articles in the national press has reported that some employers are converting their traditional defined benefit plans to an alternative form of plan called "cash balance" plans. These plans are defined benefit plans for funding purposes, but they appear to be defined contribution plans from the perspective of their participants. In these plans the worker has a notional account that is credited with a contribution and an interest accrual each year. Each year the employee receives a statement that reports the accumulated value of the cash value of the notional account. At termination the participants are typically offered a lump-sum distribution option, and anecdotal evidence suggests that the overwhelming majority take their benefits in this form. Much of the press about these plans has been quite negative, because it seems that some employers are using the conversion to save money while curtailing benefits for workers in mid-career.[53]

Much of the media discussion about cash balance plans has been misleading in its suggestion that the only reason for converting to this style of plan is to reduce pension costs; some cash balance plans have actually increased pension cost for their sponsors. It is clear, however, that some traditional plans have been shifted to the cash balance form of benefit accrual because of cost considerations. The cost savings realized in the shift away from the traditional form of defined benefit plan have been achieved by reducing benefit accruals in many cases, and in some instances these reductions have been particularly heavy for baby boom workers. But the shift to cash balance plans is only one symptom of an ailing defined benefit system that is shrinking at a faster and faster rate. From 1980 to 1985 the number of workers participating in defined benefit plans declined at a rate of 0.75 percent a year. From 1985 to 1990 the rate of decline was 1.96 percent a year, and from 1990 to 1995, it was 2.28 percent a year.[54] Indeed, the data suggest that many defined benefit plans have been terminated completely in recent years, and it is not clear that comparable defined contribution plans have replaced them in many cases.

Although every case is unique, the shrinkage of defined benefit plan coverage, whether through plan terminations or plan downsizing, is hardly surprising given the radical shifts in the economics of sponsoring a pension plan—especially a defined benefit plan—since the passage of ERISA. The ultimate irony of the conduct of pension policy over the last quarter century may be that all the

52. Schieber and Shoven (1997, p. 243).

53. For example, see Ellen E. Schultz and Elizabeth MacDonald, "Retirement Wrinkle: Employers Win Big with a Pension Shift; Employees Often Lose—'Cash Balance' Plans Save Firms Millions but Hide Pitfalls for Their Workers—A Staffer Who Did the Math," *Wall Street Journal,* December 4, 1998, pp. A1, A6.

54. Derived from U.S. Department of Labor (1999, p. 71).

efforts to enhance retirement security could actually end up reducing the retirement security of the baby boom generation. The baby boomers would be the first generation of workers to have spent virtually their whole careers under the highly regulated retirement system that exists in the United States today.

References

Achenbaum, W. Andrew. 1978. *Old Age in the New Land: The American Experience since 1970.* Johns Hopkins University Press.

Blum, Walter J. 1955. "The Effects of Special Provisions in the Income Tax on Taxpayer Morale." In U.S. Congress, Joint Economic Committee, *Federal Tax Policy for Economic Growth and Stability.* Paper submitted to the Subcommittee on Tax Policy. 84 Cong., 1 sess., pp. 251–60. Government Printing Office.

Committee on Economic Security. 1937. *Social Security in America.* GPO.

Folsom, Marion B. 1970. Oral History Collection, Columbia University, Oral History Research Office.

Graebner, William. 1980. *A History of Retirement: The Meaning and Function of an American Institution.* Yale University Press.

Greenough, William C. 1990. *It's My Retirement Money—Take Good Care of It: The TIAA-CREF Story.* Homewood, Ill.: Irwin.

Hannah, Leslie. 1986. *Inventing Retirement: The Development of Occupational Pensions in Britain.* Cambridge University Press.

Hustead, Edwin C. 1998. "Trends in Retirement Income Plan Administrative Expenses." In *Living with Defined Contribution Pensions: Remaking Responsibility for Retirement,* edited by Olivia S. Mitchell and Sylvester J. Schieber, 166–77. University of Pennsylvania Press.

Ippolito, Richard A. 1997. *Pension Plans and Employee Performance: Evidence, Analysis, and Policy.* University of Chicago Press.

James, Ralph C., and Estelle D. James. 1965. *Hoffa and the Teamsters: A Study of Union Power.* Princeton, N.J.: Van Nostrand.

Latimer, Murray Webb. 1932. *Industrial Pension Systems in the United States and Canada.* New York: Industrial Relations Counselors, Inc.

McGill, Dan M. 1955, 1979. *Fundamentals of Private Pensions,* 1st and 4th eds. Homewood, Ill.: Irwin.

McGill, Dan M., and others. 1996. *The Fundamentals of Private Pensions,* 7th ed. University of Pennsylvania Press.

Sass, Steven A. 1997. *The Promise of Private Pensions: The First Hundred Years.* Harvard University Press.

Schieber, Sylvester J. 1984. "The Evolution of U.S. Pension Policy in the Context of Tax Considerations." *Tax Memorandum* 25 (19): 235–45.

———. 1989. "Retirement System Outlook for the 1990s." Speech presented at a conference on "1990 and Beyond: Employee Benefits," sponsored by Women in Employee Benefits (later changed to Workers in Employee Benefits), Washington, November 6.

———. 1990. "Prepared Statement before the Subcommittee on Retirement Income and Employment." U.S. House of Representatives, Select Committee on Aging, July 27.

———. 1993. "Letter to the President." *Insider* (publication of Watson Wyatt Worldwide) 3 (April): 1–9.

Schieber, Sylvester J., and Patricia M. George. 1981. *Retirement Income Opportunities in an Aging America: Coverage and Benefit Entitlement.* Washington: Employee Benefit Research Institute.

Schieber, Sylvester J., and Laurene A. Graig. 1994. *U.S. Retirement Policy: The Sleeping Giant Awakens.* Washington: Watson Wyatt Worldwide.

Schieber, Sylvester J., and Marjorie M. Kulash. 1995. "Excess Pension Asset Transfers." Policy paper prepared for the Association of Private Pension and Welfare Plans, Washington (October).

Schieber, Sylvester J., and John B. Shoven. 1997. "The Consequences of Population Aging on Private Pension Fund Saving and Asset Markets." In *Public Policy towards Pensions,* edited by Sylvester J. Schieber and John B. Shoven, 219–46. MIT Press.

———. 1999. *The Real Deal: The History and Future of Social Security.* Yale University Press.

Schulz, James H., and Thomas D. Leavitt. 1983. *Pension Integration: Concepts, Issues, and Proposals.* Washington: Employee Benefit Research Institute.

U.S. Census Bureau. 1975. *Historical Statistics of the United States.* GPO.

———. 1980, 1982. *Statistical Abstract of the United States.* GPO.

U.S. Congress. Joint Committee on Taxation. 1980. *Estimates of Federal Tax Expenditures for Fiscal Years 1980–1985.* Joint Committee Print JCS8-80. Prepared for the Committee on Ways and Means and the Committee on Finance. GPO.

U.S. Department of Labor, Pension and Welfare Benefits Administration, Office of Policy and Research. 1999. *Private Pension Plan Bulletin* 8 (Spring).

U.S. Office of Management and Budget. 1999. *Historical Tables, Budget of the United States Government, Fiscal Year 2000.* GPO.

———. Various years, 1980–89. *Special Analyses, Budget of the United States Government.* GPO.

Watson Wyatt Worldwide. Various years. Survey of Actuarial Assumptions and Funding. Bethesda, Md.

Wilkin, John C., Ronald V. Gresch, and Milton P. Glanz. 1982. "Growth in Fringe Benefits." *Actuarial Note 113.* Social Security Administration, Office of the Chief Actuary (June).

3

The Shifting Structure of Private Pensions

WILLIAM G. GALE, LESLIE E. PAPKE,
AND JACK VANDERHEI

S ince the passage of the Employee Retirement Income Security Act in 1974, the private pension system has evolved along several dimensions. The single largest change has been a move away from defined benefit plans toward defined contribution plans. A second change has occurred within the universe of defined contribution plans, where 401(k) plans have emerged as the dominant form over the past twenty years. A third shift has occurred among the remaining defined benefit plans, a substantial number of which were converted to cash balance plans beginning in the mid-1990s.

These changes have drastically altered the nature of private pensions, creating a new set of opportunities and risks for workers and firms. As a result, the changes have generated expressions of both enthusiasm and concern from policymakers and participants. Some view these changes as saving the pension system, others view them as the death knell for pensions.

This paper explores several issues surrounding the changing structure of pensions. We begin by describing and contrasting the salient features of alternative types of pensions. We then document the shifting composition of pensions, investigate the extent to which new pension forms have supplemented or

We thank Brennan Kelly, Tats Kanenari, and Samara Potter for outstanding research assistance. Gale gratefully acknowledges support from the National Institute on Aging through grant number AG11836.

supplanted previously existing plans, and examine the causes and consequences of these shifts.

Alternative Pension Arrangements

In a traditional defined benefit plan, employers promise to pay a certain annual pension benefit at retirement.[1] The benefit is usually determined by a formula that depends on years of service and average salary over either the highest salary years or the final years of employment. The benefits accrued by an employee are often very low, or zero, for the first few years of the work relationship. Then, at some point the employee becomes vested and a basic level of benefits is established; after that, benefits often rise rapidly as the employee's salary and tenure with the firm continue to grow. This pattern of accrual of benefits is referred to as back-loaded, because the employee is not eligible for much of the benefit until he or she has been with the employer for some time.

The employer funds these benefits by making pre-tax contributions into a pension fund for all participants. In private sector plans, participants typically do not make contributions, though in public sector plans they often do. The employer owns the assets in the fund, directs the investments, and bears the investment risk. The Pension Benefit Guaranty Corporation (PBGC), a government agency, guarantees the benefits within limits and charges plans insurance premiums intended to cover the agency's expected costs. Benefits are often paid as an annuity, and employees typically do not have access to funds before retirement. In the event of job separation before retirement, vested benefits are usually frozen at their accrued nominal (not inflation-adjusted) levels. If the employee dies, some limited survivor annuity for the spouse is often available.

Defined contribution plans come in several varieties, each of which is quite different from defined benefit plans. Employees typically make contributions. In a 401(k) plan, the most common form of defined contribution plan, employee contributions are tax deductible. Rules regarding employer contributions vary depending on the type of defined contribution plan. Under money purchase plans, employers promise to make specified annual contributions, usually as a function of a worker's salary. Profit-sharing plans, including 401(k) plans, allow employers to vary the level of contributions on an annual basis (including zero contributions in some years), as long as the contributions are substantial and recurrent. Many firms match some percentage of employee contributions up to a specified percentage of wages.

The amount of resources available in retirement depends on the amounts contributed over the years and the investment return. Balances accrue in

---

1. There are many variations on each basic type of plan design. We will focus throughout the paper on typical formulations of each type of plan.

accounts belonging to individual workers, who almost always are able to direct the investments for employee contributions and may be allowed to direct the investments for employer contributions. Regardless of who directs the investments, the employee bears the risk of fluctuating asset values. Benefits can be paid as a lump sum or an annuity. Employees often have access to funds before retirement through loans or hardship withdrawals. In the event of early separation, workers typically have the option of rolling the funds into an individual retirement account (IRA) or cashing in the balances, subject to income taxes and penalties.

Benefits tend to be less back-loaded in defined contribution plans than in defined benefit plans. That is, they accrue more evenly over time for two reasons: vesting usually occurs sooner in defined contribution plans, and contributions typically remain the same fraction of earnings over time.

Even this short description suggests that traditional defined benefit and defined contribution plans differ in important ways and are likely to appeal to different types of workers and firms. Workers in defined benefit plans do not have to make decisions regarding participation, contribution levels, asset allocation, or the timing and nature of withdrawals, and they do not face direct investment risk. In addition, a large fraction of defined benefit pension benefits are guaranteed by the PBGC. In contrast, workers in defined contribution plans often must make active choices regarding participation, contributions, asset allocations, and withdrawals. Benefits in defined contribution plans are not guaranteed by the PBGC, and the worker bears all of the risks created by fluctuations in the market value of the account.

In traditional defined benefit plans, benefits are illiquid before retirement—employees do not have the option of cashing in funds before they reach retirement age.[2] A worker who leaves a job before retirement will find that benefits from a defined benefit program are frozen at nominal levels and typically are not portable across job changes. The benefit formulas may be difficult for workers to understand, and workers who make several job changes may be penalized significantly when the benefits are heavily back-loaded.

In contrast, defined contribution plans provide workers with more liquidity before retirement—workers can cash out the funds, subject to income taxes and penalties—and the funds are portable. Workers who leave jobs with defined contribution plans may often leave the funds at the old employer, where they may continue to grow, or they can roll the funds over into an IRA or the new employer's pension. Benefit accrual is generally easier to understand in a defined contribution plan, and such plans are typically less back-loaded, thus reducing the penalty associated with shorter tenure.

---

2. However, an employer has the right to unilaterally cash out a defined benefit pension balance that has accrued less than $5,000.

Table 3-1. *Features of Alternative Employer-Sponsored Retirement Plans*

Feature	Defined benefit plan (DB)	Defined contribution plan (DC)	Hybrid plan (tendency)
Employer contributes	Virtually always	Sometimes	Virtually always (DB)
Employee contributes	Very rarely	Virtually always	Very rarely (DB)
Participation	Automatic	Employee's choice	Automatic (DB)
Contribution level	Automatic	Employee's choice	Automatic (DB)
PBGC insurance	Yes but capped	Not needed	Yes but capped (DB)
Early departure penalty	Yes	No	No (DC)
Benefits easily portable	No	Yes	Yes (DC)
Annual communication	Benefit at end of career	Current balance	Current balance (DC)
Retirement incentives	Occur at specific ages	Neutral	Most are neutral (DC)
Accrual of benefits	Loaded to end of career	Level over career	Level or back-loaded (mixed)
Financial market risks	Employer bears	Employee bears	Shared (mixed)
Longevity insurance	Typically yes	Typically no	Not often taken (mixed)

Source: Clark and Schieber (2004).

Traditional defined benefit plans offer firms the ability to structure compensation—through pension accrual patterns—to encourage job retention at some points in the career and job departure at other points, but the plans are typically costly to administer. The typical defined contribution benefit profile presents fewer opportunities than defined benefit plans to structure benefits to encourage employee retention or retirement, but the plans may be cheaper to administer.

These trade-offs have led to the development of so-called hybrid pensions, which combine features of both defined benefit and defined contribution plans (see table 3-1). Cash balance plans are one type of hybrid plan. Legally, cash balance plans are defined benefit plans. As in a traditional defined benefit plan, in a typical cash balance plan the employer contributes funds into a general fund for all employees, owns the assets, makes the investment choices, and bears the investment risk. Pension benefits are guaranteed within limits by the PBGC.

But from an employee's perspective, cash balance plans share several features with defined contribution plans. Benefit accruals depend on annual pay credits and annual interest credits. Because benefits are a function of annual pay over the employee's entire career with the employer, cash balance plans are typically less back-loaded than traditional defined benefit plans. Benefits may be paid as a lump sum or can be annuitized. If the employee leaves the firm early, the funds may be cashed out, possibly transferred to a new employer plan, or rolled over to an IRA. Accruing benefits are reported to employees in periodic individual statements that resemble the statement one would receive from a defined contribution plan

Even so, workers will notice differences between defined contribution plans and cash balance plans. Funds in cash balance plans are typically less accessible than those in defined contribution plans for workers who remain on the job. The plan sponsor chooses how to invest the pooled pension assets and receives the return on those investments, which is unrelated to the return on the individual accounts.

The future of cash balance plans is currently unclear. Federal courts recently ruled that the cash balance plans introduced at IBM and Xerox were discriminatory on the basis of age.[3] The ruling may cause all existing cash balance plans to be viewed as discriminatory. Legal appeals and bills in Congress are pending on this issue.

Trends

Since 1974 pensions have shifted dramatically away from defined benefit plans and toward defined contribution plans. Table 3-2 shows that the number of defined benefit plans rose from about 103,000 in 1975 to 148,000 in 1985 and then fell to 56,000 by 1998.[4] Much of this change in number of defined benefit plans reflects a significant decline in such plans among small employers, but the number of large plans fell as well.[5] In contrast, the number of defined contribution plans more than tripled from 1975 to 1998, with the number of both large and small plans growing rapidly over this period.

Table 3-2 also shows that active participation in defined benefit plans changed by much smaller relative amounts than the number of defined benefit plans did. The number of active participants in defined benefit plans rose from 27 million in 1975 to just over 30 million in the early 1980s and then fell to just under 23 million in 1998, even though aggregate employment grew by 23 percent between 1985 and 1998. In contrast, active participation in defined contribution plans grew rapidly, from 11 million in 1975 to 50 million in 1998, and participation in both large and small plans rose.[6]

3. Mary Williams Walsh, "Judge Says I.B.M. Pension Shift Illegally Harmed Older Workers," *New York Times,* August 1, 2003, p. 1.

4. One handicap of using the official Department of Labor data is that the information is reported with sizable lags.

5. The number of defined benefit plans with fewer than 100 participants rose from about 83,000 in 1975 to 145,000 in 1985, but then fell to 41,000 by 1998. Larger defined benefit plans followed similar but more muted patterns, rising from 20,000 in 1975 to almost 25,000 in 1985 before declining to 15,000 by 1998 (U.S. Department of Labor 2001–02).

6. Note that workers may participate in more than one plan.

Table 3-2. *The Transition to Defined Contribution Plans*[a]

Year and item	Total	Definted benefit plans	Defined contribution plans	401(k) Plans	Definted benefit share of total (percent)	401(k) share of defined contri- bution (percent)
1975						
Number of plans	311,094	103,346	207,748		33.2	
Active participants (thousands)	38,431	27,214	11,217		70.8	
Plan assets (nominal $ millions)	259,963	185,950	74,013		71.5	
Plan assets (1998 $ millions)	787,620	563,380	224,240		71.5	
Contributions (nom- inal $ millions)	37,061	24,242	12,819		65.4	
Contributions (1998 $ millions)	112,285	73,447	38,838		65.4	
1985						
Number of plans	632,135	170,172	461,963	29,869	26.9	6.5
Active participants (thousands)	62,268	29,024	33,244	10,339	46.6	31.1
Plan assets (nominal $ millions)	1,252,739	826,117	426,622	143,939	65.9	33.7
Plan assets (1998 $ millions)	1,897,737	1,251,460	646,277	218,049	65.9	33.7
Contributions (nom- inal $ millions)	95,188	41,996	53,192	24,322	44.1	45.7
Contributions (1998 $ millions)	144,197	63,618	80,579	36,845	44.1	45.7
1998						
Number of plans	730,031	56,405	673,626	300,593	7.7	44.6
Active participants (thousands)	73,329	22,994	50,335	37,114	31.4	73.7
Plan assets (1998 $ millions)	4,021,850	1,936,600	2,085,250	1,540,975	48.2	73.9
Contributions (1998 $ millions)	201,885	34,985	166,900	134,659	17.3	80.7

Sources: U.S. Department of Labor (2001–02, tables E1, E8, E11, E14, E23).

a. Contributions and assets are adjusted to 1998 dollars using the CPI-U. See *Economic Report of the President,* table B-60, p. 345.

The massive shift toward defined contribution plans is further reflected in the growth of contributions and assets by pension type (see table 3-2). All told, in 1975 defined benefit plans dominated the pension system, accounting for roughly two-thirds of active participants, contributions, and assets. By 1998 defined contribution plans accounted for two-thirds of participants, three-fourths of contributions, and half of all pension assets.

401(k) plans have dominated the growth within defined contribution plans. Although authorized in 1978, 401(k)s did not become popular until the Internal Revenue Service (IRS) issued clarifying regulations in 1981. The growth in 401(k) plans is illustrated in table 3-2. Almost all of the net growth in the number of defined contribution plans between 1984 and 1998 was due to 401(k)s. By 1998, 401(k)s accounted for 44 percent of defined contribution plans and for about three-fourths of active participants, contributions, and assets in those plans.

It is more difficult to obtain systematic information on the trend within defined benefit plans toward cash balance plans. Until 1999 plan sponsors filing information with federal regulators did not have to provide sufficient information to identify cash balance plans, and such data are not yet publicly available. The first cash balance plan was created by BankAmerica in 1985, but the plans did not appear to attract much general interest at that time. By the late 1990s, however, cash balance plans had grown significantly. VanDerhei has summarized findings from a survey of the principal salaried retirement programs of about 1,000 major U.S. employers, in which the proportion of very large defined benefit plans that were cash balance plans rose from 6 percent in 1995 to 16 percent in 1999.[7] Data from the Department of Labor show that by 2000, about 23 percent of all workers covered by a defined benefit plan in fact had a cash balance plan, up from 4 percent in 1996–97.[8] A survey by *Pensions and Investments* magazine found that at least 325 large companies with at least $334 billion in defined benefit assets (about 15 percent of all defined benefit assets) had converted to cash balance plans.

Are the New Plans Adding to or Replacing Existing Pensions?

A key issue in assessing the changing structure of pensions is the extent to which the newly created plans represent net additions to the stock of existing pension plans or merely the substitution of one form of pension for another. Substitution at the firm level could occur through several different channels. Firms could terminate a plan and create a new one. A less drastic action would be to

7. VanDerhei (1999).
8. www.bls.gov/ncs/ebs/sp/ebrp0001.pdf.

Figure 3-1. *Private Sector Participation Rates under Primary and Supplemental Pensions Plans, 1975–98*

Percent

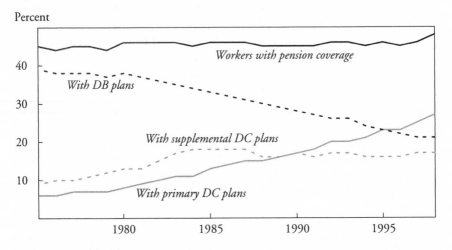

Source: U.S. Department of Labor (2001–02).

convert an existing plan to a new form. We refer to either of these options as pension replacement. In addition, however, firms could also retain, but essentially freeze, their existing pensions and put all new resources into the new plan; this would represent substitution of the new plan for the old one at the margin, even though the old plan would continue to exist. Substitution could also occur in the sense that some new plans may be established at firms that would have created other pensions if the new option had not existed.

We discuss evidence on these issues from a variety of sources: aggregate coverage rates, plan-level studies, and plan creation dates. Although the evidence is mixed, on balance the data suggest that a very significant amount of new plan creation has substituted for previously existing pensions rather than added to the net stock of pensions.

Figure 3-1 shows that the proportion of private wage and salary workers with pension coverage remained remarkably stable at around 45 percent between 1975 and 1998. However, the nature of the primary pension changed dramatically.[9] The proportion of workers with primary defined benefit coverage fell from 39 percent in 1975 to 21 percent in 1998. The proportion with defined

9. In discussing pension coverage rates, we follow the Department of Labor in classifying any defined benefit plan as the primary plan and any accompanying defined contribution plan for the same worker as a secondary plan. A defined contribution plan is considered the primary plan only if the worker has no defined benefit plan with the current employer.

contribution primary coverage rose by an almost identical amount, from 6 percent in 1975 to 27 percent in 1998. These data present a prima facie case for pension substitution among primary pension plans. In addition, supplemental defined contribution coverage doubled, from 9 percent to 17 percent of the work force.

To gain further insight, it is useful to look separately at trends from 1975 to 1985 and from 1985 to 1998. In the first period, defined benefit coverage fell by about 6 percentage points of the work force, but primary defined contribution coverage rose by 7 percentage points and supplemental defined contribution coverage rose by 9 percentage points. Thus, a little more than half of the increase in defined contribution coverage was due to supplemental coverage. This suggests that defined contribution plans were, from an aggregate perspective, both supplanting defined benefit plans (in the sense that the rise in defined contribution plans offset the decline in defined benefit plans) and also supplementing them (in the sense that there were additional supplementary defined contribution plans as well).

After 1985 the patterns change. During this period, defined benefit coverage fell by 12 percentage points of the work force. Primary defined contribution coverage rose by 14 percentage points, and supplemental defined contribution coverage actually fell by 1 percentage point. Thus, the reduction in defined benefit coverage was offset by a rise in defined contribution coverage, and the change in supplemental coverage is of little importance. These aggregate patterns suggest that there was significantly more substitution of defined contribution for defined benefit plans in the second period than in the first.

Microeconomic studies of pension replacement at the plan level generally reflect the differences found in the aggregate data for the two time periods. Kruse matched data from pension plan sponsors in 1980 and 1986 to study adoptions and terminations of different types of plans and to estimate the number of employees involved.[10] His general conclusion is that the growth in defined contribution participation during this period was primarily supplemental to defined benefit plans and did not substitute for defined benefit plans. This is consistent with the finding above that most new defined contribution plans during this period were not replacing defined benefit plans.

Results are somewhat mixed in the period since 1985, but overall they suggest significantly more substitution between defined benefit and defined contribution plans. Papke examines all employers that offered at least one defined benefit plan in 1985 and compares their pension offerings in 1985 and 1992.[11] She finds significant firm-level substitution between 401(k)s and defined benefit plans, between 401(k)s and non-401(k) defined contribution plans, and

10. Kruse (1995).
11. Papke (1999).

between non-401(k) defined contribution plans and defined benefit plans. She finds that 20 percent of ongoing sponsors dropped defined benefit plans entirely, in favor of defined contribution plans.

Papke, Petersen, and Poterba examine patterns of pension plan substitution in the later period using a direct survey of forty-three pension plan sponsors.[12] In this survey 45 percent of responding firms, representing 37 percent of 401(k) participants in the survey, indicate that another pension plan was converted to the 401(k). The survey also found that one large pension plan sponsor—accounting for 17 percent of participants—reported a termination of a defined benefit pension plan as a result of the introduction of a 401(k) plan between 1986 and 1990. In total, then, about 54 percent of participants in the sample had their pension plan replaced by a 401(k) plan.

In contrast to these findings, Ippolito and Thompson examine survival rates for 249 large defined benefit plans from 1987 to 1995.[13] After carefully tracking the history of these plans, they find that about 7 percent of the plans were converted to defined contribution plans—presumably 401(k)s—over this period. Although their estimate is lower than that reported by Papke, Ippolito and Thompson focus on a more specialized and perhaps less representative sample, and do not include analysis of conversion of other defined contribution plans to 401(k)s. Their estimate is not inconsistent with the results for defined benefit plans obtained by Papke, Petersen, and Poterba.

Poterba, Venti, and Wise find that a large fraction of new 401(k) enrollees retained defined benefit coverage.[14] This is consistent with little substitution between defined benefit plans and 401(k) plans. But it is also consistent with a scenario where firms substitute 401(k) plans on the margin for defined benefit plan improvements, as discussed below. They also find that the average annual saving rate under a typical 401(k) plan is about twice as large as the average saving rate under a typical defined benefit plan. Taken at face value, this suggests that not all 401(k)s can be substituting for previously existing defined benefit plans. At the same time, 401(k) contributions are more heavily weighted toward higher-income households than are defined benefit contributions, which complicates the interpretation of the result.

A third source of information on pension substitution comes from the reported dates of creation of various plans. As noted above, 401(k) plans proliferated after the IRS clarified its regulations in 1981. Before 401(k) plans came into existence, so-called thrift plans typically supplemented defined benefit plans. Thrifts allowed tax-deductible employer contributions, but employee contributions were made from after-tax income. When 401(k) plans—which

12. Papke, Petersen, and Poterba (1996).
13. Ippolito and Thompson (2000).
14. Poterba, Venti, and Wise (2001b).

permitted tax-deductible contributions by both the worker and firm—became available, many thrift plans were converted to 401(k)s. The 401(k) plans that result from conversion retain the creation date of the original thrift plan. We compare these dates in order to put a lower bound on the number of 401(k) plans that were replacing early defined contribution plans.

Of the roughly 200,000 401(k) plans in existence in 1995, 24,000 were created before 1979 and therefore are converted defined contribution plans. In addition, a large fraction of the almost 19,000 plans that report formation between 1980 and 1984 probably also represent conversions. Depending on the proportion of plans created in 1985–89 that were converted thrifts, by 1989 between 23 percent and 41 percent of all 401(k) plans had been converted from previously existing plans.[15]

All of the analysis above focuses on pension substitution that occurs by terminating or converting a previously existing plan. However, another alternative is that firms freeze their existing plans and instead pour marginal resources into new pensions. This would represent substitution of one pension for another at the margin but would not show up clearly in the studies described above. For example, in 1998 the state of Michigan allowed its employees to choose between the existing defined benefit plan and a new defined contribution plan. All employees hired after 1998 could participate only in the defined contribution plan.[16]

It is very difficult to obtain strong evidence on the extent to which substitution at the margin has occurred, but some suggestive evidence indicates that conversion at the margin could be widespread. VanDerhei and Olsen show that between 1985 and 1993, employers' contributions to defined contribution plans increased relative to defined benefit plans significantly more than could be explained by employment shifts since 1985.[17] Less formally, in congressional testimony on behalf of the American Savings Education Council, IBM official Donald Sauvigne noted in 1997 that IBM corporation "reduced the value of our defined benefit plan . . . yet reaffirmed its role as our base foundation retirement vehicle. Correspondingly, we increased the match in our 401(k) plan . . . and thereby rebalanced the scale of responsibility with a greater employee partnership in sharing long-term financial responsibility."[18] It is not implausible to believe that many other large firms have followed the same course.

---

15. U.S. Department of Labor (1999). A number of studies have reached similar conclusions. A survey by Buck Consultants (1989) finds that about a third of 401(k) plans were converted thrifts, and Andrews (1992) confirms this figure with Form 5500 filings. Engen, Gale, and Scholz (1996a, b) cite data from the 5500 Forms indicating that even by 1991 a large proportion of the plans and assets in 401(k)s were from plans originated before 1982.

16. Papke (2003).

17. Olsen and VanDerhei (1997).

18. Sauvigne (1997).

Although there is little systematic information on cash balance plans, all evidence to date suggests that cash balance plans came into existence through conversions of existing defined benefit plans. Thus, whether cash balance plans are substituting for existing plans or supplementing them depends on whether it is thought that the firm would have retained the original defined benefit plan or abolished it in the absence of the cash balance option. It is true that defined benefit coverage rates have declined among large firms in recent years, which suggests the possibility that large defined benefit plans may be terminated. At the same time, it is difficult to believe that the many large firms converting to cash balance plans would have simply abolished their defined benefit plans in the absence of cash balance option, which suggests that cash balance plans are usually substituting for existing plans.

Causes

Shifts in the composition of pensions have been attributed to supply-side factors—such as the changing composition of the work force across industries, government regulations and tax laws, and the effects of 401(k) plans on firms' ability to attract desirable workers—and to demand-side factors—such as increased job mobility among workers and changes in workers' preferences independent of the labor market. No single explanation is wholly satisfying. All of these factors have likely played some role. In this section we survey the key arguments.

Historically, defined benefit plans have been most prevalent in manufacturing and other "heavy" industries populated with large firms and unionized work forces. In contrast, defined contribution plans have tended to be relatively more prevalent in service industries and nonunionized industries. Thus, an obvious candidate cause for the shift from defined benefit to defined contribution plans is that the structure of the economic activity has changed, causing changes in the allocation of workers across industries.

Indeed, industrial shifts can account for a significant component of the shift toward defined contribution plans, although certainly not all of it. Clark and McDermed find that 20 percent of the decline in the defined benefit coverage rate between 1979 and 1983 can be explained by changes in the size and industrial distributions of firms.[19] Gustman and Steinmeier show that shifts in union status, firm size, and industry explain at least half of the trend toward defined contribution plans between 1977 and 1985.[20] Ippolito uses a similar procedure with improved data on union status and finds that half of the loss in defined benefit coverage between 1979 and 1987 is due to employment shifts.[21]

19. Clark and McDermed (1990).
20. Gustman and Steinmeier (1992).
21. Ippolito (1995).

Notably, all of these findings focus on the period ending roughly around 1985. As discussed above, pension patterns appear to have changed dramatically after that year.

Government regulations are another plausible candidate for causing the shift toward defined contribution plans. Government regulation of defined benefit plans is thought to be more onerous than that of defined contribution plans. This is especially true for plans with fewer than 100 employees. Cost differences between the two types of pensions for plans with more than 100 employees are small.[22] In addition, a government agency guarantees benefits in defined benefit plans and requires firms to pay premiums to maintain the insurance, and the regulations for defined benefit plans impose a complicated set of minimum funding rules, maximum funding limitations, and other rules and regulations relating to pension investments. In contrast, defined contribution plans are by definition fully funded, and because the benefits are not insured, defined contribution plans do not pay insurance premiums. The fact that defined benefit coverage has fallen faster for small employers than for large employers is consistent with regulations affecting plan type.

Further evidence is presented by Clark and McDermed, who estimate the determinants of plan choice using household data from the Survey of Consumer Finances in 1983.[23] They use the estimates, coupled with information on households surveyed in the 1979 and 1983 Current Population Surveys, to show that the predicted change in defined benefit coverage between 1979 and 1983 attributable to changes in economic and demographic variables is essentially zero. They conclude that the vast portion of the shift toward defined contribution plans during this period therefore must be due to regulation.

Still, the role of regulation in causing the shift in plan choice can be overstated. At the very least, it should be noted that the basic trend toward defined contribution plans was in place for a long time before 1974 (and ERISA). Clark and McDermed examine, among the set of plans started in different time periods and still in effect in 1985, the proportion that were defined contribution plans.[24] They report this figure as 10.4 percent for plans started before 1941. The figure rises to 16.8 percent for plans started in 1942–53, 24.8 percent for plans started in 1954–63, 31.3 percent for plans started between 1964–73, 47.4 percent for plans started between 1974–79, and 60 percent for plans started in 1980–85. Thus, ERISA may have accelerated the shift toward defined contribution plans, but a secular shift appears to have been present even before ERISA.

A third factor encouraging the shift toward defined contribution plans has to do with their potential role in enhancing the quality of the labor force. Ippolito

22. Hustead (1998).
23. Clark and McDermed (1990).
24. Clark and McDermed (1990).

argues that 401(k) plans help firms attract and retain high-quality workers.[25] He argues that workers' underlying productivity is difficult to observe but is correlated negatively with their degree of patience. Patient employees are more likely to be more productive, for a variety of reasons, and are more likely to be willing to defer their compensation. By offering a 401(k) plan with a employer match, the firm defers compensation and thus offers higher compensation to workers who are willing to save more—that is, to those who are more patient. The presence of a lump sum, available upon job exit, will make job exit relatively more attractive for impatient workers, who tend to be less-productive workers. Ippolito offers a variety of evidence consistent with this view and argues that these factors help to explain the rise of defined contribution plans in general and 401(k) plans in particular.

All of these factors discussed explain why firms would increasingly want to supply defined contribution plans. There are at least three reasons offered for why workers might demand more defined contribution coverage. The first is a set of claims that the economy now features a more mobile labor force that has shorter job tenure and therefore values defined contribution plans more than defined benefit plans, due in part to the back-loading inherent in defined benefit pensions. This view suffers from the fact that changes in job tenure alone do not appear to be anywhere near large or persistent enough to justify the massive shift in pension composition displayed in table 3-2. Median tenure for all workers barely changed over a twenty-year period, from 5.0 years in 1983 to 4.7 years in 2002. Median tenure for men fell by 1 year during this period, but median tenure for women rose slightly.[26] These trends are simply not large enough to explain the shift in pension type.

A second potential factor is that there may have been systematic changes for other (as yet unspecified) reasons in workers' tastes for defined contribution plans relative to defined benefit plans. For example, workers may prefer the notion of individual accounts or the ability to direct their own investments. It is hard to assess the mix of taste factors that may have played some role in the shift from defined benefit plans toward defined contribution plans.

The third potential reason is disarmingly simple. The shift toward defined contribution plans is almost entirely a shift toward 401(k)-type plans, which feature tax-deductible employee contributions that are generally not available in other defined contribution or defined benefit plans. The presence of the deduction may well explain a significant amount of worker interest in the plans.

Within defined benefit plans, the shift toward cash balance plans is attributable to a number of factors. First, other than freezing a defined benefit plan and creating a new defined contribution plan, the transformation of a traditional

25. Ippolito (1998).
26. Copeland (2003).

defined benefit plan to a cash balance is the most straightforward way for a firm with a traditional plan to meet any increased employee demand for plans with defined contribution features. In particular, terminating the defined benefit plan would generate very costly taxes if the firm attempts to recapture any of the excess assets. Thus, a firm might find it prohibitively expensive to terminate a defined benefit plan and replace it with a defined contribution plan. The firm can avoid the tax if it converts the final average defined benefit plan to a cash balance plan, which looks like a defined contribution plan to workers.[27]

There are several other reasons, though, why a firm might create a cash balance plan. Some employers have coupled conversion to a cash balance plan with repeal of early retirement subsidies in traditional defined benefit plans, a move that is less transparent than simply repealing the subsidies. Other employers have simply restructured their entire benefit package toward provisions with defined contribution features, simultaneously converting the traditional plan to a cash balance plan, improving the defined contribution plan and/or moving to health accounts with defined contribution features.[28]

Consequences

The shift in the nature of pension saving in recent decades may have substantial effects on workers and firms.[29] For workers the principal issues concern the level and variability of retirement income, the liquidity of the pension funds, the costs of changing jobs, and the opaqueness of the plans. For firms the key issues involve the ability to match pension characteristics to the characteristics of their work force, the ability to provide incentives to encourage workers to stay or leave, and the level of administrative costs.

Defined Benefit versus Defined Contribution Plans

There is nothing inherently more generous about either a defined contribution or a defined benefit plan. Thus, differences in retirement income generated by one type of plan versus the other will occur only if households make systematically different decisions in one type of plan or if employers somehow are able to provide lower net benefits in one type of plan.

Ultimately, whether defined contribution pension plans offer a better or worse standard of living in retirement is an empirical question to which the answer may vary by individual and plan. The empirical literature has generated mixed results. One finding of note is that given the features of pension plans in the 1980s, pension rollover rates, and job turnover rates, defined contribution

27. Ippolito and Thompson (2000).
28. Clark and Schieber (2004).
29. Munnell and Sunden (2003a) provide a comprehensive discussion of the consequences of the shift to 401(k) plans.

plans in the 1980s could generate higher retirement income on average than defined benefit plans despite the possibility of leakage of funds from the defined contribution plans, because defined benefit plans penalize workers who change jobs frequently.[30] But a different study using data from the 1990s found that 401(k) plans were on balance less generous than defined benefit plans and non-401(k) defined contribution plans.[31] A third study found that if current 401(k) contribution patterns and historical rates of returns persist, future retirees will have substantially more retirement wealth relative to lifetime earnings than current generations do.[32]

These studies need to be interpreted cautiously, however, for at least three reasons. First, the studies model outcomes for workers who save and invest in a well-informed, optimal manner. This is not only inconsistent with observed behavior, it biases the results toward overstating income from defined contribution plans. The reason is that a principal difference between the two plan types is that a worker's financial choices play a key role in determining the ultimate benefits in a defined contribution plan. The worker decides whether to participate, how much to contribute (subject to maximum limits), how to invest the fund, whether to roll over or consume pre-retirement distributions when a job change occurs, whether to borrow from the fund (if that option is available), and whether to annuitize the fund at retirement. Compared with a defined benefit plan with the same present value of benefits—if the worker were to contribute throughout his or her career—a defined contribution plan presents many opportunities for workers not to contribute in the first place, for accumulated funds to leak out before the participant's retirement, and for payments to fall short before death. Thus, worker foresight, risk tolerance, and financial sophistication can make a huge difference in retirement income from a defined contribution plan, even among workers with the same lifetime wage profile.

In contrast, retirement income from a defined benefit plan depends on a worker's years of service and some measure of highest or career earnings, but not on the workers' investment acumen. Moreover, defined benefit plans generally provide fewer opportunities to withdraw funds before retirement, through either lump sum distributions or loans. In short, retirement income in a defined benefit plan depends hardly if at all on financial decisions made by the worker—other than the decision to stay with a firm.

These differences matter for determining the relative generosity of the two plan types because there is substantial evidence that many workers lack financial sophistication, fail to plan ahead for retirement, and are ill informed of the details of their pension, including even whether it is a defined benefit or a

---

30. Samwick and Skinner (1998).
31. Even and McPherson (1998).
32. Poterba, Venti, and Wise (1998).

defined contribution plan.[33] For defined contribution plans, these problems manifest themselves in low participation rates (relative to defined benefit plans),[34] low contributions, poorly diversified portfolios (including overinvestment in the employer's stock),[35] and pre-retirement withdrawals.[36]

A second reason to treat the studies with caution is that the plans tend to pay benefits in different forms. Defined benefit plans tend to pay benefits in the form of annuities. These payments are typically not adjusted for inflation, but people do receive the payments until their death. In contrast, defined contribution plans typically provide lump-sum payments, implying that workers run the risk of running out of funds. Thus, a simple comparison of income levels in the two types of plans omits the important increased risk of outliving one's resources that defined contribution participants face. Some of the studies attempt to adjust for this factor, but the correct adjustment is unclear.

A third reason the studies should be treated with caution is that comparisons of defined contribution and defined benefit plans should not focus only on how *current* practices affect retirement outcomes. Precisely because workers have more choices in defined contribution plans, policies that affect those choices can affect the retirement income from a defined contribution plan. Changes in the default options regarding whether workers are automatically signed up and can withdraw or have to actively choose to enroll can have substantial impacts on participation rates.[37] Increased financial education can have a significant effect

---

33. See Ameriks, Caplin, and Leahy (2003); Bayer, Bernheim, and Scholz (1996); Bernheim and Garrett (1996); Bernheim, Garrett, and Maki (2001); Gustman and Steinmeier (2004); Lusardi (1999); Maki (2004); Mitchell (1988); and Starr-McCluer and Sunden (1999).

34. If large numbers of workers opt not to participate in defined contribution plans, then a comparison of potential returns from the two types of plans may be of second-order interest. Even and MacPherson (1994) find that the emergence of the 401(k) plan has reduced participation in employer-sponsored pension plans, particularly among young and low-income workers.

35. The collapse of Enron Corporation resulted in huge losses in the 401(k) plans of many former Enron workers and helped highlight problems associated with workers holding excessive amounts of their own company's stock in their 401(k)s. These holdings raise questions about the rationality of workers' investment strategies, the value of company efforts to encourage employee purchase of company stock, and the role of public policy. Workers who overly invest in company stock expose themselves to substantial amounts of risk, without a compensating higher expected rate of return on their investments (Meulbroek 2002, Poterba 2003, and Ramaswamy 2003).

36. Upon leaving a job, workers may leave their funds at their old employer, roll the funds over into an IRA, or cash out the balance. Legal rules allow workers to cash out the funds in the hope that the possibility of liquidity increases workers' willingness to contribute in the first place, but the rules also impose income tax and an early withdrawal penalty on cash-outs. Evidence suggests that most people who are given the opportunity to cash out funds do so, but most of the money that is at stake in such opportunities is rolled over. These data are reconciled by noting that the larger balances tend to be rolled over, while smaller balances tend to be cashed out. The overall magnitude of leakage attributable to early withdrawals is not large relative to retirement income, but it also appears to be the case that the groups that withdraw funds early are precisely those who would benefit most, in terms of improving the adequacy of their retirement income, by saving these funds instead. See Burman, Coe, and Gale (2000); Engelhardt (2002); and Poterba, Venti, and Wise (2001a).

37. Madrian and Shea (2001); Choi and others (2002).

on worker contribution and participation rates.[38] If certain choices are deemed undesirable—pre-retirement cash-outs of pension balances, for example—public policy can be altered to make those choices less attractive and hence less prevalent.[39] The potential for such policy changes suggests that the relative outcomes for defined contribution plans could improve over time.

Another issue concerns the variability or relative riskiness of benefits from defined benefit and defined contribution plans. It is difficult to compare the overall risk in the two types of plans because the sources of risk are so different. In a traditional defined benefit pension, the pension depends on the worker's final or highest wages and job tenure. Thus, workers are subject to risks from uncertain wages and job tenure. In a typical defined contribution plan, contributions are essentially a weighted average of wages over the career, so the risk related to final wages or job switching is not substantial. However, workers bear the risk of fluctuations in return on investments. In addition, there may be risk from overall diversification, since many employers provide financial incentives to hold company stock or may make a matching contribution in company stock. Workers with defined contribution plans who expect to purchase annuities at retirement may face interest rate risk as well. Perhaps most important, workers in defined contribution plans are much less likely to choose to annuitize their benefits and so face a substantial risk of outliving their resources. Workers in defined benefit plans, who typically receive annuities, are assured of income every year as they age, but even they face inflation risk because the annuities are almost always specified in nominal terms. In both types of plans, workers face risks because employers can change plan features in the future.[40]

The variability in returns in defined contribution plans has increased partly because of the expanded role of self-directed accounts, which allow each worker to choose his or her own allocation of assets. In 1978 only 16 percent of companies let workers direct investment of their own contributions, and 10 percent let workers direct investment of the employers' contribution. By 1994 these figures had risen to 94 percent and 74 percent, respectively, and they have stayed high since then.[41] In light of the greater heterogeneity of saving and investment behavior in defined contribution plans than defined benefit plans, it is not surprising that research has found that the advent of defined contribution plans has and will continue to skew the distribution of pension outcomes.[42]

Another important risk-related issue is that defined contribution plans are fully funded, by definition, whereas the funding status of a defined benefit plans depends on market rates of return as well as discount rates that are tied to

38. Bernheim and Garrett (1995); Clark and Schieber (1998); Muller (2000).
39. Burman, Coe, and Gale (2000).
40. See Munnell and Sunden (2003b), for example.
41. Papke (2004); Schieber, Dunn, and Wray (1998); Wiatrowsky (2000).
42. Samwick and Skinner (1998); Even and MacPherson (1998, 2003).

Treasury bond yields.[43] The simultaneous drop in the stock market and in interest rates since 2001 substantially hurt the funding status of defined benefit pensions.[44] If the current level of underfunding persists, workers face the risk that benefits accruals may be cut back or plans may actually be frozen.[45]

From the firm's perspective, a traditional argument in favor of defined benefit plans can be structured to provide incentives for workers to remain with the firm for the long term and other incentives to encourage workers to retire at propitious times. However, Ippolito has shown that to at least some extent, these same arguments can be applied to defined contribution plans.[46] Firms benefit in other ways from defined contribution plans as well. They do not have to pay premiums to the Pension Benefit Guaranty Corporation, which only guarantees benefits in defined benefit plans. To the extent that workers do not participate in a defined contribution plan, firm costs fall. Firms can both reduce their overall contribution and vary it year by year to provide more flexibility in funding a defined contribution plan than a defined benefit plan.

Traditional Defined Benefit versus Cash Balance Plans

Significant controversy has arisen over how workers are affected by the conversion of traditional defined benefit plans to cash balance plans. There is nothing inherent in the structure of cash balance plans that makes them more or less generous on average than a traditional defined benefit plan. However, for reasons discussed below, conversions have different effects on different workers.

The key issue is the impact of plan conversions on workers' retirement income. Figure 3-2 provides hypothetical, but representative, information on how pension wealth grows under different plan types as workers increase their tenure with the firm from zero to R years, where R is the number of years spent at the firm by a worker who spends his whole career there.

The line marked *DB* shows that pension wealth accrued under a traditional defined benefit plan is strongly back-loaded; the rate of accrual rises at an

43. Under a 1987 law, modified in 1994, employers use an interest rate tied to the yield on thirty-year Treasury bonds to value plan liabilities. Specifically, employers are typically required to use a range of 90 percent to 105 percent of the four-year weighted average of the yield on the bonds. As a result of abnormally low rates in recent years, plan sponsors were allowed to use a somewhat higher discount rate in 2002 and 2003. Whether this relief will be extended beyond 2003 was uncertain at the time this chapter was written.

44. Bookbinder (2003) estimates that the nation's largest corporate defined benefit plans faced more than $151 billion in unfunded liabilities in 2002, up from $108 billion the previous year. Only fourteen of the plans were fully funded in 2002 as opposed to fifty-two in 2001.

45. Sponsors with underfunded plans face considerable incentives to rectify the funding status. They may face increased premium payments to PBGC or need to make other changes to comply with accounting regulations promulgated under Financial Accounting Standards Number 87. In addition, credit rating agencies may begin explicitly to take underfunded defined benefit plans into account, in which case increased underfunding could lead to rating downgrades for the plan sponsor.

46. Ippolito (1998).

Figure 3-2. *Representative Pension Wealth Accrual under Traditional Defined Benefit and Cash Balance Plans*

Pension wealth

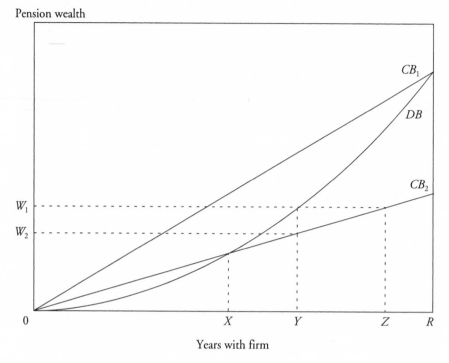

Years with firm

increasing rate as the workers' tenure rises. The line marked CB_1 shows how pension wealth grows in a cash balance plan that is just as generous as the traditional defined benefit plan for a worker who spends his whole career at the firm. Comparing the two lines yields two important points. First, for low-tenure workers, pension wealth grows faster in the cash balance plan, whereas for longer-tenure workers, pension wealth grows faster in the traditional defined benefit plan. Second, as drawn, the cash balance plan in CB_1 is more generous than the traditional defined benefit plan for workers staying for any period of time short of their entire career. Thus, a firm that converted its traditional defined benefit pension to the cash balance plan represented by CB_1 would raise its pension costs.

In contrast, the line CB_2 represents pension wealth accrual under a cash balance plan that would have the same overall costs (for a worker who would spend his or her entire career at the firm) as the traditional defined benefit plan. Examining the lines DB and CB_2 is thus more meaningful, since this comparison holds total costs constant. In this comparison, note that a worker who was planning to stay X years with the firm would do equally well under either plan (X

varies by plan). Workers with longer tenure would do better under the traditional defined benefit plan, but workers with shorter tenure would do better under the cash balance plan.

Thus, for the same overall pension costs, cash balance plans tend to tilt pension wealth more heavily toward workers with shorter tenure than do traditional defined benefit plans. Since most workers change jobs several times over their career, it is plausible that many or most workers could have more retirement income under a series of cash balance plans than under a series of traditional defined benefit plans with the same overall costs.

The discussion above focuses on the effects over the course of an entire career of being in a traditional defined benefit plan (or a series of such plans) versus the effects of being in a cash balance plan (or a series of such plans). Transitional effects, however, will also prove to be important, because workers in the labor force at the time of a cash balance conversion will spend part of their career under a traditional defined benefit plan and part with a cash balance plan. The effects of cash balance conversions on transitional workers has generated much controversy, and can be explained using figure 3-2. As before, the key feature is the different accrual patterns of the two types of plans.

Consider a worker who has job tenure of Y years when the firm converts a traditional defined benefit plan, represented by the line DB, to a cash balance plan, represented by CB_2. At first glance, the graph suggests that at the time of the conversion, the worker's pension wealth would fall from W_1 to W_2 and then would grow according to the line CB_2. However, pension law forbids companies from taking away previously accumulated benefits. This creates two changes in how the worker's pension wealth would actually evolve. First, pension wealth would not fall at the time of the conversion; if the worker retired at the date of conversion or any subsequent date, he would still receive at least the accumulated value of W_1 in pension benefits. Second, however, the worker would accrue no new pension benefits between years Y and Z. During that period, the benefits in the cash balance plan would be growing, but would still be below W_1.

As a result, the cash balance conversion penalizes this worker in two ways relative to the previously existing defined benefit plan. First, for a number of years after conversion, the worker would receive no net increase in benefits.[47] Second, in the period after year Z, pension wealth under the cash balance plan rises, but the rate of accrual is slower in the cash balance plan than it would have been under the previous plan. In short, the worker loses in the transition to a cash balance plan, because in the early part of his career—when cash balance plans have faster wealth accrual than traditional defined benefit plans—the worker was enrolled in a traditional plan. In the later years—when traditional defined

47. This period is often referred to as the wear-away period in popular discussions and the pension literature.

benefit plans have faster wealth accrual than cash balance plans—the worker was enrolled in the cash balance plan. Note also that it is workers with longer tenure (with Y years of experience at the time of transition) that are most likely to lose in the transition to a cash balance plan. These are most likely to be older workers. Of course, firms can compensate the transitional workers, or, if possible, could give them a choice during the conversion to stay with the original defined benefit structure.

Cash balance plans also affect the nature of the risks imposed on workers. Like participants in defined contribution plans, who face continual rate-of-return risk, participants in cash balance plans face interest rate risk because firms choose the interest rate credited to workers' notional cash balance.

For firms, cash balance plans offer some advantages over traditional defined benefit plans. Some have argued that firms are using cash balance plans to disguise reductions in pension benefits, in particular to reduce or eliminate subsidized early retirement benefits. Many of these subsidies were put in place years ago and may not fit well with a modern economy and labor force where productive work activity can continue well beyond age sixty-two and where labor is in relatively short supply. Of course, firms can phase out early retirement benefits under existing plans, too, but the conversion to cash balance plans may make the change more opaque to workers or reflect a change in philosophy about the nature of employer benefits and employee responsibility. As a strategy for hiding changes from workers, however, combining the phase-out of early retirement benefits with the conversion of a pension to a cash balance form could backfire, because both changes hurt older, longer-tenure workers most heavily.

Third, anecdotal, but abundant, evidence suggests that workers in the current economy appreciate and understand benefits described as a lump sum more easily than benefits described in terms of a future annuity. Firms may find it advantageous to have workers appreciate the full value of their compensation package.

Empirical evidence on all of the factors above is relatively scarce. Because a significant number of cash balance plans have emerged only in recent years, few studies have been undertaken and no comprehensive analyses are yet available. Perhaps the most comprehensive study to date, based on analysis of seventy-eight conversions to cash balance plans, found that on average employer pension costs fell by about 1.4 percent during the conversion, after considering the transitional adjustments made simultaneously with the conversion.[48] There was wide variation in cost changes over plans. About 45 percent realized cost savings in excess of 5 percent, and about 37 percent had cost increases above 5 percent. The pattern of gains and losses across workers mirrors the analysis above. Older workers at the time of the transition did less well than younger workers did. A

48. Brown and others (2000).

second analysis, based on case studies of four different conversions, finds similar qualitative effects among workers: young workers are happier with the conversions than are older workers.[49]

Conclusion

Since ERISA, the level of pension coverage has remained roughly constant, but the composition of pensions has shifted dramatically away from defined benefit pensions toward defined contribution plans in general and 401(k) plans in particular. Many of the remaining defined benefit plans have shifted to cash balance plans, which are legally defined benefit plans but share many features with defined contribution plans. The causes of this shift include changes in the size and industrial distribution of firms and in the composition of the work force, regulations that seem to weigh more heavily on defined benefit than defined contribution plans, and a desire on the part of employers to vary the level and structure of compensation in ways that will be more attractive to more productive workers than to less productive workers. Further, workers themselves may have demanded more portable pensions, or ones over which they have more control.

These massive structural changes create both new opportunities and new problems for the pension system. For workers, the change in the nature of the pension plan means accepting more of the ultimate responsibility for deciding whether to participate, how much to contribute, how to allocate investments and maintain the fund during job changes, when to withdraw funds, and whether to annuitize such withdrawals. Because investing acumen varies dramatically across workers, and because rates of return vary ex post, the shift toward defined contribution plans increases the variability of retirement outcomes. The effect of the shift on the level of retirement income is less settled. To date, the evidence suggests that average pension benefits for low-income workers may be reduced, but that there will be relatively small effects on average benefits for middle- and high-income workers. In a conversion to a cash balance plan, without compensatory benefits, workers with long tenure with the firm can lose in the transition.

These findings suggest that pensions will continue to play an important role in structuring households' and firm's choices, and retirees' well-being. But the shift in the structure of pensions also implies that laws and regulations written in the defined benefit world of the 1960s and 1970s may well be outdated. Thus, above all, the shift in the structure of pensions motivates the need for a systematic review of pension rules and regulations.[50]

---

49. Clark and Munzanmaier (2001).

50. For a sampling opinion and reviews, see the chapters in this volume by Groom and Shoven, Halperin and Munnell, and Perun and Steuerle; see also Gale and Orszag (2003).

References

Ameriks, John, Andrew Caplin, and John Leahy. 2003. "Wealth Accumulation and the Propensity to Plan." *Quarterly Journal of Economics* 118 (3, August): 1007–48.

Andrews, Emily S. 1992. "The Growth and Distribution of 401(k) Plans." In *Trends in Pensions 1992,* edited by John A. Turner and Daniel J. Beller, 149–76. U.S. Department of Labor, Pension and Welfare Benefits Administration.

Bayer, Patrick J., B. Douglas Bernheim, and John Karl Scholz. 1996. "The Effects of Financial Education in the Workplace: Evidence from a Survey of Employers." Working Paper 5655. Cambridge, Mass.: National Bureau of Economic Research (July).

Bernheim, B. Douglas and Daniel H. Garrett. 1996. "The Determinants and Consequences of Financial Education in the Workplace: Evidence from a Survey of Households." Working Paper 5667. Cambridge, Mass.: National Bureau of Economic Research (July).

Bernheim, B. Douglas, Daniel H Garrett, and Dean M. Maki. 2001. "Education and Saving: The Long-Term Effects of High School Financial Curriculum Mandates." *Journal of Public Economics* 80 (3, June): 435–65.

Bookbinder, Adin. 2003. "Largest Plans Face Liabilities of $151 billion." *Pensions and Investments* 31 (15, July 21): 1.

Brown, Kyle, and others. 2000. *The Unfolding of a Predictable Surprise: A Comprehensive Analysis of the Shift from Traditional Pensions to Hybrid Plans.* Bethesda, Md.: Watson Wyatt.

Burman, Leonard E., Norma Coe, and William G. Gale. 2000. "What Happens When You Show Them the Money: Lump Sum Distributions, Income Security, and Public Policy." Brookings and Urban Institute.

Buck Consultants, Inc. 1989. "Current 401(K) Plan Practices: A Survey Report." Secaucus, N.J. (September).

Choi, James, and others. 2002. "Defined Contribution Pensions: Plan Rules, Participant Decisions, and the Path of Least Resistance." In *Tax Policy and the Economy,* edited by James Poterba. MIT Press.

Clark, Robert L., and Ann A. McDermed. 1990. *The Choice of Pension Plans in a Changing Regulatory Environment.* AEI Press.

Clark, Robert L., and Fred Munzanmaier. 2001. "Impact of Replacing a Defined Benefit Plan with a Defined Contribution or Cash Balance Plan." *North American Actuarial Journal* 5 (1): pp. 32–56.

Clark, Robert L., and Sylvester J. Schieber. 1998. "Factors Affecting Participation Rates and Contribution Levels in 401(k) Plans." In *Living with Defined Contribution Pensions: Remaking Responsibility,* edited by Olivia S. Mitchell and Sylvester J. Schieber. University of Pennsylvania Press.

———. 2004. "The Transition to Hybrid Pension Plans in the United States: An Empirical Analysis." In *Private Pensions and Public Policies,* edited by William G. Gale, John B. Shoven, and Mark J. Warshawsky. Brookings.

Copeland, Craig. 2003. "Employee Tenure." *Employee Benefit Research Institute Notes.* 24 (3, March): 1–9.

Engelhardt, Gary V. 2002. "Pre-Retirement Lump Sum Pension Distributions and Retirement Income Security: Evidence from the Health and Retirement Study." *National Tax Journal* 55 (4, December): 665–702.

Engen, Eric, William Gale, and John Karl Scholz. 1996a. "The Effects of Tax-Based Saving Incentives on Saving and Wealth." Working Paper 5759. Cambridge, Mass.: National Bureau of Economic Research.

————. 1996b. "The Illusory Effects of Saving Incentives on Saving." *Journal of Economic Perspectives* 10 (4): 113–38.

Even, William E., and David A. MacPherson. 1994. "The Pension Coverage of Young and Mature Workers." *Pension Coverage Issues for the '90s*, edited by Richard Hinz, John Turner, and Phyllis Fernandez, 85–107. Government Printing Office.

————. 1998. "The Impact of Rising 401(k) Pension Coverage on Future Pension Income." Report submitted to Department of Labor, Pension and Welfare Benefits Administration (May).

————. 2003. "The Distributional Consequences of the Shift to Defined Contribution Plans." Miami University (July).

Gale, William G., and Peter R. Orszag. 2003. "Private Pensions: Issues and Options." In *Agenda for the Nation,* edited by Henry Aaron, James Lindsay, and Pietro Nivola. Brookings.

Gustman, Alan L., and Thomas L. Steinmeier. 1992. "The Stampede toward Defined Contribution Plans: Fact or Fiction?" *Industrial Relations* 31 (2): 361–69.

————. 2004. "What Do People Know about Their Pension and Social Security Benefits?" In *Public Policies and Private Pensions,* edited by William G. Gale, John B. Shoven, and Mark J. Warshawsky. Brookings.

Hustead, Edwin C. 1998. "Trends in Retirement Income Plan Administrative Expenses." In *Living with Defined Contribution Pensions: Remaking Responsibility,* edited by Olivia S. Mitchell and Sylvester J. Schieber. University of Pennsylvania Press.

Ippolito, Richard A. 1995. "Toward Explaining the Growth of Defined Contribution Plans." *Industrial Relations* 34 (1, January): 1–20.

————. 1998. "Disparate Savings Propensities and National Retirement Policy." In *Living with Defined Contribution Pensions: Remaking Responsibility,* edited by Olivia S. Mitchell and Sylvester J. Schieber. University of Pennsylvania Press.

Ippolito, Richard A., and John W. Thompson. 2000. "The Survival Rate of Defined-Benefit Plans, 1987–1995." *Industrial Relations* 39 (2, April): 228–45.

Kruse, Douglas L. 1995. "Pension Substitution in the 1980's: Why the Shift toward Defined Contribution Plans?" *Industrial Relations* 34 (2): 218–41.

Lusardi, Annamaria. 1999. "Information, Expectations, and Savings for Retirement." In *Behavioral Dimensions of Retirement Economics*, edited by Henry J. Aaron. Brookings.

Madrian, Brigitte C., and Dennis F. Shea. 2001. "The Power of Suggestion: Inertia in 401(k) Participation and Savings Behavior." *Quarterly Journal of Economics* 116 (4, November): 1149–87.

Maki, Dean. 2004. "Financial Education and Private Pensions." In *Private Pensions and Public Policies,* edited by William G. Gale, John B. Shoven, and Mark J. Warshawsky. Brookings.

Meulbroek, Lisa. 2002. "Company Stock in Pension Plans: How Costly Is It?" Working Paper 02-058. Harvard Business School.

Mitchell, Olivia S. 1988. "Worker Knowledge of Pension Provisions." *Journal of Labor Economics* 6 (1): 21–39.

Muller, Leslie. 2000. "Retirement Education and Pension Preservation: Does Retirement Education Teach Individuals to Save Pension Distributions?" Social Security Administration, Washington.

Munnell, Alicia H., and Annika Sunden. 2003a. "401(k) Plans: Lessons for the Future." Center for Retirement Research, Boston College.

————. 2003b. "Suspending the Employer 401(k) Match." Issue Brief 12. Center for Retirement Research, Boston College (June).

Olsen, Kelly, and Jack L. VanDerhei. 1997. "Defined Contribution Plan Dominance Grows across Sectors and Employer Sizes While Mega Defined Benefit Plans Remain Strong: Where We Are and Where We Are Going." In *Retirement Prospects in a Defined Contribution World,* edited by Dallas Salisbury, 55–92. Washington: Employee Benefit Research Institute.

Papke, Leslie E. 1999. "Are 401(k) Plans Replacing Other Employer-Provided Pensions? Evidence from Panel Data." *Journal of Human Resources* 34 (2, Spring): 346–68.

———. 2003. "Public Pensions and Pension Policy." In *Michigan at the Millennium: A Benchmark and Analysis of Its Fiscal and Economic Structure,* edited by C. L. Ballard and others, 413–34. Michigan State University Press.

———. 2004. "Individual Financial Decisions in Retirement Saving Plans: The Role of Participant-Direction." *Journal of Public Economics* 88 (January): 39–61.

Papke, Leslie E., Mitchell A. Petersen, and James M. Poterba. 1996. "Do 401(K) Plans Replace Other Employer-Provided Pensions?" In *Advances in the Economics of Aging,* edited by David A. Wise, 219–39. University of Chicago Press.

Poterba, James M. 2003. "Employer Stock and 401(k) Plans." *American Economic Review* 93 (2, May): 398–404.

Poterba, James M., Steven F. Venti, and David A. Wise. 1998. "Implications of Rising Personal Retirement Saving." In *Frontiers in the Economics of Aging,* edited by David A. Wise. University of Chicago Press.

———. 2001a. "Pre-Retirement Cashouts and Foregone Retirement Saving: Implications for 401(k) Asset Accumulation." In *Themes in the Economics of Aging,* edited by David A. Wise. University of Chicago Press.

———. 2001b. "The Transition to Personal Accounts and Increasing Retirement Wealth: Macro and Micro Evidence." Working Paper 8610. Cambridge, Mass.: National Bureau of Economic Research.

Ramaswamy, Krishna. 2003. "Corporate Stock and Pension Plan Diversification." In *The Pension Challenge: Risk Transfers and Retirement Income Security,* edited by Olivia Mitchell and Kent Smetters. University of Pennsylvania Press.

Samwick, Andrew, and Jonathan Skinner. 1998. "How Will Defined Contribution Pension Plans Affect Retirement Income?" Working Paper 6645. Cambridge, Mass.: National Bureau of Economic Research.

Sauvigne, Donald. 1997. Statement of American Savings Education Council before the House Education and Workforce Subcommittee on Employer-Employee Relations, February 12.

Schieber, Sylvester J., Richard Dunn, and David Wray. 1998. "The Future of the Defined Contribution Revolution." In *Living with Defined Contribution Pensions: Remaking Responsibility,* edited by Olivia S. Mitchell and Sylvester J. Schieber. University of Pennsylvania Press.

Starr-McCluer, Martha, and Annika Sunden. 1999. "Workers' Knowledge of their Pension Coverage: A Reevaluation." Survey of Consumer Finances Working Paper. Federal Reserve Board (January).

U.S. Department of Labor, Pension and Welfare Benefits Administration. 2001–02. "Abstract of 1998 Form 5500 Annual Reports." Private Pension Plan Bulletin 11 (Winter).

Wiatrowsky, W. J. 2000. "Putting Stock in Benefits: How Prevalent Is It?" *Compensation and Working Conditions* (Fall): 2–7.

4

Effects of Pensions on Labor Markets and Retirement

ROBERT L. CLARK AND JOSEPH F. QUINN

Employer-provided pensions represent an important part of labor compensation at many firms. From 1950 until the enactment of the Employee Retirement Income Security Act (ERISA) in 1974, pension coverage rose from approximately 25 percent of the private work force to between 45 and 50 percent, with most workers participating in defined benefit plans. Since 1974 pension coverage has remained at about half of the labor force, but there has been a dramatic shift away from defined benefit plans toward defined contribution plans.[1]

In this chapter we examine the effects pension plans have had on the labor market. In particular, we look at their effects on labor productivity and mobility during working years and on the timing and nature of retirement at the end of the work cycle. We begin by asking why workers desire employer-provided retirement plans and why firms offer them. These preferences lie behind the structure of pension plans and the incentives they create that affect worker behavior.

---

1. The employer cost for retirement and savings plans averaged 4 percent of total compensation costs for civilian workers between 1991 and 1996; see Employee Benefit Research Institute 1997, p. 17. Detailed studies of trends in pension coverage are presented in U.S. Department of Labor (1992, 1994) and Employee Benefit Research Institute (1994, 1997). The shift from defined benefit to defined contribution plans has been widely documented in studies that have examined Current Population Surveys, the 5500 tax reporting forms, the Employee Benefit Survey, and other surveys that include information on pension coverage. For further discussion of this shift, see the paper by Gale, Papke, and VanDerhei in this volume.

Economic theory suggests that firms are willing to pay workers according to the value of their productivity. Compensation can take many forms, however, with the total cost being the most important issue to the employer. If worker behavior is not affected by the type of compensation received, firms can be viewed as neutral sellers of employee benefits. In other words, all else equal, employers are willing to provide whatever combination of cash payments and benefits workers desire. This is the fundamental concept behind the theory of compensating wage differentials. The form of compensation may affect the level of productivity, however, which in turn may provide cost savings to employers. If so, a dollar of employee benefits would not require a dollar reduction in cash compensation.

The primary reason that workers prefer a portion of their total compensation to be paid in the form of pension benefits is the favorable tax treatment given to qualified pension plans. Since the 1920s the federal income tax code has contained provisions under which qualified pension contributions and the earnings of pension trusts are not subject to current taxation. Instead, benefits are taxed when received in retirement. The deferment of income tax liability enables workers to accumulate larger retirement funds through employer-provided pension plans than they could with equivalent dollars paid as current earnings. Indeed, one reason that pension coverage rates have stagnated in the last few decades may be that federal income tax reductions in the 1980s made the tax-deferred benefits of pensions less valuable to employees. The tax status of pensions suggests that variation in current tax rates across workers explains some of the differences in pension coverage rates across workers.

Moreover, since its inception in 1935 Social Security has been financed by payroll taxes paid only on cash earnings. Thus, employee compensation in the form of employer contributions to pension plans is not subject to the payroll tax, which also allows workers to accumulate larger retirement accounts than they would if they received all compensation in cash, paid payroll taxes, and then saved for retirement on their own.[2] In addition to these tax effects, workers may desire employer pensions because they facilitate retirement planning and make saving for retirement easier.

Firms offer pension plans because they can help in the management of human resources, including attracting, retaining, and eventually retiring the workers the companies desire. Some workers search out firms that provide pension plans and alter their work behavior to remain with these firms; alternatively, some workers may have a higher preference for current income over

---

2. The gain in lifetime wealth associated with pension coverage under current tax policy is neatly described in Ippolito (1986). Studies by Long and Scott (1982), Montgomery, Shaw, and Benedict (1992), and Woodbury and Huang (1991) report dramatically different tax elasticities for the demand for pension compensation.

future retirement benefits and thus tend to avoid companies with pension plans.[3] Firms may be able to achieve a lower quit rate by offering pension coverage that imposes financial penalties on workers who leave "too early." But perhaps the single most important effect of pensions from a firm's point of view is their ability to affect retirement decisions. The influence pension plans have on the timing of retirement has increased in importance since 1986, when amendments to the Age Discrimination in Employment Act outlawed mandatory retirement in most jobs. Pension plans can be structured to provide strong incentives for workers to leave the firm at specific ages, in accordance with a firm's human resource needs.

The human resource needs and objectives of companies differ. Employing high-quality workers is more important to some firms than others. Firms that face large up-front costs of hiring and training workers will want low turnover rates and may institute compensation policies to achieve this result. Companies that are concerned about an aging work force may institute policies that encourage retirement at early ages. Pension plans can play an important role in achieving these objectives.

Considerable research suggests that pensions have the desired effects, that is, workers behave as though they understand and respond to the financial incentives embedded in many pension plans. This paper presents an overview of the economic and policy research on the effect of pensions on labor mobility and retirement.[4] We attempt to identify what is known about the ways that pensions alter worker and firm decisions, what is still debated, and what key gaps in our knowledge still remain. In turn, this knowledge should help to evaluate and shape the many government tax and regulatory policies that influence a firm's decision to sponsor a pension plan.

Setting the Stage: How Pension Benefits Accrue

Before assessing the evidence on how pensions affect labor markets, it is useful to examine how pension funds can affect individual decisions. Understanding the effects of pensions on mobility and retirement requires that pensions be viewed from a lifetime perspective. The central mechanism by which pension plans affect individual decisions is the annual pension accrual. A pension plan promises a stream of future income; the present discounted value of this income flow is called pension wealth. The present value of a covered worker's expected future benefits changes each year that the worker remains on the job. The gain or loss in pension wealth from staying on the job can be seen only by evaluating

---

3. Curme and Even (1995); Ippolito (1997).

4. Earlier reviews of the role of pensions in determining labor market outcomes include Gustman, Mitchell, and Steinmeier (1994) and Dorsey (1995).

the present value of future benefits over a lifetime.[5] The change in pension wealth from working an additional year is the pension accrual for that year.

Pension plans can be broadly divided into two types: defined benefit and defined contribution. The two types of plans have different patterns of pension accrual over the lifetime of a worker and thus may be expected to affect individual decisions differently.

Defined benefit plans promise retirement benefits to workers who meet certain age and service requirements. The most common benefit formula specifies benefits as a percentage of final average salary, typically calculated over the last three or five years of service. Other benefit plans use career average earnings, and many collectively bargained plans provide a specified dollar benefit per year of service.[6]

Once an individual becomes vested in a pension, future benefits grow with additional years of service and with annual earnings. When ERISA was enacted in 1974, it required that workers be fully vested in their pension benefit after ten years of service. The law was amended in 1986 to require full vesting after five years and to permit "graded vesting," with workers achieving at least 20 percent vesting by the end of three years of service and 100 percent vesting after seven years. In most cases, defined benefit plans provide universal participation for all qualified workers.

In a typical defined benefit plan, accruals are zero until the individual achieves vesting. During the year in which a worker becomes vested, the pension accrual spikes upward. The gain in pension wealth from working that year provides the worker with an accrual representing the value of all previous years of work in determining future pension benefits. From this point on, annual benefit accruals increase steadily until the worker is eligible to retire and start receiving a pension benefit.[7] These back-loaded benefits may lead to a more stable work force for two reasons. First, the effect of having total compensation increase more rapidly with seniority offers a direct incentive to stay on the job. Second, compensation that is conditional on remaining with the firm for many years can be used to sort workers based on their own perceived probability of changing jobs. Movers will be less likely to accept employment at firms that provide a large component of compensation that is contingent on staying with the company.[8]

5. Key insights into the appropriate methods of evaluating pension benefits were developed by Burkhauser (1979, 1980) and Ippolito (1985), and these have provided much of the structure for subsequent studies of mobility and retirement.

6. U.S. Bureau of Labor Statistics (1997) provides details on the use of benefit formulas in defined benefit plans offered by medium-size and large private establishments.

7. Kotlikoff and Wise (1985) provide a comprehensive development of sample profiles of benefit accruals. See also McGill and others (1996) and Gustman and Steinmeier (1995) for calculations of benefit accruals and the concept of back-loading.

8. Salop and Salop (1976); Allen, Clark, and McDermed (1993).

Workers who change jobs, even those moving among companies with identical defined benefit pension plans, have lower total retirement benefits than workers who spend their entire career with a single company.[9] The larger the potential loss in pension benefits associated with job changes, the lower the expected turnover rate is. Firms can influence the size of the loss in pension wealth associated with changing jobs by selecting pension parameters that determine eventual pension benefits.

Pension accruals in defined benefit plans spike upward not only when workers become vested, but also when they reach the age and service requirements for early and normal retirement benefits. After the initial age of eligibility has been attained, pension accrual calculations become more complex, because higher benefits in the future derived from continued employment must be weighed against benefits forgone while the employee continues working. Typically, benefit accruals begin to decline after the age of initial eligibility for retirement and often become negative if the individual remains with the firm at older ages. A negative benefit accrual means that the present value of a worker's benefit declines with an additional year of work. This reduction in the growth rate of pension wealth—and sometimes its actual decline—provides an incentive for the worker to leave the firm. This incentive stems from a reduction in the total compensation associated with working (a pay cut), not through the paycheck, but through the details of the pension benefit calculation.

The firm can alter the size of these retirement incentives by selecting the ages for early and normal retirement and by introducing maximum benefit provisions. These pension rules encourage the firm's workers to retire at specific ages. For example, some pension plans place an upper limit on the number of years of service that can be included in the benefit calculation. If the plan states that only thirty years of service can be used in the calculation of benefit levels, then the annual benefit accrual will be much lower for workers who have more than thirty years of tenure than for those with fewer than thirty years of service. Before reaching thirty years of service, future pension benefits are increased by the additional years of service and by an increase in one's average earnings. After thirty years of service, future benefits are increased only by the higher salary average.

In defined contribution plans, both the worker and the firm make periodic contributions to the worker's retirement account; typically, a specified percentage of salary that does not vary with age or service. Unlike defined benefit plans, which usually cover all workers who meet minimum participation standards, many defined contribution plans allow workers to decide whether to participate in the plan by making voluntary contributions. In voluntary retirement savings plans, such as many 401(k) plans, workers may alter their contributions over

9. Clark and McDermed (1988).

time, and older workers tend to contribute larger percentages of their salaries than younger workers do. The rules under which these contribution decisions are made nonetheless tend to be age-neutral.

In a defined contribution pension plan, future retirement benefits depend on the size of the annual contributions and on the rate of return achieved on the accumulated assets. In most cases, the funds are vested quickly, if not immediately, and workers own their individual retirement accounts (IRAs). Annual pension accruals in defined contribution plans tend to be more uniform across years of service, although the investment returns to these accounts of course fluctuate over time and across individuals.

Because of early vesting and their ownership of their retirement account, workers in defined contribution plans tend not to suffer losses in their pension wealth when they change jobs. Individuals are typically able to withdraw their funds from their previous employer's pension plan and roll these funds into their own IRA or some other qualified pension account. Moreover, a firm cannot reduce pension wealth if a worker stays on "too long," as a firm can in defined benefit plans.

Overall, in defined benefit pension plans, pension benefit accruals generally encourage workers to remain with a company throughout most of their careers and then to retire at particular ages. Accruals in defined contribution plans are less sensitive to mobility decisions and tend to be age neutral with respect to the timing of retirement.

Pensions, Wages, and Mobility

The links among pension participation, wages, and labor market mobility are complex. Firms offer pensions as part of their compensation packages to attract, retain, and retire quality workers. The cost and value of pensions depend on whether earnings or other benefits are reduced when pensions are provided. Moreover, the value of pension coverage to workers and the cost to firms depend in part on whether pension coverage increases worker productivity through longer tenure and perhaps greater investment in human capital.

Pensions and the Level of Wages

The theory of compensating wage differentials states that, holding worker productivity constant, increases in one kind of compensation should be matched by decreases in other kinds. The theory implies that firms that offer pensions should pay lower wages than comparable firms without pensions would pay to similar workers. Empirical evidence supporting compensating differentials is inconclusive, however, with some studies finding a compensating wage differential for pensions and others finding no such effect. A survey of the literature in

1992 concluded: "Overall, the results are mixed. They certainly do not clearly support the notion of a trade-off between wages and pension benefits."[10]

Conflicting empirical results like these are often an indication that estimating the effect in question poses some difficult problems or that the available data are not adequate to address the analytical problem being considered. In this case researchers have found it difficult to take into account the technical relationship tying earnings to benefit determination, to calculate accurately the employer cost of providing pension benefits, to ensure that all fringe benefits to employees and all costs to employers are fully included in the analysis, and to control properly for other factors that might affect wage rates. Finally, high-quality workers may have higher wages *and* benefits, but the data mask the existence of compensating differentials because worker productivity at the individual level is very difficult to measure. In the face of these data shortcomings, it is not surprising that estimation of true compensating differentials has proven difficult. Moreover, the true compensating differential may be less than dollar for dollar because the productivity-enhancing aspects of pensions may reduce other labor costs.

Pensions and Productivity

Companies may adopt pensions in an effort to enhance labor productivity. Theories of firm-specific human capital suggest that firms invest more in workers who are likely to remain with the firm for longer periods of time. In this analytical framework the use of deferred payments that depend on longer job tenure can result in more investment in human capital and therefore higher productivity. Such compensation schemes might also reduce shirking on the job and promote more efficient job matches between firms that benefit from low turnover rates and workers with low turnover probabilities.[11]

Relatively few empirical studies have attempted to estimate directly the effect of pensions on firm productivity. Much of the recent work in this area has been done by Stuart Dorsey, with several different coauthors. In a 1995 review of a wide range of studies, for example, Dorsey concluded that "on balance, the literature supports the view that incentives established by nonportable benefits do enhance productivity."[12] His conclusion is based on the observation that a

---

10. Gunderson, Hyatt, and Pesando (1992, p. 147). As examples of particular studies, Clark and McDermed (1986) and Smith (1981) find evidence of significant compensating differentials associated with certain pension characteristics; Ehrenberg (1980) and Schiller and Weiss (1980) report mixed results. Mitchell and Pozzebon (1986) and Smith and Ehrenberg (1983) find no evidence of a wage-pension trade-off. Finally, Even and Macpherson (1990) report a positive relationship between pensions and the wage rate.

11. For a general discussion of firm-specific human capital theory, see Becker (1964) and Oi (1962). For discussions of how deferred payments can reduce shirking, see Becker and Stigler (1974) and Lazear (1979).

12. Dorsey (1995, p. 289).

productivity-enhancing effect is plausible given existing models of the labor market and that substantial indirect evidence supports the existence of a positive productivity effect. In a subsequent paper, Dorsey and a coauthor found a strong positive relationship between pension coverage and training on the job, providing a further link between the use of pensions as a kind of compensation and employee productivity.[13] In a recent book on pensions and productivity, Dorsey and other coauthors estimated a series of productivity models and concluded that labor appears to be more productive in firms that offer defined benefit pension plans than in firms that offer no pension at all.[14]

Because severe data limitations make estimation of direct productivity effects of pension coverage difficult, any assessment can only be described as tentative. On balance, however, the limited evidence suggests that pension coverage is associated with somewhat higher productivity and that this effect is higher in some industries than in others. In addition, the effect seems to be more pronounced in defined benefit pension plans, which typically have a vesting period in which the employee is not eligible for benefits for some time and in which the benefit level is commonly tied to the highest levels of pay received during a career; the effect is less pronounced in defined contribution pension plans, where pension contributions are often just a percentage of annual salary, paid each year, with no waiting period.

Pensions and Turnover

If workers who change jobs tend to lose pension wealth, then pension coverage should discourage labor market mobility. Indeed, empirical studies using a variety of data sets and specifications do find this negative relationship. One early study of this subject in 1982 found that pension participants were less likely to change jobs during a four-year period than were workers not covered by an employer-provided pension.[15] Numerous studies in the 1990s confirmed a link between pensions and job changes. For example, one study used the Panel Study of Income Dynamics to estimate the determinants of quit and layoff probabilities between 1975 and 1982 and found that the loss of pension wealth from changing jobs reduced turnover rates.[16]

How large is the reduction in turnover rates resulting from pensions? Lazear and Moore tackle this question by defining the "option value" associated with pension coverage as the difference between the present value of the pension at

---

13. Dorsey and McPherson (1997).

14. Dorsey, Cornwell, and McPherson (1998).

15. See Mitchell (1982). For other early studies reporting that workers covered by pensions have lower turnover rates, see Bartel and Borjas (1977) and McCormick and Hughes (1984).

16. See Allen, Clark, and McDermed (1993). Also, Cornwell, Dorsey, and Mehrzad (1991) conclude that workers covered by pension plans are less likely to be laid off than those without a pension.

the optimal retirement age and its current value. Using that value they estimate that eliminating the average worker's pension would double the turnover rate.[17] Ippolito uses data from the Pension Benefit Amounts Survey of 1978 and finds that pension plans that impose quit costs equal to one year's earnings at mid-career increase tenure at age fifty-five by more than 20 percent. He also finds that imposing losses in pension wealth has a much greater effect on discouraging turnover than does tilting the tenure-earnings profile so that new workers are underpaid and senior workers are overpaid; "pensions are important tools to obtain long-term commitments to the firm," he concludes.[18] In another study Ippolito concludes that the low quit rate among federal workers is attributable to the unusually large quit penalties in the civil service pension.[19]

This effect of pensions on mobility seems to differ according to the size of the employer. Pension coverage, whether defined benefit or defined contribution, apparently causes a greater reduction in turnover in large firms than in small firms. Among workers who are not pension participants, there is almost no association between firm size and turnover.[20]

Not all studies support the conclusion that pension coverage reduces mobility. In several papers Gustman and Steinmeier argue that pensions per se do not deter mobility. Their findings suggest that workers covered by either defined benefit or defined contribution plans have lower turnover rates than workers without retirement plans. Gustman and Steinmeier contend that if it were pension penalties that produced lower turnover, one would expect pensions to have a larger effect on turnover among participants in defined benefit plans than among those in defined contribution plans, and they find no evidence of such a differential in their analysis. Instead, they find that firms that offer pension plans also tend to pay higher wages than competing firms and they argue that it is these wage premiums that actually reduce turnover.[21] Their position has found little support among other analysts.[22]

In sum, researchers investigating how pensions alter employee wages, worker productivity, and turnover have found themselves limited by a lack of appropriate data. With these limitations firmly in mind, it is still useful to summarize the weight of the evidence in these areas. First, econometric estimates of the extent to which pensions are offset by changes in wages are mixed, and no strong statements can be made concerning size or even the direction of the pension-wage

17. Lazear and Moore (1988).

18. Ippolito (1991, p. 533).

19. Ippolito (1997).

20. Even and Macpherson (1996).

21. Gustman and Steinmeier (1993, 1995).

22. Ippolito (1994) argues against the findings of Gustman and Steinmeier, contending that the wage premium models fail to consider the supply conditions firms face and that it is an indenture premium for long tenure, instead of the wage premium, that affects turnover.

trade-off. Second, limited direct and indirect evidence indicates that workers who are covered by pension plans are more likely to engage in training and have somewhat higher productivity, although this effect may be concentrated in certain industries. Finally, it seems clear that pension participants have lower turnover rates and greater job tenure.

Access to better information should facilitate empirical studies of the labor market effects of pensions. In particular, information on coverage by type of pension and the characteristics of pension plans linked to detailed individual characteristics should stimulate new research in each of these areas.

Pensions and Retirement Decisions

There is a rich literature on the influence of pension incentives on individual retirement decisions. Extensive research along two separate tracks has shown that age-specific financial incentives to leave specific firms exist, that their magnitude can be large, and that workers seem to respond to them, often leaving the firm when the incentives dictate.

Until recently, detailed pension data were not linked to comprehensive national surveys of individuals; thus, the two main research strategies in this literature have been determined largely by data limitations.[23] One research avenue has been to delve into the details of specific employer pension plans, using administrative records and plan provisions. The advantage here is that researchers can calculate exact pension incentives for workers in a specific firm—for example, how pension wealth would change if an employee with a given earnings history worked for another year. The disadvantages are that these data sets typically contain only the most rudimentary demographic information about the workers and usually do not have important variables such as health, wealth, and family characteristics. In addition, the workers in these plans are not a representative sample of all workers covered by pensions.

The second approach has been to use one of the large microeconomic data sets such as the Retirement History Study from the 1970s, the Panel Study of Income Dynamics, and the National Longitudinal Survey of Older Men. These nationally representative surveys contain extensive information about workers and their families and some basic information about pensions, but they do not contain detailed information about the rules and regulations of the individuals' pension plans. Researchers therefore must rely on industry averages to estimate key pension parameters. Because actual pension plans are so numerous and so

23. An early exception to these data problems was the 1983 Survey of Consumer Finances (conducted by the Board of Governors, Federal Reserve System), which linked detailed pension data to a comprehensive national survey. Unfortunately, the number of older workers was quite small, limiting the usefulness of this survey for the study of retirement. For more information on this data set, see Avery, Elliehausen, and Canner (1984).

varied, these broad averages do not accurately describe the incentives encountered by any particular worker.

Fortunately, steps have been taken to address these data problems. The new Health and Retirement Study links detailed pension data obtained from employers and individual earnings records from the Social Security Administration to a wide array of individual and family demographic information. During the next decade this survey will be a valuable resource for retirement research and should help analysts identify more clearly the role of pensions in individual retirement decisions.[24]

A common starting point for determining how pensions affect retirement decisions is to estimate how much pension wealth workers would lose if they stayed with a firm "too long"—that is, past the age when the firm wants them to retire. This loss, which is equivalent to a pay cut, is an incentive for workers to retire when the firm wishes. A number of researchers have established that workers can lose significant pension wealth by staying with a firm too long. For example, one early study found that union members in the automobile industry who remained on the job from the earliest age of pension eligibility until age sixty-five lost more than half of their pension wealth by doing so—clearly a strong incentive to leave the firm and claim retirement benefits once eligible.[25]

Kotlikoff and Wise studied the retirement incentives in more than 2,300 employer pension plans in the Level of Benefits Survey conducted by the Bureau of Labor Statistics. They concluded that "typical plan provisions provide a strong incentive for retirement after the age of plan-normal retirement, and several plan types provide a strong incentive for retirement after the age of early retirement . . . . It would not be unusual for the reduction in pension benefit accrual after the age of early retirement to be equivalent to a 30% reduction in wage earnings."[26]

Kotlikoff and Wise also discovered a wide variety of incentives across firms, some encouraging retention and some departure, and they reported significant discontinuities in pension accrual, usually at the age of vesting and the ages of eligibility for early and normal retirement benefits.[27] If a firm bases its pension on twenty-five years of service, for example, rather than on an expected age of retirement, the pension gains from working longer will drop significantly after the twenty-fifth year, and workers of the same age will face very different incentives

---

24. The Health and Retirement Study, begun in 1992, is a longitudinal survey undertaken by the University of Michigan's Institute for Social Research. The first survey interviewed 12,564 respondents aged fifty-one to sixty-one, and reinterviews have occurred every two years since then. For details on this outstanding data source, see Burkhauser and Gertler (1995).

25. Burkhauser (1979).

26. Quotation from Kotlikoff and Wise (1987, pp. 330–32). See also Fields and Mitchell (1984) and Kotlikoff and Wise (1989b).

27. Kotlikoff and Wise (1989a, b).

depending on when they joined the firm. Knowing only that a person is eligible to receive a pension benefit reveals very little about the specific financial incentives that the worker is facing.

Adding Social Security to the picture can have large effects on pension accruals when pension benefits are linked to Social Security benefits, and tends to make total incentives to retire larger still. Stock and Wise estimated total annual compensation—earnings, plus or minus pension *and* Social Security accruals—for a cohort of workers in a single firm, for every age in the future.[28] They found some workers whose net compensation from working an additional year was nearly zero at age sixty-two or sixty-three; that is, the declines in pension and Social Security wealth completely offset the worker's salary, with no net gain for a year's work. This would be a significant work disincentive, to say the least.

In summary, researchers have established that many defined benefit pension plans penalize workers who remain with the firm too long. The next question is whether these incentives influence retirement behavior. Do actual retirement patterns suggest that workers understand and respond to these incentives? The available evidence suggests that these incentives are effective and that their influence is large—probably larger than that of any other single factor for those who face them.

Empirical evidence concerning the effect of pensions on the timing of retirement is of two types, and both are persuasive. The first type of findings is based on simple comparisons of retirement patterns with pension incentives by age. People tend to retire when their pension incentives dictate. But coincidence does not imply causation. Other factors are also at work, some of which may coincide with the pension incentives. The second type of evidence is based on more sophisticated econometric research that estimates how retirement decisions depend on various economic, demographic, and health-related factors simultaneously, and pensions remain important even when other factors are considered.

Analytical Evidence: Comparisons of Retirement Patterns

As an example of the first type of evidence, Kotlikoff and Wise compared the retirement rates of employees working for a Fortune 500 firm with the retirement incentives they faced.[29] Kotlikoff and Wise calculated retirement rates by age and by years of service and found dramatic changes in behavior at precisely the ages at which the retirement incentives changed, but only for those workers vested in the plan. For example, experienced workers with sufficient years of service with this firm became eligible for a special supplemental retirement

28. Stock and Wise (1990a, b).
29. This paragraph and those immediately following refer to Kotlikoff and Wise (1989a, b).

Figure 4-1. *Cumulative Retention Rates, by Age, for Workers Vested at Age 50, Based on 1981 and 1982 Hazard Rates*

Percent remaining

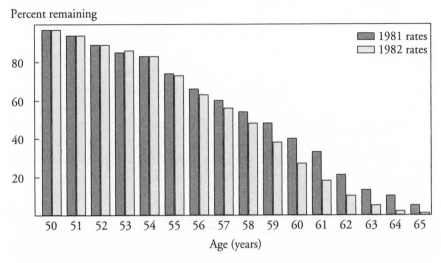

Age (years)

Source: Kotlikoff and Wise (1989a, table 10.12, p. 328); see text for explanation.

benefit at age fifty-five. As expected, almost no experienced workers left the firm at ages between fifty and fifty-four, although many workers who were not vested in the pension plan did leave at these ages. At age fifty-five, however, the retirement rates jumped significantly, but only for those vested in the plan. At age sixty, when pension accruals turned negative for those with thirty years or more of service, the retirement rate for such workers jumped again; in fact, almost one-third of those still remaining at ages sixty and sixty-one left. The increases in retirement rates at ages sixty and sixty-one were only about half as large for those who were vested but who had fewer than thirty years on the job; those workers were still accumulating service years and enjoying positive pension accruals. At age sixty-two, when workers became eligible for Social Security benefits, the retirement rate for senior workers increased to one-half of those still remaining, and remained near that level through age sixty-five.

Figure 4-1 shows the cumulative effect of these departure rates—the proportion of those vested at age fifty who would still be employed at later ages, given the age-specific retirement rates calculated for 1981. One can see the large declines at ages fifty-five, sixty, sixty-two, and sixty-five. The figure also shows the impact of a special early retirement program that was in effect in 1982 for those vested and age fifty-five or older but did not exist in either 1981 or 1983. The implementation of this early retirement plan increased the retirement rates at all ages beyond fifty-five in 1982, but not at younger ages, as expected. As seen in the right-hand bars, the declines are much more precipitous at each age after age fifty-five—by age sixty-five, only 1 in 100 remains.

In another recent study, Lumsdaine, Stock, and Wise analyzed retirement incentives and retirement behavior in a large firm and emphasized how other important factors can interact with pension incentives.[30] They also compared the retirement patterns of men and women. As in the Kotlikoff and Wise work, this study is important not because it estimates specific retirement rates at a specific firm, but because it shows that retirement incentives strongly influence behavior.

In this firm, retirement patterns also reflected the incentives specific to that pension plan. At age sixty, when workers with thirty years of service became eligible for full benefits, the retirement rate jumped from 5 to 15 percent.[31] Figure 4-2 disaggregates the departure rate from the firm by years of service and gender. The first panel shows men and women with fewer than ten years of service; the second panel, ten to twenty-nine years of service; and the third panel, thirty years or more of service. It becomes clear that the overall average retirement rate at age sixty (15 percent) is actually the average of a much larger and more abrupt increase among those with thirty years or more of service, a much smaller and more gradual increase among those with ten to twenty-nine years on the job, and no discernible effect among those with fewer than ten years of service with the firm, and therefore not yet vested in the pension. Figure 4-2 also suggests an interaction between the pension plan and Social Security. Departure rates increase dramatically at age sixty-two, to about 30 percent a year, but only for those vested in the pension plan. At age sixty-five, when strong Social Security incentives to retire also applied, between 40 and 80 percent (depending on years of service) of those remaining left the firm. That some ignored the financial incentives to retire up through age sixty-five and kept working after this age undoubtedly reflects difference in tastes or attitudes toward work. The departure rates in figure 4-2 also show almost no difference in the retirement behavior of men and women in this firm.[32]

In a later paper based on data from the same firm, Lumsdaine, Stock, and Wise simulated the impact of some hypothetical changes in pension and Social Security rules on the retirement behavior of the employees in this firm.[33] For example, if the pension plan offered positive pension accruals after thirty years of service, experienced workers would be encouraged to stay. They estimated that by age sixty-one, for example, 35 percent of those working at age fifty

30. Lumsdaine, Stock, and Wise (1994).

31. Lumsdaine, Stock, and Wise (1994, table 6.3, p. 191).

32. Coile (1999), using the new Health and Retirement Study, also reports similarities in the response of older men and women to retirement incentives. Quinn (1997, 1999a) finds very similar retirement patterns among men and women who have had long-term career jobs.

33. Lumsdaine, Stock, and Wise (1997, pp. 272–89).

Figure 4-2. *Departure Rates of Men and Women, by Age and Years of Service*

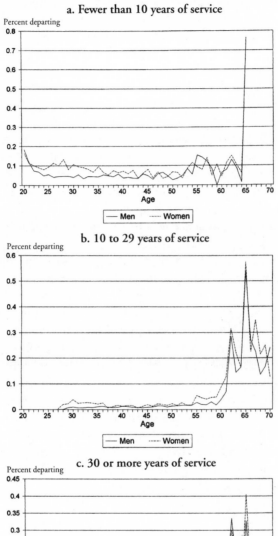

a. Fewer than 10 years of service

b. 10 to 29 years of service

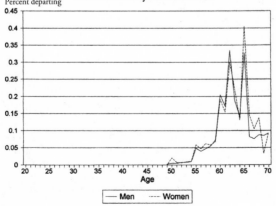

c. 30 or more years of service

Source: Lumsdaine, Stock, and Wise (1994, figure 6.4, p. 192).

would have left the firm, as opposed to 51 percent without the policy change, a difference of 16 percentage points. If the firm did not offer early retirement benefits until age sixty or sixty-two, instead of the current age of fifty-five, cumulative retirement rates by age sixty-one would drop by 17 and 43 points, respectively.

Finally, the authors demonstrated how financial incentives can render another policy, mandatory retirement, nearly meaningless. In their base case, more than 86 percent of the employees of this firm had already left by age sixty-five; only 14 percent would have been retired under a mandatory retirement policy. Before mandatory retirement policies were abolished, many people thought that they were a significant restriction on the employment opportunities of older workers. These results suggest that this conclusion was incorrect for two reasons. First, a substantial amount of what looked like the effect of mandatory retirement—that is, people retiring at exactly age sixty-five—may have actually been due to the simultaneous financial incentives built into employer pension plans and Social Security. The abolition of mandatory retirement laws did not change these incentives.[34] Second, many people were retiring before they reached mandatory retirement age. Moreover, some firms may have increased the financial incentives in their pensions plans in response to the elimination of mandatory retirement provisions, suggesting that mandatory retirement and financial incentives are alternative means to the same end.[35]

In another example using data from a single entity, Ippolito analyzed the retirement incentives faced by a sample of nearly 3,400 federal employees in 1987 and concluded that the pension system imposed large penalties for retiring before thirty years of service (the number of years required for full pension benefits) and smaller penalties for working more than thirty years.[36] He found that actual retirement behavior mirrored these incentives. Workers above age forty-five who were not yet eligible for full benefits had only a 2 percent probability of leaving the government, whereas those attaining eligibility for full benefits had a separation rate of 23 percent.

Evidence from Larger Data Sets

The general tenor of these findings regarding pension influences on employees in specific firms has been confirmed by studies using a variety of larger data sets. For example, Samwick analyzed a panel of respondents in the Surveys of

---

34. Burkhauser and Quinn (1983) came to a conclusion along these lines using a sample from the Retirement History Study. They estimated that at least half of what looked like a mandatory retirement effect actually resulted from the financial incentives built into employer pension plans and Social Security. Even this proportion was probably an underestimate, since the authors only had industry averages for pension details, rather than the real age-by-age retirement incentives that workers actually faced.

35. Luzadis and Mitchell (1991).

36. Ippolito (1997).

Consumer Finances (SCF) who were aged fifty to sixty-nine and working full time (but not self-employed) in 1983.[37] His sample consisted of 525 individuals who were observed once in 1983 and again in 1986. This was a small sample and a short duration; the data set, however, included good demographic information *and* good pension data on these individuals, thanks to detailed pension information provided by employers in a special SCF supplement, whereas previous researchers had only one or the other.

Using imputed wage histories based on age-earnings profiles by sex, race, and occupation, Samwick estimated pension and Social Security wealth in 1983 for each person in the sample and how each of these changed with additional years on the job. With this information, he then calculated year-to-year accruals. He found that accruals of retirement wealth are more important than levels of retirement wealth in explaining individuals' separations from their firms. The impact of pension accruals on separation from a firm was nearly 50 percent larger than the effect of Social Security and was statistically significant, whereas the Social Security coefficient had the expected sign but was insignificant.[38] Samwick concluded that "changes in Social Security that are typical of past and proposed legislation are simulated to have modest impacts on labor force participation of about 1 percentage point . . . . There is better evidence that the growth in pension coverage during the early postwar period contributed to the decline in labor force participation."[39] He estimates that expanded pension coverage accounted for about one-fourth of the decline in labor force participation of older men between 1955 and 1975.

A second example of a study using a broader data set is a paper by Anderson, Gustman, and Steinmeier, who applied the parameters of a structural retirement model estimated earlier to a sample of men from the 1989 Survey of Consumer Finances.[40] The authors simulated retirement behavior using the pension and Social Security rules in place in 1969, 1983, and 1989 and estimated that changes in the incentive structures of employer pensions *and* Social Security together accounted for about one-quarter of the trend toward earlier retirement observed between 1969 and 1989 among men in their early sixties.

During this time, employers with defined benefit plans introduced earlier ages of eligibility for early and normal retirement benefits and decreased the actuarial adjustments for early retirement. These changes were offset somewhat by the movement from defined benefit to defined contribution plans and a

37. Samwick (1998).
38. In Samwick's (1998) study, this comparison suffers from the fact that the Social Security variables are derived from imputed wage profiles and therefore lose much of the true variation that exists. Because of this measurement error problem, the coefficients are probably biased toward zero. This difficulty confirms the point that studies using broad data sets have difficulty in capturing the subtleties of the pension incentives that workers actually face.
39. Samwick (1998, p. 233).
40. Anderson, Gustman, and Steinmeier (1999).

policy change that required employers to continue crediting pensions for service after age sixty-five (unless the worker had reached a maximum number of years). Both of these changes should have encouraged delayed retirement, rather than the earlier retirement actually observed. This fact, and the fact that three-quarters of the change among those in their sixties remains unexplained, led Anderson, Gustman, and Steinmeier to deduce that other factors—such as rising wealth, changes in disability insurance, and differences in attitudes about work and retirement—are important in retirement decisions as well.

Coile and Gruber were among the first to use the new Health and Retirement Study to analyze the importance of Social Security and employer pensions on retirement decisions in the 1990s. They used the individual Social Security earnings records attached to the study as well as pension information that enabled them to estimate benefits (and retirement wealth) for a sample of employed men at various ages of retirement. They focused on Social Security and pension accruals and emphasized the importance of estimating the entire future pattern of accruals, not just the effects during the next year.[41]

Several important conclusions emerged from their work. Although changes in Social Security rules generally affect both the lifetime wealth of individuals and their net compensation for additional work (through accruals), the latter (the substitution effect) has a greater impact on retirement decisions than the former (the income effect). This finding leads to at least one counterintuitive conclusion: the scheduled increase in the normal retirement age from sixty-five to sixty-seven (which is equivalent to an across-the-board benefit cut) might *increase* the retirement rates of sixty-two- and sixty-three-year-olds. That could occur because the law not only increases the retirement age, but also decreases the reward for delaying receipt at those ages from the current 6.67 percent for each year of delay to only 5 percent, lowering net compensation.[42] The effect of

---

41. Coile and Gruber (2000). Calculating future Social Security or employer pension accruals requires assumptions about future earnings. Coile and Gruber assume that real earnings grow at a rate of 1 percent a year. They use a 3 percent real discount rate, and age- and gender-specific survival probabilities. The authors estimate that median Social Security accruals are positive through age sixty-four (that is, the recalculation of average earnings and the reward for delaying Social Security receipt outweigh the benefits forgone by working another year) but then turn negative at age sixty-five and continue to grow more negative with age. At every age, however, accruals are widely dispersed around the median.

42. Until recently recipients who claimed benefits at age sixty-two received 80 percent of a full "age sixty-five" benefit for as long as they received benefits; in other words, they were penalized 20 percent for claiming benefits three years early, or 6.67 percent of the full benefit a year. Under legislation passed in 1983, the normal retirement age is currently being increased from sixty-five to sixty-seven. When the normal retirement age reaches sixty-seven, the penalty will be 30 percent for claiming benefits at age sixty-two, 25 percent at age sixty-three, and 20 percent at age sixty-four. Thus the annual penalty for early retirement (or, equivalently, the reward for working and delaying receipt of benefits for one year) will be 5 percent at ages sixty-two and sixty-three and 6.67 percent from then until the normal retirement age (Social Security Administration 1998, table 2A20).

lowering net wages through the accrual process, which encourages retirement, outweighs the loss in Social Security wealth, which discourages it.

Coile and Gruber estimated that workers older than sixty-two are more responsive to retirement incentives than are younger workers, which suggests that some workers face a liquidity problem before they are old enough to receive Social Security benefits. Finally, the authors found that the magnitude of the Social Security effects declines when pensions are also incorporated into the analysis, suggesting an important interaction between the two.

It is common to assume that pensions decrease labor supply late in life. Several studies have emphasized, however, that the actual patterns are more complex. For example, in a study using the Retirement History Study from the 1970s, Ruhm estimated that pension coverage increases the probability of remaining employed at ages fifty-eight through sixty-one (by an average of about 7 percentage points), decreases it modestly for those ages sixty-two to sixty-four (by about 4 points), and then decreases it dramatically for those sixty-five through sixty-eight, by an average of about 11 percentage points, "resulting in a more complicated and ambiguous aggregate impact than is frequently realized."[43]

In sum, research during the last two decades has established that many defined benefit pension plans contain strong incentives to leave the firm at specific ages and that these incentives influence the labor supply behavior of older workers. This conclusion emerges both from studies with detailed information on specific pension plans but only limited data on the demographics of the employees and from studies with extensive demographic, economic, and family data on large representative samples but little information on the pension rules of those covered by a plan. The consensus is that defined benefit pension incentives are stronger than Social Security incentives, although there is considerable debate on the exact magnitude of both. The Health and Retirement Study contains excellent information on both and should allow researchers to make more precise estimates of the relative importance of Social Security and private retirement incentives.

Bridge Jobs: The Process of Retirement

Pension research has tended to emphasize departure from the firm as the labor market variable of interest, because pension incentives alter compensation on the career job but generally do not penalize work with other firms. Social Security research is more likely to study complete departure from the labor market, because all earnings, whether from career or subsequent jobs, are treated alike in the Social Security regulations. In many cases these two views of retirement are identical; many older Americans leave a career job and the labor market at the

43. Ruhm (1996, p. 172).

same time and retire unambiguously in one move. Considerable research, however, has established that many other workers withdraw from the labor market more gradually, utilizing "bridge jobs" between full-time career employment and complete withdrawal from the labor market.[44] For many Americans, retirement is a process, not a single event.

Some researchers have defined retirement as complete labor force withdrawal, whereas others consider as retired an older person who has significantly reduced the hours worked in any given time period. Others base retirement status on the receipt of Social Security or employer pension benefits, regardless of hours worked, and still others allow survey respondents to define themselves as retired or not. Ultimately, it is less important to define at what point along this exit route one is labeled "retired" than it is to understand the process by which people leave their career jobs and the labor market.

Bridge jobs are an important part of the exit process from full-time employment to complete retirement. The estimates of the number of workers in bridge jobs depends on how one defines the "career job" that is being left and the "bridge job" that is being entered. As a starting point, one might define a career job as a full-time job held for at least ten years. A bridge job, then, could be a part-time job of any duration, or a full-time job held for fewer than ten years. With this definition, an examination of respondents in the first three waves of the Health and Retirement Study indicates that nearly one-half of the men and women who have left a career job moved to a bridge job rather than out of the labor force. If a career job requires only eight years of tenure, then about 45 percent of those leaving a career job enter a bridge job; if a career job requires just five years of full-time work, then about 30 percent of those leaving a career job enter a bridge job.[45]

Whether a worker moves to a new job or stops working altogether after leaving a career job depends on many factors, some of which can be measured. Workers in poor health are more likely to leave the labor market entirely when they leave their career jobs, as are older workers. Those who have health insurance coverage on their career jobs and would maintain health coverage if they left (through any of a number of sources, including retiree health coverage from the firm or inclusion on the spouse's policy) are less likely to move to a bridge job than those who would lose health coverage if they left their career job or those with no health coverage to lose. There is some evidence that workers at both ends of the socioeconomic scale, measured in this case by the hourly wage rate on the career job, are more likely to take bridge jobs on the way out than are those in the middle. Apparently, some lack the resources to retire completely

---

44. Early contributors to this literature include Gustman and Steinmeier (1984), Honig and Hanoch (1985), Quinn, Burkhauser, and Myers (1990), and Ruhm (1990a, b).
45. Quinn (1999a, b, pp. 12–13).

and keep working out of economic necessity, whereas others remain in the labor force because they prefer some work to full retirement. In a recent survey by the Employee Benefit Research Institute, about 60 percent of current workers surveyed said that they thought that they would work for pay after retirement. About one-third of those suggested that they had to keep working to make ends meet, while about one-half cited "quality of life" issues as the main motivation.[46]

How do pensions affect the job exit process? The same study found that those participating in a pension plan but not yet eligible for benefits were the most likely to stay on the job and that those who were eligible for benefits at the time of the survey were the most likely to stop working by then. Defined benefit pensions had stronger effects on retirement decisions than defined contribution plans did. Eligibility for pension benefits decreased the probability of moving to a bridge job for both men and women, even though bridge jobs rarely have any effect on pension receipt. It turns out to be more difficult to predict which workers are likely to take a bridge job than which ones are likely to move out of employment altogether. Given the importance of bridge jobs in the economy and the increasingly important role they may play as the baby boom generation moves into retirement in the opening decades of the twenty-first century, additional research in this area is sorely needed.

Conclusions

Our review and analysis of the economics and policy literature on the effect of pensions on wages, productivity, turnover, and retirement provides some clear conclusions and some unanswered questions.

—Economic theory suggests that when firms allocate money to pension contributions, they allocate less to other forms of compensation. Empirical studies, however, have produced a wide range of estimates of the compensating wage differential for pensions, including positive as well as negative estimates. Are these mixed findings the result of inadequate data, or is the theory of compensating wage differentials flawed?

—Firms could make contributions to pension plans without reducing wages or other forms of compensation if there are other cost savings associated with pension coverage, such as greater productivity or increased training of pension participants. Limited evidence, both direct and indirect, provides weak support for the theory that labor is more productive in firms with pension plans.

—Another potential offset to the costs of pension contributions is lower turnover. Numerous empirical studies suggest that pension participants have longer tenure than employees not covered by a pension. Pension participants are less likely than other workers to quit or to be laid off. This longer tenure

---

46. Quinn (1999b, p. 9).

should reduce turnover and training costs and helps explain why firms might provide pension contributions without reducing wages dollar for dollar. As expected, these effects are more frequently found for workers covered by defined benefit plans.

—Defined benefit pension plans provide strong financial incentives for workers to retire at specific ages, and workers respond to these incentives. Firms can select pension provisions to discourage workers from remaining on the job after a certain age; under such provisions, workers who remain with the firm past certain ages, such as the early and normal retirement ages, typically suffer a sharp decline in expected lifetime pension benefits. A quarter century of economic research has consistently shown that pensions are a factor in workers' decisions to remain with their career employers.

—Not all workers move directly from full-time employment on a career job to complete labor force withdrawal. Many individuals leave their career employer and take on a part- or full-time bridge job. Additional research is needed to examine the transition from full-time work and the ways in which pensions affect these choices, especially the extent to which phased retirement or part-time work is influenced by pension rules and regulations.

Although many questions remain to be answered, the evidence clearly shows that pensions are an important component of compensation and that incentives associated with pension plans alter worker behavior. In general, pension participants are less likely to quit, more likely to have longer job tenure, and more likely to retire at specific ages related to their pension plans.

References

Allen, Steven G., Robert L. Clark, and Ann A. McDermed. 1988. "The Pension Cost of Changing Jobs." *Research on Aging* 10 (December): 459–71.

———. 1993. "Pensions, Bonding, and Lifetime Jobs." *Journal of Human Resources* 28 (Summer): 463–81.

Anderson, Patricia M., Alan L. Gustman, and Thomas L. Steinmeier. 1999. "Trends in Male Labor Force Participation and Retirement: Some Evidence on the Role of Pensions and Social Security in the 1970s and 1980s." *Journal of Labor Economics* 17, part 1 (October): 757–83.

Avery, Robert B., Gregory E. Elliehausen, and Glenn B. Canner. 1984. "Survey of Consumer Finances, 1983." *Federal Reserve Bulletin* 70 (September): 679–92.

Bartel, Ann P., and George J. Borjas. 1977. "Middle-Age Job Mobility: Its Determinants and Consequences." In *Men in Their Preretirement Years,* edited by Seymour Wolfbein, 39–97. Temple University, School of Business Administration.

Becker, Gary S. 1964. *Human Capital: A Theoretical and Empirical Analysis.* Columbia University Press.

Becker, Gary S., and George J. Stigler. 1974. "Law Enforcement, Malfeasance, and Compensation of Enforcers." *Journal of Legal Studies* 3 (January): 1–18.

Burkhauser, Richard V. 1979. "The Pension Acceptance Decision of Older Workers." *Journal of Human Resources* 14 (Winter): 63–75.

———. 1980. "The Early Acceptance of Social Security: An Asset Maximization Approach." *Industrial and Labor Relations Review* 33 (July): 484–92.

Burkhauser, Richard V., and Paul J. Gertler, eds. 1995. "The Health and Retirement Study: Data Quality and Early Results." *Journal of Human Resources* 30 (Supplement).

Burkhauser, Richard V., and Joseph F. Quinn. 1983. "Is Mandatory Retirement Overrated? Evidence from the 1970s." *Journal of Human Resources* 18 (Summer): 337–58.

Clark, Robert L., and Ann A. McDermed. 1986. "Earnings and Pension Compensation: The Effect of Eligibility." *Quarterly Journal of Economics* 101 (May): 341–61.

———. 1988. "Pension Wealth and Job Changes: The Effects of Vesting, Portability, and Lump-Sum Distributions." *Gerontologist* 28 (July): 524–32.

Coile, Courtney. 1999. "Retirement Incentives and Couples' Retirement Decisions." Working paper. Cambridge, Mass.: National Bureau of Economic Research (November).

Coile, Courtney, and Jonathan Gruber. 2000. "Social Security and Retirement." Working Paper 7830. Cambridge, Mass.: National Bureau of Economic Research (August).

Cornwell, Christopher, Stuart Dorsey, and Nasser Mehrzad. 1991. "Opportunistic Behavior of Firms in Implicit Pension Contracts." *Journal of Human Resources* 26 (Fall): 704–25.

Curme, Michael A., and William E. Even. 1995. "Pension Coverage and Borrowing Constraints." *Journal of Human Resources* 30 (Fall): 701–12.

Dorsey, Stuart. 1995. "Pension Portability and Labor Market Efficiency: A Survey of the Literature." *Industrial and Labor Relations Review* 48 (January): 276–92.

Dorsey, Stuart, Christopher Cornwell, and David Macpherson. 1998. *Pensions and Productivity.* Kalamazoo, Mich.: Upjohn Institute for Employment Research.

Dorsey, Stuart, and David A. Macpherson. 1997. "Pensions and Training." *Industrial Relations* 36 (January): 81–96.

Ehrenberg, Ronald G. 1980. "Retirement System Characteristics and Compensating Wage Differentials in the Public Sector." *Industrial and Labor Relations Review* 33 (July): 470–83.

Employee Benefit Research Institute. 1994. *Employment Based Retirement Income Benefits: Analysis of the April 1993 CPS.* Issue Brief 153. Washington.

———. 1997. *EBRI Databook on Employee Benefits.* Washington.

Even, William E., and David A. Macpherson. 1990. "The Gender Gap in Pensions and Wages." *Review of Economics and Statistics* 72 (May): 259–65.

———. 1996. "Employer Size and Labor Turnover: The Role of Pensions." *Industrial and Labor Relations Review* 49 (July): 707–28.

Fields, Gary S., and Olivia S. Mitchell. 1984. *Retirement, Pensions, and Social Security.* MIT Press.

Gunderson, Morley, Douglas Hyatt, and James E. Pesando. 1992. "Wage-Pension Trade-Offs in Collective Agreements." *Industrial and Labor Relations Review* 46 (October): 146–60.

Gustman, Alan L., Olivia S. Mitchell, and Thomas L. Steinmeier. 1994. "The Role of Pensions in the Labor Market: A Survey of the Literature." *Industrial and Labor Relations Review* 47 (April): 417–38.

Gustman, Alan L., and Thomas L. Steinmeier. 1984. "Partial Retirement and the Analysis of Retirement Behavior." *Industrial and Labor Relations Review* 37 (April): 403–15.

———. 1993. "Pension Portability and Labor Mobility: Evidence from the Survey of Income and Program Participation." *Journal of Public Economics* 50 (March): 299–323.

———. 1995. *Pension Incentives and Job Mobility.* Kalamazoo, Mich.: Upjohn Institute for Employment Research.

Honig, Marjorie, and Giora Hanoch. 1985. "Partial Retirement as a Separate Mode of Retirement Behavior." *Journal of Human Resources* 20 (Winter): 21–46.

Ippolito, Richard A. 1985. "The Labor Contract and True Economic Pension Liabilities." *American Economic Review* 75 (December): 1031–43.

———. 1986. *Pensions, Economics, and Public Policy.* Homewood, Ill.: Dow Jones–Irwin.

————. 1991. "Encouraging Long-Term Tenure: Wage Tilt or Pensions?" *Industrial and Labor Relations Review* 44 (April): 520–35.

————. 1994. "Pensions and Indenture Premia." *Journal of Human Resources* 29 (Summer): 795–812.

————. 1997. *Pension Plans and Employee Performance: Evidence, Analysis, and Policy.* University of Chicago Press.

Kotlikoff, Laurence J., and David A. Wise. 1985. "Labor Compensation and the Structure of Private Pension Plans: Evidence for Contractual versus Spot Labor Markets." In *Pensions, Labor, and Individual Choice,* edited by David A. Wise, 55–85. University of Chicago Press.

————. 1987. "The Incentive Effects of Private Pension Plans." In *Issues in Pension Economics,* edited by Zvi Bodie, John B. Shoven, and David A. Wise, 283–336. University of Chicago Press.

————. 1989a. "Employee Retirement and a Firm's Pension Plan." In *The Economics of Aging,* edited by David A. Wise, 279–330. University of Chicago Press.

————. 1989b. *The Wage Carrot and the Pension Stick: Retirement Benefits and Labor Force Participation.* Kalamazoo, Mich.: Upjohn Institute for Employment Research.

Lazear, Edward P. 1979. "Why Is There Mandatory Retirement?" *Journal of Political Economy* 87 (December): 1261–84.

Lazear, Edward P., and Robert L. Moore. 1988. "Pensions and Turnover." In *Pensions in the U.S. Economy,* edited by Zvi Bodie, John B. Shoven, and David A. Wise, 163–88. University of Chicago Press.

Long, James E., and Frank A. Scott. 1982. "The Income Tax and Nonwage Compensation." *Review of Economics and Statistics* 64 (May): 211–19.

Lumsdaine, Robin L., James H. Stock, and David A. Wise. 1994. "Pension Plan Provisions and Retirement: Men and Women, Medicare and Models." In *Studies in the Economics of Aging,* edited by David A. Wise, 183–212. University of Chicago Press.

————. 1997. "Retirement Incentives: The Interaction between Employer-Provided Pensions, Social Security, and Retiree Health Benefits." In *The Economic Effects of Aging in the United States and Japan,* edited by Michael D. Hurd and Naohiro Yashiro, 261–93. University of Chicago Press.

Luzadis, Rebecca A., and Olivia S. Mitchell. 1991. "Explaining Pension Dynamics." *Journal of Human Resources* 26 (Fall): 679–703.

McCormick, Barry, and Gordon Hughes. 1984. "The Influence of Pensions on Job Mobility." *Journal of Public Economics* 23 (February–March): 183–206.

McGill, Dan M., and others. 1996. *Fundamentals of Private Pensions.* University of Pennsylvania Press.

Mitchell, Olivia S. 1982. "Fringe Benefits and Labor Mobility." *Journal of Human Resources* 17 (Spring): 286–98.

Mitchell, Olivia S., and Silvana Pozzebon. 1986. "Wages, Pensions, and Wage-Pension Trade-offs." In *Explaining Patterns in Old-Age Pensions,* edited by Olivia S. Mitchell. Washington: National Institute on Aging.

Montgomery, Edward, Kathryn Shaw, and Mary Ellen Benedict.1992. "Pensions and Wages: An Hedonic Price Theory Approach." *International Economic Review* 33 (February): 111–28.

Oi, Walter Y. 1962. "Labor as a Quasi-Fixed Factor." *Journal of Political Economy* 70 (December): 538–55.

Quinn, Joseph F. 1997. "The Role of Bridge Jobs in the Retirement Patterns of Older Americans in the 1990s." In *Retirement Prospects in a Defined Contribution World,* edited by Dallas Salisbury, 25–39. Washington: Employee Benefit Research Institute.

————. 1999a. "New Paths to Retirement." In *Forecasting Retirement Needs and Retirement Wealth,* edited by Brett Hammond, Olivia S. Mitchell, and Anna Rappaport. University of Pennsylvania Press.

————. 1999b. *Retirement Patterns and Bridge Jobs in the 1990s.* Issue Brief 206. Washington: Employee Benefit Research Institute.

Quinn, Joseph F., Richard V. Burkhauser, and Daniel A. Myers. 1990. *Passing the Torch: The Influence of Economic Incentives on Work and Retirement.* Kalamazoo, Mich.: Upjohn Institute for Employment Research.

Ruhm, Christopher J. 1990a. "Bridge Jobs and Partial Retirement." *Journal of Labor Economics* 8 (October): 482–501.

————. 1990b. "Career Jobs, Bridge Employment, and Retirement." In *Bridges to Retirement: Older Workers in a Changing Labor Market,* edited by Peter B. Doeringer, 92–107. Ithaca, N.Y.: ILR Press.

————. 1996. "Do Pensions Increase the Labor Supply of Older Men?" *Journal of Public Economics* 59 (February): 157–75.

Salop, Joanne, and Steven Salop. 1976. "Self-Selection and Turnover in the Labor Market." *Quarterly Journal of Economics* 90 (November): 619–27.

Samwick, Andrew A. 1998. "New Evidence on Pensions, Social Security, and the Timing of Retirement." *Journal of Public Economics* 70 (November): 207–36.

Schiller, Bradley R., and Randall D. Weiss. 1980. "Pensions and Wages: A Test for Equalizing Differences." *Review of Economics and Statistics* 62 (November): 529–38.

Smith, Robert S. 1981. "Compensating Differentials for Pension and Underfunding in the Public Sector." *Review of Economics and Statistics* 63 (August): 463–68.

Smith, Robert S., and Ronald G. Ehrenberg. 1983. "Estimating Wage-Fringe Tradeoffs: Some Data Problems." In *The Measurement of Labor Cost,* edited by Jack Triplett, 347–67. University of Chicago Press.

Social Security Administration. 1998. *Annual Statistical Supplement to the Social Security Bulletin.* Washington.

Stock, James H., and David A. Wise. 1990a. "The Pension Inducement to Retire: An Option Value Analysis." In *Issues in the Economics of Aging,* edited by David A. Wise, 205–29. University of Chicago Press.

————. 1990b. "Pensions, the Option Value of Work, and Retirement." *Econometrica* 58 (September): 1151–80.

U.S. Bureau of Labor Statistics. 1997. *Employee Benefits in Medium and Large Private Establishments, 1995.* Government Printing Office.

U.S. Department of Labor, Pension and Welfare Benefits Administration. 1992. *Trends in Pensions 1992.* GPO.

————. 1994. *Pension Coverage Issues for the '90s.* GPO.

Woodbury, Stephen A., and Wei-Jang Huang. 1991. *The Tax Treatment of Fringe Benefits.* Kalamazoo, Mich.: Upjohn Institute for Employment Research.

5

The Effect of Pensions and 401(k) Plans on Household Saving and Wealth

WILLIAM G. GALE

One of the most important and controversial aspects of the pension system is its effect on private saving, wealth accumulation, and retirement preparedness. Although traditional pensions and other tax-deferred vehicles, like 401(k) plans and individual retirement accounts (IRAs), clearly make up a sizable share of households' wealth in the pre-retirement years and during retirement, it is less clear how much of that wealth represents incremental balances that would not have existed in some other form in the absence of pensions.

The saving incentive programs mentioned above raise private saving to the extent that households finance their own contributions with reductions in consumption or increases in labor supply; that is, to the extent that households choose to reduce their current living standards. To the extent that households finance their own contributions by shifting into the account existing assets or current-period savings that would have been set aside even in the absence of the incentive, or by increasing their debt, saving incentives do not raise private saving. Likewise, there is no increase in private saving to the extent that households respond to employer-provided pensions or contributions with reductions in their other saving or increases in their borrowing.

I thank Eric Engen, Peter Orszag, John Karl Scholz, Timothy Taylor, and Mark Warshawsky for helpful comments, and the National Institute on Aging for research support.

103

Although a number of prominent economic theories have implications for the effects, if any, of pensions and tax-deferred saving on wealth accumulation, and how these analyses should be modeled, ultimately the question is empirical in nature. Moreover, it has taken on added importance in recent years, for at least two reasons. First, with individuals living longer and retirement ages not rising very fast, many or most people now face the prospect of a lengthy retirement period, for which they will need to find sources of income. But with projected financial shortfalls in Social Security and Medicare suggesting the possibility of significant benefit cuts, the financial status of the elderly in the future will depend heavily on private saving for retirement. Second, federal subsidies for new pensions cost almost $100 billion per year, or almost 1 percent of GDP. Subsidies of this magnitude deserve careful scrutiny.

This paper addresses two key questions about the effects of pensions on saving. First, to what extent do traditional pensions and defined contribution plans raise aggregate wealth? The earliest research on both traditional defined benefit pensions and defined contribution or 401(k) plans appeared to demonstrate very strong effects on private wealth and saving. These efforts, however, were marred by a series of econometric and statistical problems. More recent research using improved econometric and statistical methods has found significantly smaller effects of tax-preferred saving vehicles on private saving and wealth, and in some cases no net effects at all.

The second question is the target-effectiveness of pensions. That is, to what extent do the net tax benefits of pensions accrue to those who need to save more for retirement (or would need to save more in the absence of pensions), and to what extent are the increases in wealth caused by pensions accruing to those households? These issues receive far less attention than the overall impact of pensions on aggregate saving, but arguably are at least as important. Increasing the level of saving in the economy can have positive long-term growth effects, but for retirement income policy, who receives the benefits of pensions and whose saving actually rises is a central concern. If it were known, for example, that pensions and 401(k)s raised the wealth of the Forbes 400 (the richest members of society) but not anyone else, it would be hard to claim that broad retirement policy goals were being met.

Although the example just given is extreme, it is nonetheless the case that pension benefits are skewed toward more affluent households. Evidence shows that these households would be more likely to be saving adequately for retirement even without pensions, and that they disproportionately use pensions as a tax shelter—that is, to divert other savings—rather than to raise their overall level of saving. In sharp contrast, pension benefits are meager among lower- and middle-income households. More often, these households are not saving adequately for retirement; when they do use pensions, however, the net effect is usually to raise their retirement wealth.

Thus, while it is clear that private pensions as currently designed can raise private wealth to some extent, the benefits stemming from increases in wealth are diluted by the substantial shifting of other assets and savings into tax-preferred accounts and the significant mismatch between who receives current pension subsidies and who needs to save more for retirement. Moreover, tax subsidies for pensions cost the government money.

Two policy implications of these conclusions are worth noting. First, expanding pension coverage or contributions or both among low- and moderate-income households would be an effective way to raise their net saving and aggregate private wealth and to make the distribution of wealth more equal. Second, raising contribution limits for pensions or 401(k) plans would be unlikely to raise private saving very much. Only people who already contribute to the limit would be directly affected, and those households predominantly have very high income. According to the evidence, their contributions are more likely to represent the shifting of funds that already have been or would anyway have been saved, rather than the accumulation of new net saving. These findings also leave an ambitious agenda for new research and policy examining the role of alternative incentive, information, and default structures for tax-preferred saving.

Defined Contribution Plans

In defined contribution plans, employers or employees, or both, contribute a specified portion of a worker's current salary into an account belonging to the individual worker. In the most common defined contribution arrangement, the 401(k) plan, employees' contributions are also excluded from current personal income tax. The employer's contributions may be independent of the worker's contributions, but many companies match a percentage of the worker's contribution. Workers typically direct the investments themselves. At retirement, the worker receives the account balance as a lump sum or converts it to annuity, and pays income taxes on any withdrawals. Employees generally may borrow against these accounts or make hardship withdrawals before retirement. Those who leave their jobs before retirement typically may roll the funds into an IRA or cash out the balances. If the funds are withdrawn before the legislated ages, workers are subject to penalties in addition to income taxes.

Although the effect of 401(k) plans on household wealth seems straightforward, several factors make this a difficult problem. First, saving behavior varies significantly across households. Households that participate in, or are eligible for, saving incentive plans have systematically stronger tastes for saving than do other households. Thus, a simple comparison of the saving behavior of households with and without saving incentives will be biased toward showing that the incentives raise saving.

Second, saving and wealth are net concepts: If a household borrows $1,000 and puts the money in a saving incentive account, net private saving is zero. The data indicate that households with saving incentives have taken on more debt than other households. Hence, studies should focus on how saving incentives affect wealth (assets minus debt), not just assets. Moreover, because financial assets are small relative to total assets, studies that focus only on the effects of saving incentives on financial assets may have particularly limited significance.

Third, since the expansion of 401(k)s starting in the early 1980s, financial markets, pensions, and Social Security have undergone major changes. If one ignores interactions among these changes and saving incentives, one can overstate the effects of the incentives on saving.

Fourth, saving incentive contributions are generally tax deductible and saving incentive accounts represent pre-tax balances; one cannot consume the entire amount, because taxes and perhaps penalties are due upon withdrawal. In contrast, contributions to other accounts are generally not deductible and one may generally consume the entire balance in a taxable account. Therefore, a given balance in a saving incentive account represents less saving (defined either as reduced previous consumption or reduced available balances for consumption) than an equivalent amount in a conventional account.[1] Failure to correct for this factor will tend to overstate the amount of saving by 401(k) households, and hence overstate the effects of 401(k) plans on saving.

There is a sizable literature examining the effects of 401(k) plans on household wealth accumulation.[2] A major theme of this chapter is that analyses that ignore these issues overstate the effect of saving incentives on saving. In particular, Engen, Scholz, and I show that accounting for these factors largely or completely eliminates the estimated positive impact of saving incentives on saving found in the literature up to the mid-1990s.[3] This chapter summarizes more recent work on 401(k)s and places it in the context of earlier findings.

Cross-Sectional Analysis

A key issue in the analysis of 401(k) plans is how best to control for heterogeneity in tastes for saving across different groups and over time that may be correlated with 401(k) eligibility and participation. One approach to this problem has been to use cross-sectional variation in eligibility for 401(k)s. In this approach, the effects of 401(k)s are identified by the assumption that 401(k) eligibility is uncorrelated with unobserved tastes for saving, after controlling for certain factors. If eligibility is exogenous with respect to tastes for saving, then

1. Gale (1995); Poterba (2004).
2. This literature is reviewed extensively in Engen, Gale, and Scholz (1996a, 1996b), Poterba, Venti, and Wise (1996a, 1996b), and Bernheim (1999).
3. Engen, Gale, and Scholz (1996a, 1996b).

higher financial assets or wealth for eligible households relative to ineligible households would imply that 401(k)s raise saving. Poterba, Venti, and Wise, for example, perform a cross-sectional analysis using data from several waves of the Survey of Income and Program Participation (SIPP) in the 1980s and 1990s.[4] Based on the premise that eligibility is exogenous with respect to tastes for saving, once one controls for income, they find that almost all 401(k) balances represent increases in wealth.[5]

More recent work has addressed in detail some of the problems that arise in cross-sectional analysis and has found significantly smaller effects of 401(k)s on saving. Benjamin, using the 1991 SIPP, employs propensity-scoring methods to classify households and address the potential correlation between 401(k) eligibility and households' unobserved tastes for saving.[6] His analysis shows that the underlying assumption of Poterba, Venti, and Wise's cross-sectional analysis is false, thus invalidating their results. He goes on to show that about half of 401(k) balances represents new private saving, and one-quarter represents net additions to national saving (after adjusting for the fact that tax exclusions for 401(k) contributions reduce government revenues). Likewise, Engelhardt, using a cross-sectional sample from the 1992 Health and Retirement Study, finds positive effects of 401(k)s on financial assets but not on broader measures of wealth that include pension wealth.[7]

Successive Cross-Sectional Analysis

Poterba, Venti, and Wise also propose a second approach that compares the evolution of asset balances over time for successive cross-sections of "similar savers"—for example, the group of eligible households.[8] In this test, the effects of 401(k)s are identified by the assumption that the only significant difference between the overall samples of eligible households in earlier and later years is that the latter have had increased years of exposure to 401(k)s (and IRAs). Thus, if the eligible households in later years have higher financial assets as a group than those in earlier years, controlling for household characteristics, the conclusion would be that 401(k)s raise saving.

A variant on this approach that allows for events during the period in question to affect saving is to use the group of ineligible families over time as a control group. In this approach, the effects of 401(k)s are identified by the assumption that nothing that changed over the sample period (other than the

4. Poterba, Venti, and Wise (1995).

5. Their assumption, and other issues that arise with cross-sectional tests, are discussed in Engen, Gale, and Scholz (1996a, 1996b) and Bernheim (1999).

6. Benjamin (2003).

7. Engelhardt (2001).

8. Poterba, Venti, and Wise (1995).

advent of 401(k)s had a *differential* impact on the group of eligible households relative to the group of ineligible households. Thus, if assets rose more for the group of eligible households over time than for the group of ineligible households, the difference would be interpreted as the positive effect of 401(k)s on wealth accumulation.

Using these two approaches, Poterba, Venti, and Wise (1995) conclude that 401(k)s raise the financial assets of eligible households. Engen and I use the same approaches and find that while 401(k)s raised financial assets, they did not raise the overall net worth (a broader wealth measure) of eligible households.[9]

Remarkably, Poterba, Venti, and Wise's criticisms of Engen's and my estimates, which use wealth (including housing equity) as the dependent variable, almost exactly parallel the criticisms by Engen, Scholz, and me of Poterba, Venti, and Wise's estimates, which use financial assets as the dependent variable.[10] In each case, the argument is that (a) eligible households *as a group* began the sample period with higher earnings and applicable measures of wealth than ineligible households; and (b), outside factors caused changes in wealth *across earnings classes* that were confused with the effects of 401(k)s. The outside factors caused financial assets to grow in arithmetic terms for high earners relative to low earners over this period, leading Engen, Scholz, and me to argue that the Poterba-Venti-Wise tests using financial assets overstated the impact of 401(k) plans. In contrast, other outside factors caused housing wealth to fall in arithmetic terms for high earners relative to low earners, leading Poterba, Venti, and Wise to argue that the Engen-Gale tests using broad wealth measures that include housing understated the impact of 401(k)s.

In later work, Engen and I address these issues.[11] To separate the effects of 401(k) eligibility from changes in other factors that affect wealth and that have different effects at different earnings levels, we examine the effects of eligibility within each earnings class over time. rather than for the groups as a whole over time. Engen's and my model generalizes both Poterba, Venti, and Wise's successive cross-section analysis and the earlier Engen-Gale model. We explicitly test and reject both of those frameworks, thus invalidating the earlier results. Our more general model generates estimates that about 30 percent or less of 401(k) contributions represent net additions to private saving.[12]

9. Engen and Gale (1995, 1997).

10. Poterba, Venti, and Wise (1996a, 1996b) critique Engen and Gale (1995, 1997); Engen, Gale, and Scholz (1996a, 1996b) critique Poterba, Venti, and Wise (1995).

11. Engen and Gale (2000).

12. An important issue for interpreting these and earlier results in the literature is whether and how average tastes for saving shifted over time for different groups. Engen and Gale (2000) provide new evidence, based on a test proposed by Bernheim (1999), consistent with the view that average tastes for saving across eligible and ineligible households did *not* shift over time in a way that would bias the results toward finding no effect of 401(k)s on wealth.

Effects of Defined Benefit Plans on Household Wealth

In a defined benefit plan, employers commit to paying workers with sufficient job tenure an annual retirement benefit that usually depends on the number of years of service and a measure of a worker's average salary. A typical formula might provide an annual benefit equal to 1 percent multiplied by the number of years the worker stayed at the firm times the average salary over the worker's five highest-paid years at the firm. The employer funds these benefits by making contributions to a pension fund for all employees. Employees typically do not make contributions or have access to the funds before retirement. Employer contributions and the buildup of investment returns inside the account are tax-free; employees pay income tax when the benefits are paid.

Because defined benefit plans were the dominant form of pensions until the 1980s, there have been many studies of their effects on household wealth.[13] The literature can be summarized in two simple statements. First, the vast majority of studies finds that defined benefit pensions are either mostly or wholly new wealth.[14] Second, much of this literature—in particular, almost all of the studies that find the largest "new wealth" effects—suffers from a series of econometric problems that impose systematic biases toward finding that pensions raise wealth. Hence, this literature is uninformative.

This section discusses those biases, ways to adjust for the biases, and the literature that has done so in various ways. Many of the same biases occur in the estimation of defined contribution plans' effects on wealth, as discussed above, and these will be noted only briefly here.

Econometric Issues

Two econometric concerns are similar to those mentioned in the analysis of defined contribution plans, but nevertheless are worth emphasizing here. First, households with higher tastes for saving may be more attracted to jobs with defined benefit plans or jobs with more generous pension plans. To the extent that such a correlation exists and is not corrected in the analysis, the results will be biased toward showing a more positive effect of pensions on wealth than truly exists.[15] Most studies of the effect of defined benefit pensions on wealth have not corrected for this correlation. Several authors, however, use legislative changes in

13. See Gale (1995, 1998) for background on the issues raised in this section.
14. Gale (1995) reviews the literature to the mid-1990s; this chapter discusses subsequent contributions.
15. Johnson (1993), using experimental data from the Health and Retirement Study, finds that workers with high risk aversion or lower time preference rates are more likely to be covered by pensions.

pension benefits as a way to isolate variation in pension wealth from individual tastes for saving.[16] Notably, these two studies find smaller effects of defined benefit pensions on saving than do most other studies, as discussed below.

Second, narrow measures of nonpension wealth bias analyses toward overstating the effect of pensions on wealth. In general, studies that focus on narrow measures of saving or wealth have found little if any offset, while the largest offsets are found in studies that look at broad measures of nonpension wealth.[17] For example, Avery, Elliehausen, and Gustafson estimate that each dollar of pension wealth reduces households' financial assets (a narrow measure of nonpension wealth) by 11 cents, but reduces a broad measure of the household's nonpension wealth by 66 cents.[18]

In contrast to a defined contribution plan, in which a worker has an established balance at any point in time, in a defined benefit plan, a worker has the right to a deferred benefit that is payable as an annuity. This difference raises two additional econometric concerns for the analysis of defined benefit plans.

First, the construction of measures of pension wealth for participants in defined benefit plans is problematic. In a defined benefit plan, pension wealth is the discounted value of future pension income flows adjusted for mortality, inflation, and other factors. The future pension income flow, in turn, depends on the worker's salary history, future salary growth, current and future tenure at the firm, and features of the pension plan. Thus, defined benefit pension wealth for current workers is almost surely measured with error. Measurement error is important because estimates of pension wealth that are unbiased but measured with error will lead to overestimates of the effects of pension on wealth. One way to reduce the severity of this problem is to use data on the pension income of retirees, since this can presumably be measured more precisely than the expected benefits of workers in the future.[19]

The second issue that does not arise with defined contribution plans is the need to adjust for the fact that defined benefit wealth is a present value of future income flows, whereas other wealth is usually represented as a balance at a point in time. This fact, coupled with the fact that a defined benefit plan is part of an

16. Attanasio and Brugiavini (2003), Attanasio and Rohwedder (2003).

17. Cagan (1965), Katona (1965), Venti and Wise (1996), and Samwick (1995) use narrow measures of nonpension wealth and find little offset; Munnell (1976) and Dicks-Mireaux and King (1984) use broad measures of saving and wealth and find significant offsets. The relation between broad wealth measures and estimated offsets is not exact, however: some studies that use broad measures find little offset, for example, Blinder, Gordon, and Wise (1980) and Diamond and Hausman (1984).

18. Avery, Elliehausen, and Gustafson (1986).

19. Venti and Wise (1996) and Gale, Muller, and Phillips (2005) use this approach.

Table 5-1. *Underestimating the Pension Offset*[a]

Income and wealth	Worker A		Worker B	
	Period 1	*Period 2*	*Period 1*	*Period 2*
Cash earnings, pension	100	10	100	0
Consumption	55	55	50	50
Nonpension wealth[b]	45	0	50	0
Pension wealth[b]	10	0	0	0
Offset				
True offset	−1			
Estimated offset	−0.5			
Estimated/true	0.5			

a. True offset is 100 percent.

b. Wealth measures are reported at the end of the period.

employee's total compensation, leads to a fundamental source of bias.[20] In regressions that control for cash earnings and pension wealth, the coefficient on pension wealth will pick up the standard substitution effect or offset between pensions and other wealth, but it will also pick up an income or wealth effect associated with *raising* the household's total compensation by adding a pension.[21] As a result, these estimates will systematically overstate the effect of pensions on wealth—that is, they will understate the true level of offset.

Table 5-1 provides an example of this bias. The interest, discount, and inflation rates are set to zero, for simplicity. Worker A has total compensation in period 1 of 110 units, of which 100 units are paid as a cash wage and 10 are paid as deferred compensation.[22] He optimizes by smoothing consumption over time at 55 units per period, and so holds 45 units of nonpension wealth at the end of period 1. Worker B has the same cash wages of 100 in period 1, but no

20. An additional complicating factor is that current defined benefit pension wealth can be measured either as the level of benefits a worker would receive if he or she stopped working today or as the level of benefits that would be received if he or she continued to be employed at the firm until retirement. In this chapter, as in most of the literature, the latter definition is used.

21. A related point, but not a necessary condition for the results that follow, is that the burden of financing "employer-provided" benefits tends to fall largely on workers through reduced cash wages; see Gruber and Krueger (1991), Montgomery, Shaw, and Benedict (1992), and Gruber (1995). That is, pensions are a form of deferred compensation rather than added compensation.

22. To be consistent with a variety of studies, the cash wages may be thought of as current cash earnings, age-adjusted cash earnings, or lifetime cash earnings.

pension. He smooths consumption at 50 units per period and holds 50 units of nonpension wealth at the end of period 1.

Now consider the results of estimating the pension offset on these two workers at the end of period 1, controlling for cash wages. Since worker A has 10 more units of pension wealth (calculated as the present-discounted value of all future pension income) and 5 fewer units of nonpension wealth than worker B does, the estimated offset would be 50 percent.[23] However, the true offset—the reduction in nonpension wealth from deferring a part of compensation, holding total compensation constant—is 100 percent.

To clarify that the true offset is 100 percent in this example, note that if worker B earned 110 in wages in the first period, he would consume 55 in each period, the same as worker A. Thus, changing the composition of compensation from wages to pensions has no effect on the consumption, a finding that implies (indeed defines) the idea that pension wealth is completely offset by reductions in other wealth.

These results have an intuitive explanation: controlling for cash earnings, the pension represents added compensation, rather than a change in the composition of compensation. Let $N(A)$ be the number of years that a worker of age A has been covered by a pension plan, and let T be $N(A)$ plus the remaining lifetime of the worker. In the years before retirement, a true offset of 100 percent implies an estimated offset of only $N(A)/T$ at age A; more generally, for *any* value of the true offset, the estimated offset will be $N(A)/T$ times as large in absolute value.[24] In this example, the worker spends the added compensation evenly over the T periods from the beginning of coverage to the end of life. At age A, the worker has been in the plan for $N(A)$ years, and has spent $N(A)/T$ of the pension wealth. This spending is financed by reductions in nonpension wealth. He thus has $N(A)/T$ less in nonpension wealth per dollar of pension wealth, so that the estimated offset is $N(A)/T$, even though the true offset is 100 percent.[25]

In earlier work, I generalize this finding to a multiyear model of household saving and consumption and show that the bias can be removed by adjusting the measure of pension wealth used in the regression. In the example above, multiplying pension wealth by $N(A)/T$ yields an estimated effect that equals the true effect. In a more general model, a more complex adjustment is required.

---

23. Let the estimating equation be $W = \alpha E + \beta P$, where W is nonpension wealth, E represents cash earnings (net of employer-provided pensions), and P is pension wealth. The equations would be $45 = \alpha 100 + \beta 10$ for worker A, and $50 = \alpha 100$ for worker B. These equations imply estimates of $\alpha = 0.5$ and $\beta = -0.5$.

24. Gale (1998).

25. This intuition applies until retirement. After retirement, pension and nonpension wealth fall at the same rate, so that the estimated offset remains constant but is still biased; see Gale (1995).

With such adjustments, my own empirical work as well as studies by Attanasio and Brugiavini and Attansio and Rohwedder all find much smaller effects of defined benefit pensions on wealth than did previous studies.[26]

It is worth highlighting the presence of several other biases in the literature. Measuring defined benefit wealth in pre-tax terms overstates the impact of such plans on wealth for the reasons described above. Likewise, studies that omit the worker's age, expected lifespan, and expected retirement age can generate extremely misleading estimates of the impact of defined benefit plans on wealth. Specifically, these studies can lead to the conclusion that defined benefit pensions actually *raise* the amount of nonpension wealth, even if the true effect is that every dollar of defined benefit wealth *reduces* nonpension wealth by a full dollar.[27]

Previous Studies

The following review focuses only on studies of the effects of defined benefit pensions that have made adjustments to pension wealth. In studies using a sample of forty- to sixty-four-year-olds from the 1983 Survey of Consumer Finances, I find a range of effects, depending on the specification.[28] Using a standard specification, I find offsets between 0 and 10 percent, consistent with much of the literature. After adjusting pension wealth as described above, however, I finds offsets that range between 40 and 80 percent.

Attanasio and Brugiavini use variation in pension wealth across households created by the Italian pension reforms of 1992.[29] This variation largely affects households as a function of the age of the head of household in 1992 and his or her occupation, and so is plausibly exogenous with respect to tastes for saving. They adjust pension wealth in a special case of the manner described in my own work.[30] Their results indicate that pension wealth is a substitute for other savings, especially for households in the middle years of their life cycle. In various parameterizations, they find that between 30 percent and 70 percent of defined benefit pension wealth is offset by reductions in other wealth.

---

26. Gale (1998), Attanasio and Brugiavini (2003), and Attanasio and Rohwedder (2003). Controlling for total resources would seem to be an alternative approach, but as discussed in Gale (1998) it is not valid in the presence of less than perfect offset. In a study of the effects of Social Security on wealth, Bernheim (1987) controls for lifetime resources inclusive of Social Security and pension benefits. He finds much larger offsets for Social Security wealth than most previous studies. Bernheim and Scholz (1993b) make a similar point, noting that other things equal, an increase in pension wealth raises lifetime resources and also shifts resources toward retirement.

27. See Gale (1995).

28. Gale (1995, 1998).

29. Attanasio and Brugiavini (2003).

30. Gale (1998).

Attanasio and Rohwedder conduct a similar analysis, using pension reforms in the United Kingdom to generate estimates of the effects of changes in defined benefit pension wealth that are plausibly uncorrelated with unobserved individual tastes for saving.[31] They find that between 55 and 75 percent of earnings-related pension wealth results in lower saving for households headed by persons aged between 32 and 64 years. They find no offset for younger households, but these households account for only a small portion of pension accruals.

Two other studies make adjustments to pension wealth that differ from those dictated by the theory laid out in my study.[32] Gustman and Steinmeier perform a careful and comprehensive analysis of pensions and wealth accumulation using the Health and Retirement Study.[33] They find large effects of pensions on wealth accumulation, with more than half of pensions representing new saving in virtually all of the estimates and up to 100 percent or more representing new saving in some of the specifications.

However, they define current defined benefit wealth as a fraction of the defined benefit wealth the worker would receive if he stayed at his current job until retirement: the ratio of years worked in the plan to date to the years that the worker would have been in the plan if he stayed until retirement. This approach overstates defined benefit wealth relative to the adjustments examined in my work, and by a potentially large margin, biasing their estimates upward.[34] In addition, their estimates contain a second source of upward bias because they do not adjust for the tax-preferred status of pensions.

Khitatrakun, Kitamura, and Scholz use data from the Health and Retirement Survey on pensions and lifetime resources.[35] They adjust defined benefit pension wealth along the lines indicated in my study, but they also adjust defined contribution wealth to equal its expected value at retirement, which significantly complicates the interpretation of the results. They find no offsets between pensions and other wealth at the median of the wealth distribution, but they note the difficulties of interpreting these results when the data contain a combination of credit-constrained and unconstrained households.

---

31. Attanasio and Rohwedder (2003).

32. Gale (1998).

33. Gustman and Steinmeier (1998).

34. See Gale (1998). Gustman and Steinmeier adjust defined benefit pension wealth by the fraction $(A - B)/(R - B)$, where A is current age, B is the age of the worker when he began to participate in the pension plan, and R is 62, the age of early retirement. Gale (1998) adjusts by $(A - B)/(D - B)$, where D is the expected age at death. Thus, for example, for a worker who started in his or her current job at age 50, is currently 60, and will live until 80, the Gustman-Steinmeier adjustment factor would be 0.833, whereas my adjustment factor would be 0.333, less than half as large.

35. Khitatrakun, Kitamura, and Scholz (2000).

The Adequacy of Saving and the Heterogeneous Effects of Pensions on Wealth

The preceding sections have discussed the aggregate effects of pensions on private wealth. Once a variety of econometric issues have been addressed, the evidence suggests that only a relatively small portion of the existing wealth accumulated in defined benefit and defined contribution plans represents net additions to private savings.

The goal of the pension system is to help households achieve *adequate* (as opposed to unlimited) retirement income. A well-designed system of retirement saving incentives would (a) provide benefits mainly to households who were otherwise not saving enough for retirement, and (b) structure tax-deferred saving plans in a way that would increase the wealth of households that did participate and receive benefits. This section therefore addresses three related issues: Who is not saving adequately for retirement? Who benefits from pension plans? And, whose wealth increases due to pension plans?

Although there is some controversy on the subject, most studies have found that at least some U.S. households are saving too little and therefore will arrive at retirement with insufficient wealth to maintain their current living standards. Not surprisingly, these studies typically find that the problem is more serious among families with modest incomes and with low levels of education. In contrast, families with high income and extensive education appear to be doing quite well.[36]

The broad pattern of distributional benefits from pensions is also clear: High-income households are more likely to be covered by a pension. If they are eligible, they are more likely to participate. The share of salary contributed rises with earnings, which implies that the actual amounts put in rise more than proportionally as income rises. As a result, the benefits of the pension system are concentrated among higher-income households.

In short, high-income households (or generally more-advantaged households) are better prepared for retirement than are other households, and high-income households receive more pension benefits than do other households. If pensions and 401(k)s were generating new wealth for high-income households, this would explain one result (that high-income households are better prepared for retirement) in terms of the other (that they also receive more pension benefits), and this would be very encouraging news for the efficacy of pensions and 401(k)s in raising saving.

36. See, for example, Banks, Blundell, and Tanner (1998), Bernheim (1992), Bernheim and Scholz (1993a), Engen, Gale, and Uccello (1999, 2005a, 2005b), Moore and Mitchell (1997), Mitchell, Moore, and Phillips (1998), and Warshawsky and Ameriks (1998).

Unfortunately, the literature has come to almost exactly the opposite conclusion: namely, that pension wealth and 401(k) balances tend *not* to increase wealth among high-income, high-education, or otherwise advantaged households (for example, those who have other types of saving incentive assets), but to raise wealth among lower-income or less-advantaged households. This result is common to studies both of 401(k) plans and of defined benefit plans.[37] This is plausible, since such households would find it easier to substitute existing taxable assets or current-period saving that would have been done anyway into the tax-preferred accounts. By doing so, they obtain the tax subsidy without having to incur any painful loss of consumption or leisure. Even the studies that find only a small share of overall contributions represents net additional saving indicate that pensions and 401(k) plans can help raise wealth accumulation by low- and middle-income households, which often have little in the way of other assets. Since more advantaged households possess the vast majority of pension and 401(k) wealth, the finding that these households tend to substitute other saving into tax-preferred forms helps explain why the overall response of saving to pensions is so anemic.

In summary, the results regarding (a) the distribution of pension benefits, (b) the differential effects of pensions on saving across income and demographic groups, and (c) the composition of who is saving adequately for retirement match up in an interesting way. Higher-income (or generally more-advantaged) households are generally saving adequately for retirement and are most likely to utilize pensions, but their pension contributions represent less new saving and more asset shifting (and hence, more tax avoidance) than do the pension accumulations of lower earners. Conversely, lower-income households are less likely to be saving adequately for retirement and are less likely to have pensions than are higher earners, but their pension contributions are more likely to represent net additions to savings. If the goal of pension and 401(k) benefits is to raise the adequacy of saving for retirement among the American population, they do not appear to be well targeted.

Conclusion

This survey leads to two principal conclusions. First, current pension arrangements do have limited effects on private wealth. Second, a large share of the benefits from current pension rules are directed toward households that do not need them in the first place and use them to shelter funds rather than to raise their saving. This suggests that the benefits of pensions are significantly diluted.

37. On 401(k) plans, see Benjamin (2003), Engelhardt (2001), and Engen and Gale (2000). On defined benefit plans, see Bernheim and Scholz (1993a, 1993b), Gale (1998), and Gale, Muller, and Phillips (2005).

A complete policy evaluation, however, would incorporate several other factors. For example, to the extent that saving incentives do raise private saving, do they do so at an acceptable cost? Contributions to saving incentives and investment earnings are typically tax deferred, and thus reduce public saving (increasing the budget deficit) in the short run. The long-run impact on public saving is less obvious; if the incentives increase private saving, they may also increase future income and tax revenue. Saving incentives only succeed in a meaningful sense if they raise national saving—that is, if they raise private saving by more than they reduce public saving. Although this issue is beyond the scope of the present discussion, it is an important caveat in evaluating alternative pension policies. In addition, even if saving incentives do not raise saving at all, there may be equity reasons for providing access to saving incentives to certain groups, such as households that do not have pension coverage. Issues relating to the equity and efficiency of tax-based saving incentives more generally are also beyond the scope of this chapter.

The conclusion that less than half, and quite possibly a quarter or less, of pension and 401(k) wealth represents increases in private savings or net worth (and a correspondingly even smaller portion represents increases in national saving) fits nicely into the hierarchy of responses of economic behavior to tax rules developed by Slemrod and Auerbach.[38] They find that decisions concerning the timing of economic transactions are the most clearly responsive to tax considerations. The next tier of responses include financial and accounting choices, such as allocating a given amount of savings to tax-preferred versus other assets. The least responsive category of behavior consists of agents' real decisions, such as the level of saving. This is consistent with the view that tax-preferred saving opportunities generate a substantial amount of balances in tax-preferred accounts but have a small effect on overall wealth accumulation.

These results leave an ambitious agenda for future research. Better pension designs could be obtained if it were understood why existing saving incentives appear not to have worked well to date, and why the incentives appear to have more positive effects on the wealth of less-advantaged households. It may be that 401(k)s raise saving for low-income groups by providing cheap access to the stock market.[39] Alternatively, illiquid retirement saving might be a poor substitute for other saving for households with little wealth, who need the savings for precautionary reasons.[40] If so, then, to the extent that low-earning households do contribute to such plans, their contributions are more likely to be new saving. A third possibility is that higher earners or high-saving households are simply more economically sophisticated, and hence have both the resources and the

38. Slemrod (1992) and Auerbach and Slemrod (1997).
39. Carney and Gale (1999).
40. Samwick (1995).

wherewithal to take advantage of sheltering strategies that allow them to capture the tax benefits of 401(k)s without sacrificing living standards.

The virtual absence of randomized experiments is perhaps the biggest obstacle to evaluating policies toward tax-preferred saving. Although there have been a few experiments to date, a broader set of randomized trials could help clarify why and how tax-preferred saving incentives could be made to function more effectively.[41] Promising possibilities that are currently being explored for improving the design of tax-preferred saving plans include altering their default or incentive structures and increasing the information and education available to participants and the planning undertaken by them.[42] This is an exciting new direction for research and policy toward pensions.

References

Ameriks, John, Andrew Caplin, and John Leahy. 2003. "Wealth Accumulation and the Propensity to Plan." *Quarterly Journal of Economics* 118 (3): 1007–47.

Attanasio, Orazio P., and Agar Brugiavini. 2003. "Social Security and Households' Saving." *Quarterly Journal of Economics* 118 (3): 1075–119

Attanasio, Orazio P., and Susann Rohwedder. 2003. "Pension Wealth and Household Saving: Evidence from Pension Reforms in the United Kingdom." *American Economic Review* 93 (5): 1499–521.

Auerbach, Alan J., and Joel Slemrod. 1997. "The Economic Effects of the Tax Reform Act of 1986." *Journal of Economic Literature* 35 (2): 589–632.

Avery, Robert B., Gregory E. Elliehausen, and Thomas A. Gustafson. 1986. "Pensions and Social Security in Household Portfolios: Evidence from the 1983 Survey of Consumer Finances." In *Savings and Capital Formation,* edited by F. Gerard Adams and Susan M. Wachter. Lexington: Lexington Books.

Banks, James, Richard Blundell, and Sarah Tanner. 1998. "Is There a Retirement-Savings Puzzle?" *American Economic Review* 88 (4): 769–88.

Bayer, Patrick J., B. Douglas Bernheim, and J. Karl Scholz. 1996. "The Effects of Financial Education in the Workplace: Evidence from a Survey of Employers." Stanford University.

Benjamin, Daniel J. 2003. "Does 401(k) Eligibility Increase National Savings? Evidence from Propensity Score Subclassification." *Journal of Public Economics* 87 (5–6): 1259–90.

41. Duflo and others (2005) examine how randomized variation in matching rates on contributions to IRAs affect willingness to contribute to the IRA and the amount contributed. Mills, Gale, and Patterson (2005) evaluate the effects of individual development accounts on wealth in a randomized trial.

42. On the role of defaults, see Madrian and Shea (2001), Choi and others (2001a, 2001b, 2003), and Thaler and Benartzi (2004). For background on incentives, see Duflo and others (2005) and Gale, Gruber, and Orszag (2005). The role of information, planning, and financial education is discussed by, among others, Ameriks, Caplin, and Leahy (2003), Lusardi (2001), Bayer, Bernheim, and Scholz (1996), Bernheim and Garrett (2003), and Bernheim, Garrett, and Maki (2001).

Bernheim, B. Douglas. 1987. "The Economic Effects of Social Security: Toward a Reconciliation of Theory and Measurement." *Journal of Public Economics* 33 (3): 273–304.

———. 1992. "Is the Baby Boom Generation Preparing Adequately for Retirement?" Technical Report. Merrill Lynch (September).

———. 1999. "Taxation and Saving." Working Paper 7061. Cambridge, Mass.: National
Bureau of Economic Research (March).

Bernheim, B. Douglas, and Daniel M. Garrett. 2003. "The Effects of Financial Education in
the Workplace: Evidence from a Survey of Households." *Journal of Public Economics* 87
(7–8): 1487–519.

Bernheim, B. Douglas, Daniel M. Garrett, and Dean Maki. 2001. "Education and Saving:
The Long-Term Effects of High School Financial Curriculum Mandates." *Journal of Public
Economics* 80 (3): 435–65.

Bernheim, B. Douglas, and John Karl Scholz. 1993a. "Private Pensions and Household Saving." Mimeo. University of Wisconsin.

———. 1993b. "Private Saving and Public Policy." In *Tax Policy and the Economy*, vol. 7,
edited by James Poterba, pp. 73–110. MIT Press.

Blinder, Alan S., Roger H. Gordon, and Donald E. Wise. 1980. "Reconsidering the Work
Disincentive Effects of Social Security." *National Tax Journal* 33 (4): 431–42.

Cagan, Phillip. 1965. *The Effect of Pension Plans on Aggregate Saving: Evidence from a Sample
Survey.* Columbia University Press.

Carney, Stacie, and William G. Gale. 1999. "Asset Accumulation in Low-Income Households." In *Benefits and Mechanisms for Spreading Asset Ownership in the United States,*
edited by Thomas M. Shapiro and Edward Wolff. New York: Russell Sage Foundation.

Choi, James J., and others. 2001a. "Defined Contribution Pensions: Plan Rules, Participant
Decisions, and the Path of Least Resistance." Working Paper 8655. Cambridge, Mass.:
National Bureau of Economic Research (December).

———. 2001b. "For Better or for Worse: Default Effects and 401(k) Savings Behavior."
Working Paper 8651. Cambridge, Mass.: National Bureau of Economic Research (December).

———. 2003. "Passive Decisions and Potent Defaults." Working Paper 9917. Cambridge,
Mass.: National Bureau of Economic Research (August).

Diamond, Peter A., and J. A. Hausman. 1984. "Individual Retirement and Savings Behavior." *Journal of Public Economics* 23 (1/2): 81–114.

Dicks-Mireaux, Louis, and Mervyn King. 1984. "Pension Wealth and Household Savings:
Tests of Robustness." *Journal of Public Economics* 23 (1/2): 115–39.

Duflo, Esther, and others. 2005. "Saving Incentives for Low- and Middle-Income Families:
Evidence from a Field Experiment with H&R Block." Brookings (September).

Engelhardt, Gary. 2001. "Have 401(k)s Raised Household Saving? Evidence from the Health
and Retirement Study." Center for Policy Research, Maxwell School of Citizenship and
Public Affairs, Syracuse University (June).

Engen, Eric M., and William G. Gale. 1995. "Debt, Taxes and the Effects of 401(k) Plans on
Household Wealth Accumulation." Mimeo. Brookings (October).

———. 1997. "Debt, Taxes and the Effects of 401(k) Plans on Household Wealth Accumulation." Mimeo. Brookings (May).

———. 2000. "The Effects of 401(k) Plans on Household Wealth: Differences across Earnings Groups." Brookings (August).

Engen, Eric M., William G. Gale, and John Karl Scholz. 1996a. "The Illusory Effect of Saving Incentives on Saving." *Journal of Economic Perspectives* 10 (4): 113–38.

———. 1996b. "The Effects of Tax-Based Saving Incentives on Saving and Wealth." Working Paper 5759. Cambridge, Mass.: National Bureau of Economic Research (September).

Engen, Eric M., William G. Gale, and Cori Uccello. 1999. "The Adequacy of Household Saving." *Brookings Papers on Economic Activity,* no. 2: 65–187.

———. 2005a. "Lifetime Earnings, Social Security Benefits, and the Adequacy of Retirement Wealth Accumulation." *Social Security Bulletin* 66 (1): 1–20.

———. 2005b. "Effects of Stock Market Fluctuations on the Adequacy of Retirement Wealth Accumulation." *Review of Income and Wealth* 51 (3): 397–418.

Gale, William G. 1995. "The Effects of Pensions on Wealth: A Re-Evaluation of Theory and Evidence." Brookings (June).

———. 1998. "The Effects of Pensions on Household Wealth: A Reevaluation of Theory and Evidence." *Journal of Political Economy* 106 (4): 706–23 (August).

Gale, William G., Jonathan Gruber, and Peter Orszag. 2005. "Improving Opportunities and Incentives for Saving by Middle- and Low-Income Households." Brookings (September).

Gale, William G., Leslie Muller, and John W. R. Phillips. 2005. "Effects of Defined Benefit Pensions and Social Security on Household Wealth: Evidence from a Sample of Retirees." Brookings (February).

Gruber, Jonathan. 1995. "The Incidence of Payroll Taxation: Evidence from Chile." Working Paper 5053. Cambridge, Mass.: National Bureau of Economic Research (March).

Gruber, Jonathan, and Alan B. Krueger. 1991. "The Incidence of Mandated Employer-Provided Insurance: Lessons from Workers' Compensation Insurance." In *Tax Policy and the Economy*, vol. 5, edited by David Bradford, pp. 111–44. MIT Press.

Gustman, Alan L., and Thomas L. Steinmeier. 1998. "Effects of Pensions on Savings: Analysis with Data from the Health and Retirement Study." Working Paper 6681. Cambridge, Mass.: National Bureau of Economic Research (August).

Johnson, Richard W. 1993. "The Impact of Worker Preferences on Pension Coverage in the HRS." Health and Retirement Study Working Paper 94-018. Ann Arbor, Mich.: PSC Publications (December).

Katona, George. 1965. *Private Pensions and Individual Saving.* University of Michigan Press.

Khitatrakun, Surachai, Yuichi Kitamura, and John Karl Scholz. 2000. "Pensions and Wealth: New Evidence from the Health and Retirement Study." Mimeo. University of Wisconsin, Madison.

Lusardi, Annamaria. 2001. "Explaining Why So Many People Do Not Save." Working Paper 2001-05. Center for Retirement Research, Boston College (September).

Madrian, Brigitte C., and Dennis F. Shea. 2001. "The Power of Suggestion: Inertia in 401(k) Participation and Savings Behavior." *Quarterly Journal of Economics* 116 (4): 1149–87.

Mills, Gregory, William G. Gale, and Rhiannon Patterson. 2005. "Effects of Individual Development Accounts on Household Saving Behavior: Evidence from a Controlled Experiment." Abt Associates (April).

Mitchell, Olivia, James Moore, and John Phillips. 1998. "Explaining Retirement Saving Shortfalls." Philadelphia: Pension Research Council.

Montgomery, Edward, Kathryn Shaw, and Mary Ellen Benedict. 1992. "Pensions and Wages: An Hedonic Price Theory Approach." *International Economic Review* 33 (1): 111–28.

Moore, James F., and Olivia S. Mitchell. 1997. "Projected Retirement Wealth and Savings Adequacy in the Health and Retirement Survey." Working Paper 6240. Cambridge, Mass.: National Bureau of Economic Research (October).

Munnell, Alicia H. 1976. "Private Pensions and Saving: New Evidence." *Journal of Political Economy* 84 (5): 1013–32.

Poterba, James M. 2004. "Valuing Assets in Retirement Saving Accounts." Working Paper 10395. Cambridge, Mass.: National Bureau of Economic Research (March).

Poterba, James M., Steven F. Venti, and David A. Wise. 1995. "Do 401(k) Contributions Crowd Out Other Personal Saving?" *Journal of Public Economics* 58 (1): 1–32.

———. 1996a. "How Retirement Programs Increase Savings." *Journal of Economic Perspectives* 10 (4): 91–112.

———. 1996b. "Personal Retirement Saving Programs and Asset Accumulation: Reconciling the Evidence." Working Paper 5599. Cambridge, Mass.: National Bureau of Economic Research (May).

Samwick, Andrew A. 1995. "The Limited Offset between Pension Wealth and Other Private Wealth: Implications of Buffer-Stock Saving." Dartmouth College (December).

Slemrod, Joel. 1992. "The Economic Impact of the Tax Reform Act of 1986." In *Do Taxes Matter? The Impact of the Tax Reform Act of 1986*, edited by Joel Slemrod. MIT Press.

Thaler, Richard H., and Shlomo Benartzi. 2004. "Save More Tomorrow: Using Behavioral Economics to Increase Employee Saving." *Journal of Political Economy* 112 (1), part 2: S164–68.

Venti, Steven F., and David A. Wise. 1996. "The Wealth of Cohorts: Retirement Saving and the Changing Assets of Older Americans." Working Paper 5609. Cambridge, Mass.: National Bureau of Economic Research.

Warshawsky, Mark J., and John Ameriks. 1998. "What Does Financial Planning Software Say about Americans' Preparedness for Retirement?" New York: TIAA-CREF Institute (July).

6

Deregulating the Private Pension System

THEODORE R. GROOM AND JOHN B. SHOVEN

I n the early part of the twentieth century, most workers died with their work boots on. Employee pensions were regarded as a "fringe" benefit in the true sense of the word. They were not considered to be fundamental to the basic employee-employer relationship but instead were viewed as gratuities or rewards for faithful long-term service and were often contingent on remaining with the same employer until retirement. At least as early as 1913, however, employee pensions were recognized as deferred compensation paid for entirely by the labor of employees, and today pension benefits paid under employer retirement plans are generally considered to be simply one form of compensation for labor.[1]

The genesis of the tremendous growth of pensions in this century was the favorable tax treatment given to qualified retirement plans compared with other forms of saving; favorable treatment of pensions was provided initially by a set of IRS rulings in the 1920s and then by provisions of the 1942 Revenue Act. The massive growth in pensions began with the sharply increased marginal tax rates introduced in 1942 and with the wage and price controls during and after World War II. Both management and unions viewed the introduction and enhancement of pension benefits as a way around the wage and salary regulations. Many laws regulate pensions, but the Internal Revenue Code has provided the principal legal framework for the last fifty years. Herein lie both the strength and the fundamental weakness of the private pension system.

---

1. DeRoode (1913, p. 287).

The strength emanates from the fact that amounts that qualify for favorable tax treatment are essentially not taxed until retirement payments are made and income is consumed. For pension savings, the extra layer of personal tax that is otherwise imposed on saving is avoided, and there is neutrality between current and deferred consumption. That is, assets in qualified pension accounts are taxed in a manner consistent with a consumption tax. As a result, qualified retirement savings have become the single largest source of personal savings. Of course, a large fraction of pension assets are corporate equities, whose return has already been subject to the corporate income tax. Therefore, even pension assets are not taxed on a true consumption tax basis. The weakness—the cloud behind this rainbow—stems from the perception of pension savings as a tax preference or tax expenditure, in which the government is considered to be forgoing tax revenue that would have been derived from a tax based on a broad definition of income. In this analytical framework, an attempt is then made to justify the tax expenditure by examining whether the retirement plan serves the general public interest. To ensure that certain public goals are met, policymakers have used law and regulation to impose an extraordinarily complex regime of limitations and restrictions. These restrictions add costs to the retirement system and divert savings from the retirement system to other purposes. The complex regulatory environment has much to do with the decline in traditional defined benefit plans and the lack of progress in pension coverage generally.

We believe that the concept of a tax preference or expenditure defined against the starting point of a broad income tax should not be used to evaluate the private retirement system. In our view the appropriate base is a consumption tax, and from that standpoint the current tax treatment of the private retirement system makes perfect sense. Moreover, the existing private retirement system is based on the flawed judgment that the labor force and society at large benefit from retirement savings programs that are highly structured by the government. The private retirement system would be aided by its extensive deregulation, including the elimination of most of the current detailed tax requirements as well as other burdensome aspects of government regulation not necessary to ensure the fundamental integrity of the system. The growth of the private pension system can be stimulated by adopting neutral tax rules within broad limits to promote retirement saving, fostering continued public financial education about retirement income, and allowing Adam Smith's "invisible hand" to encourage employers and workers to pursue their enlightened self-interest.

Social Security and Private Pensions: Two Legs of the Three-Legged Stool

An evaluation of public policy toward private pensions is impossible without examining the other elements of retirement income provision in the United

Table 6-1. *Projected Replacement Rates for Long-Career Single Individuals under Existing Social Security Law*[a]

Percent

Year of birth	Year age 65	Low earner	Average earner	High earner	Maximum earner
1935	2000	57.2	42.5	34.4	25.3
1940	2005	54.7	40.7	33.4	25.6
1945	2010	52.4	39.0	32.2	25.3
1950	2015	51.8	39.0	32.2	25.8
1955	2020	48.7	38.5	31.8	25.6
1960	2025	48.7	36.2	29.9	24.1
1965	2030	48.7	36.2	29.9	24.1

Source: Advisory Council on Social Security (1997).

a. These replacement rates take into account the recent revisions to the Consumer Price Index.

States. Employer-sponsored pensions are almost never expected to be the sole source of support of retired workers. For at least the past fifty years, the American system of retirement income provision has depended on three important components: Social Security, public and private pensions, and voluntary household saving. None of the components has been expected to provide adequate retirement income alone. The relative importance of each leg of the three-legged stool differs greatly, depending on the economic circumstances of households.

For the vast majority of Americans, Social Security provides the first tier of retirement security. By design, the system offers both a higher rate of return and larger replacement ratios for workers with low lifetime incomes. The projected replacement rates (Social Security benefits relative to final annual wage income) for single individuals retiring at age sixty-five are shown in table 6-1.

Many analysts who study life-cycle consumption behavior believe that to maintain a particular standard of living, household retirement income needs to be roughly 75 to 80 percent of pre-retirement income. Several factors account for the 20–25 percent drop in required income, among them the fact that retirees no longer need to contribute to private pensions, pay Social Security and Medicare taxes, or make work-related purchases such as transportation and clothing. The fact that Social Security income is untaxed for low-income retired households and more lightly taxed than wage and salary income for all taxpayers is another contributing factor.

If Social Security in the next few years will be replacing a little more than half of final preretirement income for low-income single individuals, as shown in table 6-1, and if it takes 75–80 percent of pre-retirement income to maintain a standard of living, then Social Security will be providing low-income households with approximately two-thirds to three-fourths of the resources they need to maintain their pre-retirement standard of living. By a similar calculation,

Social Security provides approximately half of the resources for median-income individuals and perhaps one-third of the necessary resources for high-income participants. This leaves a smaller role for pensions and private saving for low-income households, who are trying to spread their resources over their lifetimes, than for higher-income households.

In thinking about these broad averages, it is important to remember that the specific circumstances or needs of each particular household may be quite different. For example, a household in retirement with a paid-off mortgage (and Social Security) requires far smaller pension benefits to maintain its standard of living than a household that pays rent or still has major monthly house payments. Clearly, "one size fits all" solutions to pension participation and benefits are not appropriate.

Because Social Security is the first leg of the retirement income stool, the way its projected solvency problems are resolved is extremely important. The replacement rates shown in table 6-1 are based on current law, but Social Security's trustees forecast that the system cannot remain solvent without significantly changing current law. The system has both a defined benefit structure and a defined payroll tax revenue source. The solvency problem boils down to the fact that revenues are projected to fall short of benefit payments by 2018 and the Social Security trust fund—formally, the Old Age, Survivors, and Disability Insurance Trust Fund—is projected to be depleted by 2042. At that time, payroll tax revenues are projected to be only 70 percent of systemwide benefit payments. To bring the system back into long-run solvency, either contributions must be increased or benefits reduced. No other solution, such as investing the trust fund in equities, will ensure the solvency of this essential program.[2] Either choice will affect the future role of employer-based pensions. If contributions are increased and benefits preserved, the need for private pensions will be, if anything, reduced. The reduction comes about because the increased contributions would lower the standard of living during working years, thereby reducing the necessary retirement resources to maintain the lower pre-retirement standard of living. Conversely, if Social Security achieves long-run solvency by cutting benefits (perhaps by further increasing the "normal" retirement age, increasing the taxation of benefits, or changing the number of years of earnings factored into the benefit formula), the need for private pensions will be greatly expanded. Pension policy reform cannot be determined in isolation from Social Security reform.

One proposal that would cure Social Security's solvency problem without reducing benefits is described in a recent book by Sylvester J. Schieber and John B. Shoven.[3] The program, named "Personal Security Accounts 2000," would

2. For a detailed analysis of Social Security investing in private securities, see MaCurdy and Shoven (1999).

3. Schieber and Shoven (1999).

require employers and employees to make a combined additional contribution of 2.5 percent of payroll. This additional contribution would be matched dollar for dollar by the government, resulting in total contributions of 5 percent of covered earnings. Although the structure of benefits would be radically changed, the overall level of benefits would be maintained. The new benefit structure would give every individual who worked a full-length career $500 a month (in 1999 dollars, about $550 in 2003, indexed for wage growth during the work career and for inflation during retirement) plus the proceeds of the 5 percent individual account. The first-tier benefit of $500 a month, which would be received by everyone regardless of earnings, would maintain and strengthen the progressivity of the current Social Security program. This benefit level would automatically increase for younger cohorts as the level of real wages rises. Our point here is not to advocate this particular plan, but to emphasize that a plan that seeks to maintain currently legislated levels of benefits must raise contributions in some way by at least as much as the 2.5 percent of payroll in the Schieber-Shoven proposal.

An Overview of the Private Pension System

The importance of the three-legged stool in funding retirement was recently documented in two papers that analyzed data from the Health and Retirement Study (HRS), conducted by the National Institute on Aging.[4] These data are undoubtedly the best available information on the income and wealth holdings of those born between 1931 and 1941 and therefore now approaching and entering retirement. Table 6-2, taken from Gustman and Steinmeier, shows the average and median components of wealth for the HRS households.[5] The numbers are based on 7,607 household surveys and use the HRS sample weights to represent the entire cohort of those aged fifty-one to sixty-two in 1992. The figures are striking. Average pension assets (including individual retirement accounts, or IRAs) amount to almost 30 percent of average total household wealth and exceed the mean present value of future Social Security benefits. Of course, a number of these distributions are skewed. Yet even for households in the middle of the wealth distribution, average pensions and IRA assets exceed 25 percent of total wealth. Average pensions and IRA assets exceed average house values and real estate assets in both columns of numbers. Nonpension financial assets are relatively unimportant.

Gustman and others also used the HRS data to give a picture of the distribution of pension assets across households.[6] Overall, 65.6 percent of households

4. Gustman and others (1999); Gustman and Steinmeier (1998).
5. Gustman and Steinmeier (1998).
6. Gustman and others (1999).

Table 6-2. *Components of Household Wealth in the Health and Retirement Sample, 1992*[a]

Item	Mean		Mean in 45–55th wealth percentiles	
	1992 dollars	*Percent*	*1992 dollars*	*Percent*
Pension assets	124,991	25.4	73,571	22.0
IRA assets	19,613	4.0	10,259	3.1
Social Security	116,455	23.7	128,084	38.2
House value	78,826	16.0	63,389	18.9
Real estate	39,227	8.0	9,484	2.8
Business assets	39,724	8.1	6,776	2.0
Financial assets	42,140	8.6	19,687	5.9
Retiree health insurance	8,461	1.7	9,122	2.7
Other	22,383	4.6	14,638	4.4
Total	491,821	100	335,009	100

Source: Gustman and Steinmeier (1998).
a. Percentages are rounded.

had positive pension wealth. This number is significantly higher than the approximately 50 percent of the work force that is covered by a pension at any point in recent history, for two reasons. First, some people have a pension for part of their career. Second, many two-worker households will have claim to at least one pension. The relative importance of pensions in household wealth as a function of relative wealth is shown in table 6-3. Pension participation is very low for those in the bottom decile of the wealth distribution. More than one-third of the households in the tenth to twenty-fifth percentiles of wealth have pension wealth, and on average pensions account for a nontrivial 7 percent of their total wealth. The figures are even more impressive for the second quartile (twenty-fifth to fiftieth percentiles), where more than two-thirds of the households have pension wealth and pensions account for 15 percent of total wealth. None of the figures in table 6-3 include IRA accounts. Our conclusion is that pensions are widely held by households across the wealth spectrum, although not in the bottom 10 percent, and to some extent not in the tenth to twenty-fifth percentiles.

Figure 6-1 documents the remarkable growth of the aggregate assets in pension funds. The figure plots pension assets as a percentage of total assets of households and nonprofit institutions as compiled by the Flow of Funds Accounts of the Federal Reserve.[7] Pension assets have increased from barely more than 1 percent of household net worth in 1945 to almost 34 percent by the second quarter of 2003. No other category of household wealth has grown nearly as much. By the second quarter of 2003, the roughly $11 trillion of assets in pensions exceeded the replacement cost of all household residential structures

7. Board of Governors of the Federal Reserve System (1999).

Table 6-3. *Pension Participation and Importance across the Wealth Distribution*

Wealth percentile	Percent with pension	Pension wealth as a percentage of total wealth
95–100	65	19
90–95	82	31
75–90	86	31
50–75	83	24
25–50	67	15
10–25	37	7
5–10	11	2
0–5	4	13

Source: Gustman and others (1999).

in the United States, which the Federal Reserve estimated as $9.085 trillion. Cumulatively, pensions are extremely large and play an immensely important role in the overall economy.

In fact, pensions are the primary source of saving and investment funds for the nation. The real net wealth of households and nonprofit organizations increased by roughly $11.5 trillion between 1988 and 1998. Real pension wealth grew by about $5 trillion over the same interval, meaning that almost 45 percent of the growth in real household net wealth was attributable to growth in real pension assets. By some measures, pension funds have generated roughly all of the domestically generated investment funds over the past fifteen years. In short, pensions are the major source of saving in the economy and are an extremely important source of wealth appreciation.

Several factors account for this massive growth in the importance of pension funds. First, the fact that the pension system in the United States is relatively young (being primarily a post–World War II phenomenon) has been a factor in the buildup of assets. Funded pensions, unlike the largely pay-as-you-go Social Security system, generate net saving and build up large asset bases while they are maturing. Second, America's uneven demographics—with low birth rates in the 1930s and early 1940s followed by the baby boom and then the baby bust—has affected private pensions and Social Security alike. Funded pensions face the same demographic and economic future as Social Security—and some of the same strains.

In earlier work, Schieber and Shoven tried to project how private pensions would cope with the retirement of the baby boom generation, particularly in the years 2010 through 2050.[8] Social Security's finances are expected to be destabilized during this period, with the number of workers per retiree falling from 3.2 to 2.0. Schieber and Shoven forecast that at some point, private

8. Schieber and Shoven (1997).

Figure 6-1. *Pension Fund Reserves as a Percentage of Household and Nonprofit Organization Net Worth, 1945–98*

Percent

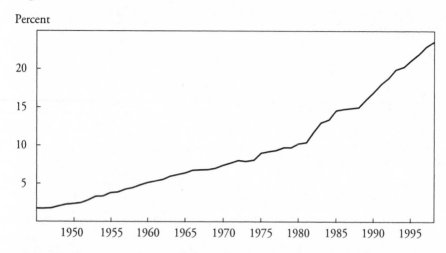

Source: Data are derived from the Federal Reserve's Flow of Funds Accounts (Board of Governors 1999) and refer to all funded pension plans, including those of state and local governments.

pensions will change from a huge source of saving for the economy to a huge source of dissaving—that is, pensions will change from being a net acquirer of financial assets to being a net liquidator of stocks and bonds. The gradual decline in pensions as a source of saving has already begun but will become much more dramatic in the second decade of the century. Sometime early in the third decade, the pension system will become a net seller of financial assets and the forecast, based on the current structure of pension contributions and benefits, is that it will continue in this mode as far into the future as can be seen.

Although defined contributions plans are not immune to demographic forces, the problem is potentially much more severe for defined benefit plans. If defined benefit plans left their benefit formulas and funding practices unchanged, they would likely face the same solvency problems as Social Security. The choice will also be the same: either reduce the benefit formula for newly accruing benefits, or dramatically increase contributions. Already vested benefits would remain secure.

One interpretation of the current move toward substituting cash balance plans for defined benefit ones is that some firms are already attempting to slow the growth in their pension obligations. It is also likely that demographic forces will continue to favor the growth in defined contribution plans relative to defined benefit ones.

The impact of these changes on asset prices, and the possibility of an "asset meltdown" has attracted significant attention. One way to look at the funded pension system is that retired individuals sell their pension assets to younger workers accumulating pension portfolios. With each retiree only having 2.0 workers to sell to, rather than 3.2, one could imagine asset prices falling by more than one-third.

But jumping to this conclusion would be incorrect. For a number of reasons, the effects are likely to be more modest. First, as the demographics shift, firms will recognize that many of their shareholders are in the stage of their lives when they want cash. In response, firms can increase their cash payouts to shareholders—dividends and share repurchases—thereby reducing the need for retirees to sell assets in the market. Of course, the money has to come from somewhere, and the likely source is from reduced retained earnings and corresponding investment projects. The impact of the decline in the saving of pension funds will thus be partially reduced by a decline in the demand for investment funds.

There are other reasons to dismiss the real doomsday interpretation of the impact of the baby boomers' retirements on asset markets. The retirement of the boomers certainly is not going to be a surprise to markets. Its impact is already being weighed by financial markets and will be assessed for something like the next fifty years. Even a fall in asset prices by one-third (relative to where they would be headed without the demographic effects) would only modestly change asset returns when spread over several decades. A reasonable assessment of the magnitude of the effect would be that asset returns could average 1.0 or 1.5 percentage points below normal for the second and third decades of the twenty-first century. This would mean that real equity returns might average approximately 6 or 7 percent rather than the 8 percent or so that they have averaged during the past seventy-five years. We would not classify this as a calamity or "asset meltdown," although these returns are almost certainly less than what people might expect based on returns in the boom periods of the 1980s and 1990s. If these lower returns do materialize, both defined benefit and defined contribution plans would be affected, and people would have to accumulate more funds if they wished to sustain their life-styles after retirement.

Trends in Plan Design

Any effort to understand the pension system must confront the constantly shifting landscape of the pension world. Numerous trends in the composition of pensions over the last several decades have altered the economics of pensions.

The Switch to Defined Contribution Plans

Along with the massive growth of pension assets, there has been a dramatic shift from traditional defined benefit pensions to defined contribution plans. The magnitude of the shift can be seen in figure 6-2, which shows the assets behind each of the two types of pensions. This shift has almost certainly been caused by

Figure 6-2. *Assets in Private Defined Benefit (DB) and Defined Contribution (DC) Plans, 1985–98*

Billions of dollars

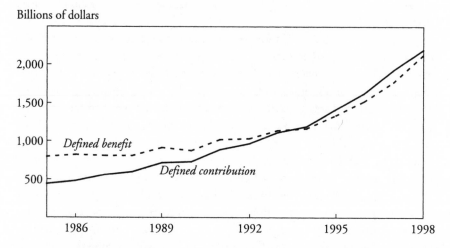

two factors: the relative administrative and regulatory complexity (and costliness) of defined benefit plans compared with defined contribution plans, and the increased mobility of the American work force.

In some defined contribution plans, the plan sponsor makes or controls investment decisions. The defined contribution world, however, is increasingly dominated by plans where individual participants make the overall portfolio allocation decisions. In IRA, 401(k), 403(b), 457, and Keogh accounts, the individual directs where the money is invested. The question many observers have asked is whether people are sufficiently knowledgeable about financial markets to make reasonable choices. The question may have arisen out of concern that individuals would be too conservative in directing their retirement money, placing too much in short-term debt instruments and guaranteed investment contracts. That is, individuals would underestimate the long-term advantages of equity investments. The aggregate figures, however, show that these concerns are misplaced. The equity exposure of defined contribution pension accounts is actually slightly greater (at $2,198 billion, or 59 percent) than the professionally managed defined benefit accounts ($2,132.5 billion, or 58 percent).[9] These figures do not

9. The principal source for these aggregate figures is the Federal Reserve's Flow of Fund Accounts, 1991–98 (Board of Governors 1999). The percentages include assets in equities or equity mutual funds, with the latter derived by assuming pension plan ownership of corporate equity mutual funds in the same proportion as all mutual fund ownership, as shown in Investment Company Institute (1999).

mean that particular individuals are not making serious errors, but on average people do appear to be allocating their investments reasonably.

This dramatic shift in the form of pensions, from defined benefit to defined contribution, makes it appropriate to reexamine the entire pension regulatory system. As just one example, the Pension Benefit Guaranty Corporation (PBGC), which provides insurance for defined benefit pensions, is literally irrelevant to defined contribution pensions.

Cash Balance Plans

A recent—and controversial—change in plan design is the introduction of cash balance plans. These are defined benefit plans that express each participant's accrued benefit as a balance that is available for distribution in a lump sum. Unlike a defined contribution plan, the accrued benefit accumulates at a specified and guaranteed rate of interest, and benefits tend to accrue as a constant percentage of compensation. The plans are attractive to younger workers because of the visibility and portability of their benefits and, in some cases, because benefits accrue more rapidly during the early years of employment than in the typical defined benefit plan.

The problem arises when a traditional defined benefit plan converts to cash balance. Most traditional defined benefit plans are based on a formula related to final pay and, as a result, accrue benefits quite rapidly in the later years of employment. When a plan converts, rules prohibit employers from reducing currently accrued benefits but not future accruals. The bottom line is that older employees tend to receive a lower overall benefit under a cash balance plan than they might have under the traditional defined benefit plan.

Although the disappointment of older employees is readily understandable, no one has a guarantee as to future compensation or accrual of future benefits. The problems with respect to cash balance conversions have been exacerbated— it is alleged—by the failure of plan sponsors to describe fully and fairly the consequences of conversions to all employees.

Employer Stock-Based Plans

When ERISA was enacted, one concern was that defined benefit plans could become too heavily invested in employer stock and real estate, with the result that upon the insolvency of the employer, employees would lose both their jobs and their accrued pension benefits. As a result, these plans were generally limited to investing no more than 10 percent of plan assets in employer securities and real estate. The federal tax code, however, permits—indeed encourages— nearly unlimited investment in employer stock in other plans, including employee stock ownership plans (ESOPs), a variety of 401(k) and other defined contribution plans in which employer stock is a permissible option, and stock purchase plans that permit employees to purchase stock at 85 percent of current value without current income realization.

Many new Information Age companies do not sponsor defined benefit plans, and employer stock is a major asset of other plans provided to employees. In many cases, the rapid growth in stock values has made millionaires out of thousands of employees and, understandably, these plans have become wildly popular. A classic example is Microsoft, which has no defined benefit plan; nearly 50 percent of 401(k) investments chosen by employees is in Microsoft stock. The result of this trend has been a tremendous increase in employer stock ownership by employees. According to one estimate, employees own more than 8 percent of the market capitalization of U.S. companies.[10]

The downside of this trend may be that employees have inadequately diversified their retirement savings and, as originally feared in the case of defined benefit plans, some employees may be overexposed to the future success of their employer. The collapse of Enron, and the resulting effects on workers who lost both their jobs and much of their retirement accounts at the same time, typifies these concerns.

Nonqualified Plans

One of the effects of the short-sighted techniques of the deficit reduction legislation from the early 1980s through the early 1990s was to increase revenues by limiting participation in qualified retirement plans by highly compensated employees. Because tax-favored retirement plans do not adequately meet the needs of high-income company decisionmakers, the number of nonqualified plans has grown significantly in recent years as companies address the reduction in qualified plan limits. For example, one study found that the year after Congress reduced the compensation limit from $200,000 to $150,000, the number of companies with nonqualified deferred compensation plans tripled, from 20 percent to 67 percent.[11] Additional studies have documented further growth in nonqualified plans as more sponsors adapted to the legislative changes.[12]

The trend toward nonqualified plans is widely regarded as an unfavorable development for low- and middle-income employees. Not only do these employees not participate in nonqualified plans, but these programs further separate the interests of the company's decisionmakers from those of rank-and-file employees. Moreover, the additional cost of maintaining nonqualified arrangements may actually decrease company resources that could be dedicated to the qualified plans of all workers.

---

10. National Center for Employee Ownership (www.nceo.org/library).

11. Lissy and Morgenstern (1995, p. 3).

12. According to one article, 74 percent of Fortune 1000 companies offered nonqualified plans in 1995, up from 62 percent in 1994. "Trends and Surveys," *Employee Benefit Plan Review,* September 1996, p. 556.

The Complex Legal and Regulatory Environment Governing Pensions

The primary legal structure for defining economic rights in a market economy is the contract, which also governs most aspects of the employment relationship. For employee benefits, however, the contract is largely replaced by an extraordinarily complex federal legal system. The primary structure for the regulation of pensions is provided by the federal income tax system on the theory, described later, that pensions are tax preferences or indirect government expenditures.

In total, four government agencies regulate the pension system under multiple sets of federal laws. The Internal Revenue Service administers the tax rules. The Department of Labor administers rules relating to fiduciary conduct, disclosure of information to plan participants, and enforcement of rights. The PBGC (set up by ERISA) administers the rules intended to insure the safety of defined benefit promises. The Securities and Exchange Commission regulates investment products offered to some participant-directed retirement options.

Generally, collectively bargained pension plans are also subject to regulation under the Taft-Hartley laws. Under most circumstances pension plans are not subject to state regulation. Some providers of pension benefits, however, most notably insurance companies, are subject to state regulation on the adequacy of their reserves and are required to contribute to guaranty funds to ensure that promised benefits will be paid. Another important source of regulation for pension plans for publicly held companies are the accounting rules, administered by the Financial Accounting Standards Board, that govern financial reporting of expenses and liabilities associated with pension plans.

The many levels of regulation impose direct and indirect costs on plan providers. Generally, teams of lawyers, actuaries, accountants, and financial and investment advisers or managers are necessary to establish and operate qualified retirement plans. Filings must be made routinely with the Internal Revenue Service and other regulatory agencies, and plans and their sponsors are subject to regular audit. Investment managers must constantly review routine investment decisions to ensure compliance with prohibited transaction rules. Mergers, acquisitions, and rehabilitation of troubled companies may hang on some arcane nuance of pension law.

The complex regulatory structure of ERISA also touches directly on the lives of the supposed beneficiaries of this system. ERISA regulates some of the terms of the allocation of retirement benefits upon divorce and allocates retirement income between husband and wife. It also defines how rapidly the retirement nest egg must be consumed and, indirectly, what portion may be left to children upon death.[13]

13. Section 414(p) of the tax code sets forth in two and one-half pages of small print the requirements that domestic relations orders dividing the property of divorced spouses must satisfy to be enforceable against employee benefit plans. The code also requires benefits to be paid as joint

The costs imposed by ERISA are frequently blamed for the decline of the defined benefit plan. A less discussed, but perhaps more important, issue is the extent to which ERISA imposes opportunity costs and interferes with the creativity of the market system by interfering with choices relating to the form and amount of saving.

An interesting comparison is provided by the different ways the legal system treats retirement income saving and saving for homeownership. Both forms of saving are considered to be tax-favored. Home ownership is somewhat more favorably treated because not only is interest on homeownership debt tax-deductible, but the imputed rent of the home is never taxed and gains on sale of homes are largely untaxed. The federal tax system does not, however, limit the homeownership deduction by complex deduction limits and nondiscrimination rules.[14] The federal tax system does not require homes to be jointly owned or specify how the home must be divided on divorce, nor in general does federal law supplant contractual and state law by a complex system of federal regulation.

Major Issues in Pension Reform

Any reform of the pension system has to deal, explicitly or implicitly, with several major issues. These include whether the underlying tax structure of the pension system should be based on income or consumption, and the impact of the reform on pension coverage and the adequacy of benefits.

Income versus Consumption Tax Base

Frequently the pension system is evaluated and reforms are recommended based on the assumption that all income, broadly defined to include all capital income, should be taxed currently. A corollary belief is that provisions of the tax code relating to the pension system are tax preferences and tax expenditures by the government.

We begin with a different frame of reference—namely, that consumption provides a fairer and more neutral basis for taxation than income. Since compensation set aside for retirement is essentially taxed when consumed, we are unmoved by criticisms of the private system that stem from its perceived failure to tax income currently. The problem with the existing income tax system is

---

and survivor annuities in some circumstances, unless waived by the participant's spouse. This rule applies even if the benefit was accrued during a previous marriage and is waived in a prenuptial agreement. The minimum distribution rules influence the pattern of lifetime consumption and affect estate planning.

14. Under section 163(h) of the tax code, the amount of home mortgage indebtedness for which interest is deductible is generally limited to $1,000,000 for married persons filing joint returns. Of course, housing, as well as employment, are subject to equal opportunity rules—nondiscrimination rules of a different sort.

that it taxes saving too much and provides too many incentives for current consumption rather than provision for retirement.

Logically, these beliefs would lead us to favor substitution of a consumption tax for the current income tax. That is unlikely to happen, however, and probably should not happen, because of the political and practical problems of making the transition to an entirely different system from the one now in place. In any event, the current system is only partially an income tax; most commentators regard it, more accurately, as a hybrid income-consumption tax system. We would even go so far as to assert that the current personal tax system is closer to a consumption tax than to an income tax. After all, the two biggest financial assets owned by most households are their home and their pension. Neither is taxed by income tax principles. In fact, owner-occupied housing is taxed even more favorably than would be supported by a consumption tax. Human capital investments—particularly higher education—are also largely taxed according to consumption tax principles. The largest cost of higher education is the forgone earnings during that time period, and that cost is effectively tax deductible.

In contrast the "tax expenditure" system measures costs relative to a comprehensive income tax system. In other words, it measures the costs of deviations from a system that the country has been moving away from. If one takes consumption as the appropriate tax base, then the current tax treatment of pensions is exactly appropriate, and the tax expenditure of the treatment is zero. The current tax treatment can also be defended without reference to tax theory. There is widespread belief that the private retirement system in the United States works well in both providing retirement security and contributing to personal savings. The direction in which the United States should move is to expand and improve this system.

Budgetary Effects

Current budgetary procedures treat pensions as a tax preference that costs about $200 billion annually. This calculation is based on the income tax forgone on current contributions to pension plans and on the earnings of pension assets, which are excluded from taxation under current law, minus the income tax paid on current pension distributions. Current tax expenditure "scoring" distorts the true economic effect of saving through qualified plans in three ways.

First, even under the assumption that all income should be taxed, the scoring is faulty because it calculates revenue changes over a budget cycle of five to, at most, ten years (depending on which house of Congress or agency of government is doing the scoring). Tax incentives for qualified plans should be scored across a long-term horizon, considering the current tax expenditure in light of its future recapture. Tax incentives for qualified pension assets merely defer taxation until the time of consumption and allow earnings to accumulate to create larger taxes at that time, thereby simply collapsing the double tax on individual income and earnings upon those savings. The future tax payments on pension assets are a huge asset for the federal government. The government will ultimately capture roughly one-fourth of the total in pension accounts, giving it an "off the books" asset of almost $3 trillion.

Second, current scoring fails to consider how tax expenditures will pay for themselves through increased productivity (through increased saving, higher capital-labor ratios, and higher real wages). Whether pensions increase national saving in the short run is controversial and ambiguous. There is general agreement, however, that savings are enhanced more over the long run when the kind of asset-swap strategy of taking advantage of the tax law is not feasible.[15] The preliminary analysis of the HRS data by Gustman and Steinmeier indicates that pensions add to total household wealth by at least fifty cents on the dollar.[16] One can interpret this kind of analysis as trying to figure out whether society gets a good return on the tax preference granted to pensions. Third, our view is that pensions are not really tax advantaged at all. They are taxed appropriately, whereas "bank account saving" and other conventionally taxed saving are overtaxed by the current tax system.

Distributional Effects

Current distributional analysis of tax expenditures for pensions does not accurately portray their effects. Under the progressive American income tax regime, any tax incentive or expenditure necessarily benefits high-income individuals by more in absolute dollars, because they pay a greater proportion of the national tax burden than do rank-and-file employees. But analysis of the distributional effects of tax incentives for qualified plans should focus on who benefits from plan participation and resultant retirement savings, not merely on the amount of the tax expenditure. In a 1994 study the Wyatt Company found that the most significant beneficiaries of retirement plans are workers with annual incomes of $15,000 to $50,000. These families paid slightly more than one-third of all federal income taxes but received almost two-thirds of pension accruals.[17] Another study, an analysis of the March 1998 Current Population Survey, found that of married couples currently receiving pension benefits, 57 percent had incomes below $40,000 and nearly 70 percent had incomes below $50,000. Among widow(er)s currently receiving retirement benefits, 55 percent had incomes below $25,000. More than 50 percent of pension benefits (in terms of pension dollars) go to the elderly with adjusted gross incomes below $30,000. Of those active workers currently accruing retirement benefits, nearly 45 percent had earnings below $30,000 and more than 66 percent had incomes below

15. Hubbard and Skinner (1996).
16. Gustman and Steinmeier (1998).
17. Schieber and Graig (1994).

$50,000.[18] Any way you look at it, middle-class Americans account for the bulk of pension participants.

Federal law with respect to retirement income favors low-income groups even more dramatically when Social Security benefits (and potential taxes on such benefits) are taken into account. That is because all of the tax benefits that high-income recipients receive under the private retirement plan system are more than offset by losses that such recipients incur under the Social Security program. Even if the current limits on contributions to pension plans were loosened, workers in families with less than $50,000 of income would continue to receive the large bulk of benefits.

Pension Coverage

At any particular time, fewer than half of all U.S. workers are covered by private pension plans. The story is quite different, however, when workers' entire life spans are considered. A Wyatt study indicates that nearly 70 percent of workers are covered by private plans at some time during their working lives. This proportion is consistent with the HRS data and appears to be growing. Given the heterogeneity of workers' circumstances and reliance on Social Security to provide minimal retirement benefits, it is unreasonable to expect that the private system would or should provide universal coverage for all workers.

Diversity of Plan Limits and Restrictions

Currently ERISA provides for different maximum annual benefit accruals for defined benefit and defined contribution plans; different funding requirements for defined benefit and defined contribution plans; and separate contribution limits for 401(k) and 403(b) plans, 457 plans, traditional IRAs, Roth IRAs, Simplified Employee Pensions, and SIMPLEs, as well as separate eligibility and contribution limits for traditional and Roth IRAs.

Although diversity of plan types permits an employer to choose the type of benefit that best meets its employees' needs (and the employer's ability to meet that obligation), the myriad limits and restrictions make some employer-sponsored plans more attractive on a tax basis than other employer-sponsored plans with the same coverage goals, thereby violating the tax policy doctrine of neutrality. There is no tax or public policy reason to permit a small firm worker to defer only $6,000 in annual compensation under a SIMPLE plan or to allow a state government employee to defer $8,000 under a 457 plan when a worker in a large firm may defer up to $10,000 in annual compensation under a 401(k) plan. Tax policy demands that tax benefits be distributed in a neutral, uniform manner.

18. Mulvey (1999).

We believe that only one fundamental distinction should be made between pension plans—those plans that cover a broad base of employees and those that involve individualized participation decisions. The classic example here is the difference between a plan that mandates employer contributions based on a fixed benefit formula and an individual retirement account. We believe that there should be two sets of plan limits and restrictions: one set for plans with broad-based participation (including elective plans with broad-based participation) and the other for plans with individual participation.

Within retirement savings policy there exists a tension between the grant of tax incentives to qualified plans to encourage plan sponsorship and the limits and discrimination rules enacted to ensure that these benefits are fairly distributed. Plans with broad-based participation are not prey to abuse by highly compensated executives and should have relaxed limits that encourage increased saving, whereas plans with individualized participation should have lower limits.

Directions for Reform

The role of social insurance is to provide a safety net—some assurance of outcome in a complex society where there can be faultless failure. How rich should the safety net be?[19] The best way to resolve this issue is to have each generation responsible for its own insurance by providing an actuarially balanced system and minimizing intergenerational transfers. Limiting intergenerational transfers requires the generation that votes for more benefits to support payment for those benefits and introduces a modicum of discipline into the system. Social insurance necessarily involves redistribution of income and assurance of minimal levels of benefits, whether earned or not. Reasonable people will continue to disagree over the appropriate level of social insurance. That debate is aided by confining resolution of social issues to the Social Security system, rather than by overlaying a second level of redistribution of wealth within the private pension system.

Restructuring U.S. retirement policy to eliminate legal and regulatory barriers to retirement savings should be a high priority for Congress for two reasons. First, expansion of qualified plans can serve as a practical substitute for fundamental tax reform based on a consumption model because pensions are already taxed on that basis and can therefore be expanded without addressing the difficult transitional issues that are involved in converting the entire system to a consumption tax. Second, U.S. saving rates are too low, and present generations that are relying on those saving rates will have inadequate retirement income.

19. Robert Myers, a former chief actuary of the Social Security Administration, says that Social Security benefits should be high enough that the vast majority of people (90 percent) do not need supplementary public assistance. President's Commission on Pension Policy (1981).

Expansion of qualified plans will increase saving and the retirement security of future retirees.

Over the years Congress has enacted a host of limitations and hurdles that impede saving for retirement. Moreover, a maze of costly and complex regulations promulgated by three large bureaucracies further discourages the formation of pension plans. To promote new retirement saving, U.S. pension laws should be fundamentally revised. Most of the rules that discourage new pension saving are in the tax code and regulations issued by the Internal Revenue Service. Additionally, the fiduciary rules administered by the Department of Labor and the rules relating to termination of defined benefit plans administered by the PBGC contribute to the cost and complexity of current law. Virtually all of the tax rules are based on the mistaken belief that limits should be placed on the benefits of executives and other highly compensated workers, to limit tax abuse and promote an equitable distribution of the tax incentive to lower-paid workers.

The significant and overlapping limits on benefits that may be paid to high-income workers have some negative effects. These limitations may make pension plans significantly less attractive to the decisionmakers in a firm and actually reduce the availability of pensions to the rank-and-file workers. Moreover, limiting pension plan saving runs counter to the underlying themes supporting consumption taxes. It is unfair to tax twice income that is saved (when it is first received and again when earnings on investments of that income are taxed), while taxing income that is consumed only once. Saving benefits the entire society by providing the capital necessary to increase productivity and the standard of living of everyone, and it is an unwise policy to penalize "excessive" saving. Increased retirement saving is necessary to maintain the standard of living of future retirees.

To increase the attractiveness of qualified pension plans, reform proposals should focus on increasing incentives to save and on reducing costly and redundant regulation. The private system should continue to be voluntary, giving individuals and employers the opportunity to provide for their retirement, but leaving maximum flexibility as to the type, form, and contents of the arrangement. Creativity of markets, self-reliance, and individual responsibility are better values to foster than reliance on the state for well-being.

Proposals for Fundamental Changes to the Private Retirement System

These considerations lead us to propose significant changes in the direction and composition of rules regarding private pensions. Our proposals would increase pension coverage and participation and raise retirement income by stripping away the cumbersome and counterproductive rules that inhibit the growth of pensions currently.

Removing Tax Law Restrictions

Most of the current criticism of the private pension laws involves the tax provisions contained in the Internal Revenue Code. Here we describe five changes to the tax code that would remove many restrictions that impede retirement income saving.

—*Eliminate complex nondiscrimination rules.* Section 401(a)(4) of the tax code requires that plans "not discriminate in favor of highly compensated employees." In interpreting this phase the Treasury Department has issued several hundred pages of regulations that impose complex numerical testing requirements intended to determine whether benefits actually received by participants are nondiscriminatory. In addition, special mathematical tests—known as the actual deferral percentage (ADP) test and the actual contribution percentage (ACP) test—are established for 401(k) and 401(m) plans. The complexity and enormous costs of these nondiscrimination tests are not justified and discourage employers, particularly smaller businesses, from maintaining pension plans. We advocate substituting a rule that each feature of a plan be currently or effectively available to all workers. Under our proposal, plans that are designed to be available for all workers would be exempt from current nondiscrimination rules, top-heavy rules, and the myriad limits on amounts that can be contributed or received in benefits. Everyone should be able to contribute amounts sufficient to maintain pre-retirement standards of living.[20]

—*Eliminate current liability limitations on funding.* Defined benefit plans should be funded to satisfy the accrued liabilities that may be expected to emerge under the plan. Most defined benefit plans provide a benefit that is tied into the salary level of the participant during the participant's highest earning years, which are frequently the participant's final years of work. For tax purposes, however, plans are permitted to fund only a percentage of current liabilities, that is, the level of liabilities that would be incurred if the plan were terminated. The Omnibus Budget Reconciliation Act of 1987 restricted funding to 150 percent of current liabilities, and 1997 amendments liberalized the current liability limitation to 170 percent by 2005. For some plans 170 percent of current liabilities is still less than 100 percent of accrued liabilities. We advocate sole reliance on a funding standard based on projected liabilities rather than on shutdown liabilities.

—*Eliminate limits on employer contributions and benefits under qualified plans.* The tax code places numerous limitations and penalties on the amount employers may contribute to qualified plans and the amount employees may receive. These limits include a $12,000 limit (in 2003) on elective deferrals to a 401(k) plan; a $200,000 limit (in 2002) on the amount of compensation that can be

20. See President's Commission on Pension Policy (1981).

taken into account for contributions and benefits under a defined contribution plan; a limit on contributions to defined contribution plans equal to the lower of 100 percent of W-2 pay or $40,000 (for 2002); and a limit on annual pension benefits from defined benefit plans equal, in 2002, to the lesser of $160,000 or 100 percent of the participant's average compensation (not exceeding $200,000) for the participant's three consecutive years of highest compensation.

In general, limits on contributions and benefits should be eliminated so long as the pension plan is designed and made available to participants in a nondiscriminatory manner. The only limits that we would impose would be general ones intended to ensure that savings were limited to amounts necessary to replace pre-retirement standards of living. We would retain a contribution limit of 25 percent of earnings for defined contribution plans and would restrict defined benefit plans to replacing 100 percent of pre-retirement compensation with full inflation indexation. These limits would not be binding for most participants in any reasonable pension plan, but would prohibit a few wealthy people from using pensions as a massive tax shelter.

For those plans that permit individuals to choose whether to participate—401(k) plans, tax-deferred annuity plans, IRAs, and Keogh plans—we would allow contributions up to $15,000 annually (indexed for inflation).

The myriad conflicting and ever-decreasing contribution and benefit limits are clearly inconsistent with the policy of promoting retirement saving and limit the pool of available national saving. Moreover, under our approach, workers would have the added ability to save on a tax-preferred basis for retiree medical expenses, long-term care, and medical savings accounts. All employees should be able to maintain their pre-retirement standard of living in retirement. The current rules merely stimulate nonqualified plans, and that has adverse effects on the formation and structure of qualified plans.

—*Liberalize antireversion rules.* When ERISA was enacted, it provided that if a defined benefit plan terminated with assets in excess of liabilities, the excess would revert to the plan sponsor. In 1990 Congress amended the tax code to impose a 50 percent excise tax penalty on such reversions. This excise tax and related rules should be eliminated. The punitive tax discourages contributions and encourages conservative investment strategies designed to avoid special minimum funding obligations rather than maximizing investment return. Employers view defined benefit funding as one-sided; they face downside risks for underfunding, but upside benefits for overfunding are limited.[21] Some plans have developed investment strategies that emphasize the downside risk by matching plan liabilities with fixed income investments in circumstances where

---

21. Overfunded amounts are reflected on financial statements prepared under generally accepted accounting procedures and do reduce future contribution obligations, but they cannot be invested in the employer's business.

equity investments would optimize economic returns. Given the perception of one-sidedness, most new firms choose not to offer defined benefit pension plans.

   —*Eliminate minimum distribution requirements.* Code section 401(a)(9) contains complicated minimum distribution rules that generally require plans to begin distributions to participants no later than April 1 of the year following the year in which they reach age seventy and one-half and to complete distributions within certain specified periods. These rules apply even to participants who are active employees. Because active employees normally continue to accrue benefits, very complex rules must be followed to calculate the required minimum distributions and avoid the double payment of benefits. If minimum distributions are not made in a timely manner, the plan may be disqualified, and the affected participant is subject to a punitive excise tax of 50 percent of the amount of the shortfall.

   The administrative and record-keeping costs associated with complying with the minimum distribution rules are significant. These rules were enacted to ensure that plan participants receive their benefits during their retirement years rather than using the plan as an estate planning tool by accumulating benefits in the plan and then leaving the benefits to their beneficiaries. This problem is quite limited in scope, however, since substantially all participants receive their benefits during their lifetimes, particularly if they have retired from work. Moreover, this issue is addressed in large part by other provisions of the code. Importantly, the elimination of minimum distribution rules may affect the timing of federal tax revenues, but it would not affect the present value of federal tax receipts. Under our plan, amounts undistributed on the death of a participant would be income in respect of a decedent, and the federal government's taxes would increase in proportion to increased returns that are earned. Our recommendation is that the minimum distribution rules should be eliminated entirely as they apply to qualified plans and other tax-favored retirement plans.

ERISA's Fiduciary Regulation and Defined Benefit Insurance Scheme

Changes are also needed in the provisions of ERISA that regulate fiduciary conduct and insure the solvency of defined benefit plans. Titles I and IV of ERISA were controversial at the time of their enactment and in major respects involved congressional judgments in favor of experimental governmental regulation of pension markets. Title I was intended to ensure the integrity of employee benefit plans by substituting for contractual principles a new federal system for enforcing rights under the plans; the Department of Labor was given the primary responsibility for defining and enforcing Title I. Title IV provided for federal insurance of defined benefit plans through a new government corporation, the Pension Benefit Guaranty Corporation. The PBGC was also given a significant role in regulating insured plans, plan sponsors, and third parties dealing with plans.

   The specific objectives of Title I and Title IV have been largely accomplished. Today, there is widespread confidence that pension and profit-sharing plans are honestly run. Adopting uniform federal rules that apply to trust funds that invest large sums on a global basis has been beneficial to both business and labor. A central feature of Title I is its establishment of federal fiduciary rules, and the law's emphasis on fiduciary obligations to participants has had a salutary effect in situations where before ERISA some trust fund assets had been diverted to further union or employer interests. Title IV has successfully delivered PBGC payments to beneficiaries of terminated plans. Unfortunately, it is also true that these objectives have been accomplished at excessive cost through overregulation.

We advocate reforms in three major aspects of ERISA:

—*Reduce the regulatory role of the Department of Labor under ERISA.* Title I provides redundant regulation of fiduciary and other transactions with benefit plans. In the first instance, it codifies preexisting law requiring fiduciaries to be prudent and loyal to the interests of plan participants and beneficiaries. As previously noted, applying a uniform set of federal standards to these transactions is beneficial and helps ensure the integrity of these funds. Unfortunately Congress added a second set of rules—the prohibited transaction rules. At best, these rules are duplicative, as in the case of the rules of section 406(b), which prohibit self-dealing, conflicts of interest, and bribery of plan fiduciaries, conduct already prohibited by the general fiduciary standards of section 404 of ERISA.[22] At worse, these rules prohibit a wide variety of transactions by "parties in interest"—persons presumed to be "plan insiders," but actually defined to include tens of thousands of individuals with some direct or indirect relationship to the plan.[23] Although ERISA provides an exemption procedure to separate the wheat from the chaff, the procedure is time consuming and costly. Moreover, even where it is practical to obtain exemptions, regulators frequently impose conditions on the terms of the transactions themselves, requiring additional disclosures, approvals, or other changes in contract terms than the parties to the transactions—often financially sophisticated persons—would have negotiated in the marketplace.

There are other potential criticisms of Title I and the Labor Department's administration of it.[24] ERISA requires the filing of various reports with participants and the department, which are expensive to prepare and in some respects

22. ERISA, section 404(a)(1) provides that "a fiduciary shall discharge his duties, with respect to a plan solely in the interest of the participants and beneficiaries and . . . for the exclusive purpose of . . . providing benefits to participants and their beneficiaries . . . and with the care, skill, prudence, and diligence under the circumstances then prevailing that a prudent man acting in a like capacity and familiar with such matters would use in the conduct of an enterprise of a like character and with like aims . . . ."

23. The term "party in interest" includes the sponsoring employer and or union or service provider to an employee benefit plan; their employees, officers, and directors; certain relatives of service providers and employers and defined affiliates or partners. See ERISA, section 3(14).

24. While we disagree with a number of judgments made by Labor Department regulators, on the whole they do a creditable job of administering the statute Congress has enacted. The principal fault is not with the regulators, but with the statutory rules Congress enacted.

of doubtful utility. As is true with every regulatory agency, the Labor Department is occasionally overzealous in its enforcement. For example, the department recently insisted on maintaining a lawsuit against plan fiduciaries after the lawsuit had been settled by the parties with federal court approval.[25]

—Encourage participant education and provide uniform regulation and compliance procedures for participant-directed accounts. In view of the growth of individual account plans in which participants direct investments, the importance of increasing the investment sophistication and literacy of participants has been generally recognized. This is reflected in the Department of Labor's Interpretive Bulletin 96-1, which generally encourages plan sponsors to provide a variety of investment educational services, including investment allocation models and interactive investment materials, without being classified as an ERISA fiduciary by virtue of having done so.[26] It is reflected also in the substantial increase in educational programs offered participants by plan sponsors and by various providers of financial products.

Participant educational efforts may be encouraged in several other ways. Legislation adopted by Congress in 1999 but subsequently vetoed by President Clinton included a provision "clarifying" that the cost of employer-provided "retirement advice" is excluded from income.[27] It is not clear that this provision covers advice with respect to selection of plan investments, but presumably it does. We see no reason, however, to distinguish between employer-provided investment advice relative to plan investment decisions and advice paid for by participants in employer plans and IRAs. Individuals who directly pay for investment advice with respect to their retirement accounts should be able to deduct the cost of such advice without regard to the limit of 2 percent of adjusted gross income currently imposed on miscellaneous deductions.

Moreover, the selection of providers of investment advice by plan sponsors is currently regarded as a fiduciary act and subjects the sponsor to fiduciary liability if the selection is not prudent or involves self-dealing. Concern about possible liability for providing advice inhibits plan sponsors from providing such services. It would be reasonable to use a good faith, rather than a fiduciary, standard to limit liability of plan sponsors who select providers of investment advice.

The scheme for enforcing rights of plan participants should also be reviewed and made uniform. Currently, the Department of Labor regulates fiduciary acts by fiduciaries of employee benefit plans, and both individual participants and the Department of Labor can sue in federal courts to enforce their rights. In the

---

25. *Herman v. South Carolina National Bank,* 140 F. 3d 1413 (11th Cir., 1998).

26. 29 C.F.R. 2509.96-1.

27. H.R. 2488, Taxpayer Refund and Relief Act of 1999 (TRRA 1999). The pension provisions of this bill have been subsequently added to minimum wage and other proposals. As this is written in late 1999, these provisions are expected to resurface as legislation considered during 2000. Hence we continue to refer to the pension provisions of TRRA 1999.

case of an IRA, however, the participant is relegated to rights provided by state laws (and possibly federal securities laws) and is frequently required by the terms of the financial arrangement to take claims to arbitration. Although the IRS may impose taxes for violations of the prohibited transaction rules for IRAs, that power is infrequently used and does not restore the participant's loss in any event. If a mutual fund is offered to an IRA participant, a prospectus that satisfies 1933 Securities Act requirements must be provided. No such requirement necessarily applies to a participant in a 401(k) plan. Participants are generally unaware that their rights change in subtle, yet important, ways when they withdraw funds from a qualified retirement plan and roll them over to an IRA. It would appear desirable to consolidate regulation of participant investment decisions in a single federal regulatory agency and to provide uniform enforcement rights for participants of individually directed account plans, whether the plan is a 401(k), an IRA, or a tax-deferred annuity.

—*Revamp the Pension Benefit Guaranty Corporation.* Any questions relating to the wisdom of some Title I provisions or the Labor Department's administration of it pale in significance to questions that relate to the insurance termination provisions of Title IV and the PBGC's administration of it.

Before ERISA was enacted, workers' rights to receive promised defined benefits were limited by the amount of assets held in the pension trust. When a business failed, workers not only lost their jobs, but their pension benefits also were at risk. Several highly publicized cases, such as the failure of Studebaker, where workers lost both their jobs and their pensions, were a major factor leading to the legislation. Quite commonly, collectively bargained plans also had large unfunded liabilities because of the practice of providing pension credits for service before the establishment of the plan and lengthy amortization of the resulting liabilities. For different reasons, both unions and employers were indifferent to the unfunded liabilities that were created. Unions used the promise of providing past service credits as an organizing tool, and employers thought their obligations to these plans were limited to the amount currently required to be contributed under the collective bargaining agreements.

ERISA dealt with these issues by requiring faster funding of liabilities. To ensure that benefits would be paid within prescribed levels, a system of plan termination insurance was enacted. Under this system each defined benefit plan pays an insurance "premium" on a per capita basis into either a multiemployer or single employer fund. Annual premiums range from a low of $2.60 a participant for multiemployer plans to $19 a participant for fully funded single employer plans. Additional premiums for underfunded single employer plans were previously capped at $53 a participant, but are now based on the amount of the plan's unfunded benefit liability. Employers are also subject to liability on termination of the plan, initially up to one-third, but now up to the full amount of their net worth.

Leaders of organized labor vigorously sought enactment of the plan termination insurance system as a way of bailing out seriously underfunded plans in dying industries. A classic example at the time was pension plans for drivers engaged in home delivery of milk, a disappearing occupation where possible future contribution levels were hopelessly insufficient to amortize unfunded liabilities.[28] Especially in its early days the plan termination system served as a means of subsidizing dying industries and pension plans through wealth transfer from healthy industries and plans. The system was also viewed as a wealth transfer system from prudently managed retirement systems to systems that were imprudently (or even fraudulently) managed. From the standpoint of well-funded and well-managed plans, premium payments to the PBGC effectively became a tax on maintaining a defined benefit plan. Naturally, many firms switched to defined contribution alternatives.

One of the major activities of the PBGC is what it describes as loss prevention. The PBGC maintains an early warning system to monitor the potential insolvency of several hundred major underfunded defined benefit plans. The agency has statutory authority to terminate plans when it determines that any one of four statutory standards is met, including a "reasonable-unreasonable" test. Under this test, the PBGC may terminate a plan if "the possible long-run loss of the corporation with respect to the plan may reasonably be expected to increase unreasonably if the plan is not terminated."[29] The mere threat of involuntary plan termination poses a severe risk to a business, since upon termination the PBGC may impose liens against plan sponsors and affiliates equal to the unfunded liability of the plan as measured by conservative PBGC standards and immediately become the company's largest creditor and threaten its viability. Using the threat of pension plan termination, and nothing more, the PBGC has taken increasingly aggressive steps to intervene in proposed corporate spin-offs and asset sales where the PBGC has concluded that the transaction might reduce the amount the agency may collect on its claims in the event of a later pension plan termination. The PBGC's standards for measuring unfunded liability are very conservative, so much so that the PBGC has threatened plan termination in cases where, under generally accepted accounting procedures, the plan was in a surplus position. The PBGC has used its powers under this provision to interfere with many normal corporate transactions and has extracted additional contributions to plans and other corrective actions in these cases under the guise of protecting the system.[30]

---

28. Leslie (1992, p. 939).

29. ERISA, section 4042(a)(4).

30. For a description on how this process works, see the comments by Diane E. Burkley (1992, 1994), a former deputy executive director and chief negotiator of the Pension Benefit Guaranty Corporation.

It is time to review the appropriateness of plan termination insurance from top to bottom. In view of the increased funding of defined benefit plans, is the system needed at all? Alternatively, could the interests of participants be adequately protected by increasing the priority of plans' claims to employer assets in the event of insolvency? While we believe abolition of the PBGC should be considered, at a minimum two lesser steps should be taken to reduce its regulatory role.

First, the PBGC should be required to purchase market annuities for all pension plans that terminate. This approach could be the first step toward privatizing PBGC functions. Annuity purchases could reduce the PBGC's deficit because annuities purchased may reflect a better price than the "price" the terminated plan was booked at. Moreover, true market valuation rates would establish a much better measure of the PBGC deficit, which would assist policymakers in evaluating future PBGC legislation. Finally, such a change could substantially reduce the number of staff (currently several hundred) necessary to administer the insurance program.

Second, the PBGC's authority to interfere with arm's-length business transactions should be restricted. The agency's authority to use the "reasonable-unreasonable" test should be abolished. Alternatively, greater procedural protections should be made available to companies subject to PBGC oversight.

The Halperin-Munnell Proposal Compared with Groom-Shoven

Daniel Halperin and Alicia Munnell have written a companion paper for this volume with their prescription for future public policy toward pensions. They have observed the same history of developments regarding employer-provided pensions that we have but come out with a very different set of recommendations on future policy directions. Halperin and Munnell advocate progressive, matching contributions, fully or partially financed with a new 5 percent tax on the annual earnings of pension assets. Their overriding concern is the distribution of pension benefits and their perception that the pension system has failed to provide pension benefits for the lower half of the wealth distribution. Table 6-3 shows that the pension system actually extends further into the lower tail of the wealth distribution than Halperin and Munnell suggest, with two-thirds of households in the 1931 to 1941 birth cohort and in the second quartile of wealth having some pension wealth.

We differ from Halperin and Munnell in both philosophy and implementation of pension policy. We support a policy that ensures equal opportunity and access to pensions. They support a policy of equal or even universal participation. They support concentrating tax-qualified pension benefits among the rank and file. We think that saving—both pension saving and saving in general—by even the rich and wealthy is a good thing that benefits society as a whole. We see no reason to restrict pensions for the affluent. Halperin and Munnell see liberalized pensions as enlarging an already gaping tax loophole. We see raising the limits on pension contributions as healthy for the economy and as movement toward tax reform. They explicitly advocate that the federal government should provide all of the necessary retirement income for low-lifetime-income households to maintain their standard of living in retirement. We think that this approach would turn Social Security and their USA Account plan into welfare, with all of the baggage that goes with that label. They think that traditional defined benefit plans are better than 401(k) plans and that policy should be tilted to favor the former. We advocate a level playing field for the two types of plans, and in some ways our proposal to deregulate pensions could allow defined benefit plans to stage a comeback. But we do not think that drastic measures should be taken to prevent defined benefit plans from diminishing, or even disappearing. They advocate that all pension payouts be in annuity form. We advocate eliminating the minimum distribution requirement. All in all, the two proposals are largely diametrically opposed.

The most dramatic proposal Halperin and Munnell make is for a new tax on pension earnings, a proposal that stems from their view that the ideal world would feature a comprehensive income tax. From our perspective, however, the change would represent extraordinarily bad policy, for several reasons.

First, the tax would add a new distortion between consumption while working and saving for retirement. Even a 5 percent earnings tax on pension assets can increase the cost of retirement by 15 percent. If the nominal return on assets averages 10 percent a year, then the 5 percent tax amounts to a wealth tax of 0.5 percent a year, or 50 basis points. If the average money is in a pension plan for thirty years, the annual tax of 50 basis points reduces the money available for retirement by 15 percent. If nominal asset returns average only 8 percent, then the effective price increase for retirement funds is roughly 12 percent.

Second, the tax would violate the implicit contract offered by past pension legislation. The deal has always been tax-deferred contributions and tax-free earnings followed by fully taxable withdrawals. Now, Halperin and Munnell propose to tax earnings inside the pension. If this proposal were implemented, who could be certain that the rate would remain at 5 percent? Rational workers would realize that saving with pensions is risky because the government can change the rules whenever it wants. The result? Less saving and a poorer economy.

Third, the implied tax increase is substantial. Pension assets total $11 trillion. If pension assets were to earn an average nominal return of 8 percent, then the 5 percent of earnings tax would cost $44 billion a year.

Fourth, the social return to saving exceeds the private return to saving (partially because the corporation income tax generates $150 billion a year). Why would the country finance a prosaving plan for the poor with an antisaving tax on the assets in pension accounts? Even if one buys into the redistributionary consequences of the Halperin and Munnell proposal, raising the marginal tax rates on wage income for the well-to-do would be superior to reducing pension and saving incentives.

Fifth, the tax would add another layer of complexity. One aspect of pensions that is simple today is their taxation. All withdrawals are fully taxed, but no taxation is imposed on earnings of the assets. There is no need to keep track of dividends, interest, capital gains, and so forth. There is not even a need to get a precise market value of assets each year. Will this Halperin and Munnell tax apply equally to rental income, asset appreciation, realized and unrealized capital gains, spin-offs, and all the other ways in which value can be stored or transferred? Will real estate holdings inside a pension be depreciated? What about investments in venture capital funds and other assets that are not marked to market daily. Halperin and Munnell give no guidelines on how they plan to calculate the tax base for their new tax.

It is not surprising that we are unpersuaded by the advantages of Halperin and Munnell's proposals. We favor equal opportunity and consumer sovereignty. They favor more equal outcomes and more government involvement in allocating resources.

Summary and Conclusions

The employer-sponsored pension system is one of the big successes for the U.S. economy in the second half of the twentieth century. Pensions now represent almost 25 percent of total household wealth in the country and account for most of the aggregate private saving. Approximately two-thirds of households nearing retirement have a pension asset. Average pension assets at retirement exceed the average value of homes. They also exceed the average present value of future Social Security benefits.

Despite this generally rosy picture, there are serious problems with the pension system. Employer-provided pensions are faced with incredibly complex and expensive regulation imposed by at least four separate government agencies. Partly as a result of this overregulation, firms are abandoning traditional defined benefit pension plans in favor of the simpler and less-regulated 401(k) and defined contribution plans. Nondiscrimination tests, intended to ensure that rank-and-file workers participate on a fairly even footing with highly compensated employees, are so complex and difficult to meet that they discourage pensions altogether. Pension coverage has been stalled for the past two decades, at about 50 percent of the work force. Limits on pension contributions are extremely uneven across workers and across plan types and have been sharply reduced in real terms over the past twenty years in a misguided attempt to balance the budget by curtailing the mismeasured and exaggerated tax expenditure associated with pensions.

We advocate a significant deregulation of pensions. We support liberalizing and leveling contribution limits. We document that the U.S. tax system is already closer to a consumption tax than it is to a comprehensive income tax, and we argue that this is a good thing. A consumption tax is economically preferable particularly because it allows people to allocate their resources over their lifetimes without distortionary taxes. In the consumption tax framework, pensions do not represent a tax expenditure at all.

We would base pension regulation on the principle that all workers in a firm should have an equal opportunity to participate in the firm's pension plan. We would not mandate equal participation, but simply equal opportunity to participate. We would eliminate the minimum distribution requirement, leaving people free to choose their own pattern of pension withdrawals. In general, we would radically liberalize and simplify pension regulation. The likely result would be more pensions, more saving, and a stronger economy.

References

Advisory Council on Social Security.1997. *Report of the 1994–1996 Advisory Council on Social Security,* vol. 1: *Findings and Recommendations.* Government Printing Office.

Board of Governors of the Federal Reserve System. 1999. *Flow of Funds Accounts of the United States: Balance Sheets for the U.S. Economy 1945–98.* Washington (June 11).

Burkley, Diane E. 1992. "Remarks to the Wings Club." New York, March 18.

———. 1994. "Increased PBGC Intervention in Corporate Spinoffs, Divestitures, and Other Transactions." *Employee Benefits Journal* 19 (March): 5–12.

DeRoode, Albert. 1913. "Pensions as Wages." *American Economic Review* 3 (June): 287–95.

Gustman, Alan L., and Thomas L. Steinmeier. 1998. "Effects of Pensions on Savings: Analysis with Data from the Health and Retirement Study." Working Paper 6681. Cambridge, Mass.: National Bureau of Economic Research.

Gustman, Alan L., and others. 1999. "Pension and Social Security Wealth in the Health and Retirement Study." In *Wealth, Work and Health: Innovations in Measurement in the Social Sciences,* edited by James P. Smith and Robert J. Willis, 150–208. University of Michigan Press.

Hubbard, R. Glenn, and Jonathan S. Skinner. 1996. "Assessing the Effectiveness of Saving Incentives." *Journal of Economic Perspectives* 10 (Fall): 73–90.

Investment Company Institute. 1999. *1999 Mutual Fund Fact Book.* Washington (May).

Joint Committee on Taxation. 1999a. *Description of Revenue Provisions Contained in the President's Fiscal Year 2000 Budget Proposal.* JCS1-99. Government Printing Office (February 22).

———. 1999b. "Estimated Budget Effects of the Conference Agreement for H.R. 2488, JCX-61-99 R (www.house.gov/jct/x-61-99r.pdf [Aug. 5,1999]).

Leslie, Douglas L. 1992. *Cases and Materials on Labor Law: Process and Policy.* 3d ed. Boston: Little, Brown.

Lissy, William E., and Marlene L. Morgenstern. 1995. "Nonqualified Defined Contribution Plans Burgeon." *Compensation and Benefits Review* 27 (May–June): 12.

MaCurdy, Thomas, and John B. Shoven. 1999. "Asset Allocation and Risk Allocation: Can Social Security Improve Its Future Solvency Problem by Investing in Private Securities?" Working Paper 7015. Cambridge, Mass.: National Bureau of Economic Research (March).

Mulvey, Janemarie. 1999. *Analysis of the March 1998 Current Population Survey.* Washington: American Council of Life Insurers.

President's Commission on Pension Policy. 1981. *Coming of Age: Toward a National Retirement Income Policy.* GPO.

Schieber, Sylvester J., and Laurene A. Graig. 1994. *U.S. Retirement Policy: The Sleeping Giant Awakens.* Bethesda, Md.: Watson Wyatt Worldwide.

Schieber, Sylvester J., and John B. Shoven. 1997. "The Consequences of Population Aging on Private Pension Fund Saving and Asset Markets." In *Public Policy Towards Pensions,* edited by Sylvester J. Schieber and John B. Shoven, 219–45. MIT Press.

———. 1999. *The Real Deal: The History and Future of Social Security.* Yale University Press.

7

Ensuring Retirement Income for All Workers

DANIEL I. HALPERIN AND ALICIA H. MUNNELL

The Employee Retirement Income Security Act (ERISA) of 1974 did what it was supposed to do—protect promised pension benefits under defined benefit plans offered by private employers. But ERISA did not address what has become the primary problem today, namely, gaps in coverage—the absence of promised benefits in the first place. It has become increasingly clear that private pension plans will never cover the entire work force; at any point in time more than 50 percent of American workers are not covered by a pension plan. Although more will be covered at some time during their work lives, ensuring wider and deeper coverage is the most important challenge facing private pensions.

The time has come to assess what voluntary private pension arrangements can and cannot accomplish. The existing system, which combines generous tax incentives and complex regulation, does not appear to make anyone happy. Employers and the pension industry complain that reporting requirements and regulations make pensions unduly expensive to administer. Critics complain that few of the substantial tax incentives that flow into the pension system end up reaching low-income workers. The solution to this widespread dissatisfaction may well require reducing aspirations for employer-sponsored plans—alleviating some of the regulation and limiting some of the tax preferences—and providing additional retirement income for lower-paid workers directly.

The authors thank Jeremy Zipple for his excellent research assistance.

It does not make sense, however, simply to throw more money at the current system. As a society, we need to rationalize the commitment of public resources to supplementary retirement income beyond personal savings and Social Security. In this paper we approach such a rationalization by identifying the goals of pension policy, assessing the extent to which the current system achieves those goals, exploring options to remedy the defects in the current system through marginal adjustments, and then examining the options for major restructuring.

What Are the Goals of Pension Policy?

The approach of federal pension policy as far back as the 1940s has been to provide tax incentives that will encourage highly paid employees to support the establishment of employer-provided pension plans that provide retirement benefits to the rank and file. The tax incentives arise because under the Internal Revenue Code, employer contributions to an employee's pension plan are deductible as a business expense when made, and the employee is not taxed until receipt of pension benefits. In addition, the pension fund is not taxed on its earnings. These provisions, which permit tax deferral on both employer contributions and the earnings on those contributions, are equivalent to exempting from taxation the earnings on the money that would have been invested after tax, assuming the employee remains in the same tax bracket. In 2001 the Office of Management and Budget estimated that the revenue loss associated with the favorable tax provisions for pensions was $92 billion.[1]

The problem is that policymakers have never defined very clearly what sort of pension coverage they expected to result from the favorable tax treatment of pensions. The "rank and file" was not defined until 1986, when legislation set an upper income limit for this group ($85,000 in 2001). But if the rank and file is meant to include those who end up in the bottom 40 percent of the income distribution after retirement, then pension policy has failed. A look at the income distribution for those over age sixty-five in 1998 showed that pensions accounted for only 3 percent of the retirement income of the lowest quintile and 7 percent of the income of the second-lowest quintile. These percentages have changed very little over time. Meanwhile, those in the second-highest and highest quintiles received 24 percent and 20 percent of their (considerably higher) retirement income from pensions, respectively.[2]

The lack of pension income at the low end of the income scale raises two questions. Do these low-income individuals need additional income, or does Social Security provide an adequate level of replacement? If additional retirement income is needed, are employer-sponsored pension plans the best way to provide it?

1. U.S. Office of Management and Budget (2000, table 5-3, p. 117).
2. Social Security Administration (2000c).

Table 7-1. *Hypothetical Monthly Benefit Amounts and Earnings Replacement Rates under Social Security, January 2000*

Worker benefit	Age sixty-two		Age sixty-five	
	Benefit (dollars)	Replacement rate (percent)	Benefit (dollars)	Replacement rate (percent)
Low earner	518	45.6	598	52.6
Average earner	853	33.8	987	39.1
Maximum earner	1,241	20.5	1,433	23.7

Source: Monthly benefit amounts are taken from Social Security Administration (2000b, p. 16). Replacement rates are calculated based on the estimated average wage index for 1999, taken from Social Security Administration (2000a, p. 1), assuming 45 percent of the average for the low earner and Social Security maximum taxable earnings ($72,600) for the maximum earner.

Ideally, retirement benefits should enable workers to maintain the same standard of well-being in retirement as they enjoyed while they were employed. Most analysts assume that retirement income does not need to replace 100 percent of pre-retirement earnings because of lower clothing and transportation expenses as a result of not working, the reduction in taxes, particularly the payroll tax, and less need to save. As a rough benchmark, retirement income equal to 80 percent of pre-retirement earnings should be more or less adequate.

The Social Security Administration calculates benefits and replacement rates under Social Security for individuals and families with hypothetical earnings histories; some examples are given in table 7-1. These numbers may overstate, in at least two ways, the extent to which earnings are replaced by Social Security benefits. First, many commentators assume retirement at age sixty-five, but in fact most workers retire earlier and receive lower benefits and lower replacement, as shown in table 7-1. Second, "average earner" in tables like this one implies that replacement rates are being measured for someone in the middle of the earning distribution for all retirees. But the middle of the earning distribution for people near retirement is higher than for the population as a whole ($32,188 for full-time workers aged fifty-five to sixty-four, compared with $29,900 for all full-time workers), and as the table shows, the higher the earnings, the lower the replacement.

Those who argue that Social Security alone is adequate for low-income workers sometimes point out that the benefits and replacement rates in table 7-1 do not reflect the fact that spouses with no earnings or low earnings are eligible for benefits up to 50 percent of the worker's. They add a spouse's benefit to the 53 percent replacement rate for low-income workers shown in the table and conclude that the combined benefit meets the suggested replacement rate. This calculation is misleading for two reasons. First, relatively few spouses are entitled to a full spousal benefit. In 1999, for example, 62 percent of female Social

Security beneficiaries aged sixty-two and older were receiving wives' or widows' benefits, but only 35 percent of all women in that age group had no earnings history and were entitled to the full wife's or widow's benefit. In the remaining cases, the wife's earnings would have to be taken into account when measuring replacement. Second, if one is going to carry out an adjustment for spousal benefits, one should also adjust for the other factors just mentioned, such as those who retire before age sixty-five, that tend to make the replacement rates in table 7-1 upwardly biased estimates.

Ultimately, of course, the real issue is not about the estimation procedures used by the Social Security Administration to generate the data shown in table 7-1, but about the actual replacement incomes that people experience. The second series of interviews in 1994 for the new Health and Retirement Study (HRS), which includes participants aged fifty-three to sixty-three, provides data to estimate replacement rates for those opting for early retirement. Within this group Social Security replacement rates averaged 55 percent for *couples* in the lowest quintile of the income distribution.[3] These numbers are consistent with data from the 1982 New Beneficiary Survey, which suggested that the actual replacement rate for couples in the lowest quartile was 58 percent.[4] Thus, it would appear that low-income workers, just like their higher-income counterparts, do not receive enough from Social Security to avoid a decline in economic well-being upon retirement and thus need supplementary pension income.

Indeed, to add emphasis to this conclusion, it is worth noting that the dollar amounts of Social Security benefits for workers with histories of low wages are clearly inadequate by current measures of poverty. For example, a low-income worker retiring in January 2000 at age sixty-two would have received only $6,216, significantly below the official 1999 poverty threshold of $7,990 for an aged individual. Even if that worker's spouse received the full 50 percent spouse's benefit, the combined amount of $9,324 falls short of the $10,070 poverty threshold for an aged couple. Thus, without additional income, many low-income elderly, even with a lifetime of covered employment, live below the poverty line in retirement.

---

3. The replacement rate in this calculation is the ratio of benefits in the year of retirement as a percent of earnings in the previous year. Where only one member of the couple was receiving benefits, the recipient was treated as a single individual and the benefit was related to the beneficiary's pre-retirement earnings. This sample excluded people still working, so that benefits are not affected by the Social Security earnings test. The Health and Retirement Study was conducted by the University of Michigan's Institute for Social Research.

4. Grad (1990, p. 13) reports two different Social Security replacement rates, one using the average of the five years of highest earnings as the denominator, and the other using the five years of earnings just before retirement. These rates were 39 percent and 77 percent, respectively. The number reported in the text is the average of these two. The New Beneficiary Survey was conducted by the Social Security Administration.

The need for additional retirement income does not mean that an extension of employer-sponsored pensions or some form of mandatory universal pensions is the answer. Some advocates of extended pension coverage argue as if private pensions were a way for employers to give something to their employees. Economists typically maintain, however, that the introduction of a pension implies a reduction in cash compensation, even if it takes some time for the adjustment to occur.[5]

The potential trade-off between higher pensions and lower wages may be somewhat more complicated than a simple one-for-one offset, however. For example, by reducing employee turnover or shirking or by facilitating retirement of less productive workers, the introduction of a deferred compensation arrangement might increase productivity and thus make employers willing to increase total compensation.[6] Alternatively, because of the favorable tax treatment of pensions, the employer has somewhat more money to play with than if it paid all compensation in cash; the firm could retain this windfall as profit or share some of it with employees, thereby raising total compensation. Even if the trade-off between pensions and wages occurs in the aggregate, it may not happen on a person-for-person basis. For example, raising pensions for minimum wage workers cannot lead to a reduction in wages, because the employer cannot reduce wages below this level. Similarly, plans must cover at least some lower-paid employees to qualify for special tax treatment. But those employees may have no interest in saving for retirement, so plan sponsors may have to use some of the tax benefits to increase the total compensation of "reluctant savers," those who do not much value this deferred compensation.

Even though introducing pensions or raising the levels of existing pensions might not lead to a full reduction in wages for low-income workers, it would certainly lower wages somewhat. The welfare implications of such a reduction depend on whether the worker is a temporarily low-paid employee or one who will experience a lifetime of low income. Although the United States is a mobile society, a significant portion of the population has persistent low earnings. For example, of those who started in the lowest quintile of the income distribution in 1974, 42 percent were still in the lowest quintile seventeen years later in 1991, and another 23 percent had moved up only to the second-lowest quintile, according to data from the University of Michigan's Panel Study of Income

5. Some early studies, such as Schiller and Weiss (1980) and Smith and Ehrenberg (1983), found little evidence of a trade-off between pensions and wages. These studies, however, employed models that examined only period-by-period trade-offs of wages for pensions. More recent studies have examined the trade-off over several time periods. Such studies, which include Montgomery, Shaw, and Benedict (1992) and Gunderson, Hyatt, and Pesando (1992), find a pension-wage trade-off of roughly one for one over the worker's lifetime.

6. See Sass (1997) for a discussion of the original reasons for the introduction of deferred compensation arrangements.

Table 7-2. *Earnings for Full-Time Workers at Selected Percentiles, 2000*[a]
Dollars

Percentile	Upper limit
10	14,404
25	19,604
50	29,900
75	44,668
90	66,924

Source: U.S. Department of Labor, Bureau of Labor Statistics (2000).
a. Annual earnings are calculated by multiplying weekly earnings by fifty-two.

Dynamics.[7] This country's tax policy for low-wage workers—at least for those with children—is designed to raise take-home pay, not to reduce it. For a family with two children, the earned income credit (EIC) in 2000 provided a refundable tax credit of 40 percent for incomes up to $9,720 (a maximum of $3,888), which was then phased out gradually between incomes of $12,690 and $31,152. Further, the poverty level for a four-person household with two children was $16,895 in 1999. Thus, it probably does not make sense to increase the pensions—and thereby reduce the wages—of low-skill workers earning, roughly speaking, $20,000 or less. The only reasonable way to improve retirement benefits for low-income households such as these is to increase their lifetime income through some redistributive device, not through the extension of employer-provided pension plans.

Suppose an annual income of $20,000 is the minimum income level at which society might wish to start encouraging households to save more out of current income. If this income level is the lower bound of rank-and-file workers, what should be the upper bound? The question has no definitive answer, but we can suggest some indicators. In 2000, 90 percent of full-time workers earned below $66,924 (table 7-2). Also in 2000 the maximum income taxable under Social Security was $76,200, which reveals something about how society views compulsory contributions to retirement. As noted earlier, the Internal Revenue Code currently defines the top of the rank and file as those employees earnings no more than $85,000 in 2001; above that level employees are considered "highly compensated." Thus, a broad definition of the rank and file might run from the edge of poverty to the edge of wealth. This group, while it might not save if given the option, can afford to defer current compensation in exchange for income when it stops working, and employer-sponsored pension plans provide a disciplined mechanism through which it can save for retirement.

7. Gottschalk (1997, p. 37).

ERISA Successes and Remaining Challenges

ERISA's principle objective in 1974 was to secure the rights of pension plan participants, so that a greater proportion of covered workers would receive their promised benefits. It was a response to failings and abuses in defined benefit pension plans, which covered the majority of workers at the time. Before the legislation was enacted some employers had imposed such stringent vesting and participation standards that many of their workers reached retirement age only to discover that because of some layoff or merger, they had never become eligible for a pension. Even workers who satisfied their plans' requirements had no assurance that accumulated pension assets would be adequate to finance benefits. A few pension plans were administered in a dishonest, incompetent, or irresponsible way. Managers of other plans engaged in forms of financial manipulation, such as concentrating investments in the stock of the plan-sponsoring company, which—although not illegal—also jeopardized the welfare of plan participants. The net effect of these problems was that plan participants were at the mercy of plan sponsors. ERISA was designed to change the balance of power.

Most observers agree that ERISA has succeeded in meeting its stated objective of strengthening workers' claims on benefits. Participation and vesting standards enabled workers to establish a legal right to benefits. The implementation of funding and fiduciary standards helped to ensure that money would be available to pay these benefits. ERISA also established the Pension Benefit Guaranty Corporation (PBGC), which administers a mandatory pension insurance program to protect most workers who participate in defined benefit pension plans against the loss of their basic retirement benefits should their plans be terminated. As a result of these changes, more workers covered by private sector programs received benefits, and many got larger benefits than they would have in the absence of ERISA.

Although the legislation was successful, in terms of today's pension landscape its focus was limited. First, ERISA falls short of ensuring that expected retirement protection actually materializes. Although questions of pension portability and inflation protection were discussed during the deliberations, the final legislation either did not address those questions at all or addressed them in a very limited fashion. Other issues, such as the conditions under which cashing out of lump-sum benefits should be allowed, received almost no attention.

Furthermore, although ERISA made portions of the private pension system work better, it left the matter of coverage unresolved. Only 50 percent of wage and salary workers in the private sector between ages twenty-five and fifty-four were covered by a pension plan of any sort, according to a Current Population Survey with a pension supplement (May 1993) (table 7-3). The percentage of the private work force covered by any type of employer-sponsored retirement plan has not increased since the late 1970s. Moreover, in view of the enormous

Table 7-3. *Pension Coverage by Employer-Sponsored Plans of Wage and Salary Workers Aged Twenty-Five through Fifty-Four, Selected Years*

	Percent covered			
Plan	1979	1983	1988	1993
All workers	58	54	54	55
Private	52	48	48	50
Public	83	78	82	80
Coverage status under				
401(k) type plans		8	17	
Defined benefit plans			37	28
Both defined benefit and 401(k) plans		9	10	

Source: Woods (1994, pp. 15, 20).

expansion of defined contribution plans, especially 401(k) and similar plans, coverage under traditional defined benefit plans declined from 37 percent of total participants in 1988 to only 28 percent in 1993.[8] A large proportion of those still covered by defined benefit plans are probably public employees because public plans are more likely than private plans to be defined benefit.

The framers of ERISA recognized the lack of coverage as a serious problem, but they shied away from mandating coverage in any way and believed in encouraging the growth of employer-sponsored plans. In addition, for those workers whose employers did not provide a plan, ERISA authorized the individual retirement account (IRA). Although eligibility was limited initially to those without pensions, it was expanded in 1981 to encompass all workers, including those currently covered by pension plans. It soon became evident, however, that while IRAs were offered to all, they were being used primarily by higher-income people. Moreover, the data revealed that IRAs did little to expand pension coverage. For example, in 1998 more than half of the 28 percent of total households with IRAs also had pension coverage (table 7-4), which means that only an additional 13 percent of households had picked up pension coverage through IRAs, leaving nearly 40 percent with no pension provisions at all.[9] Moreover, for

8. Woods (1994, table 6, p. 20).

9. The 40 percent figure is derived by subtracting those with employer-provided pensions or IRAs from the total. The 1993 Current Population Survey found that 49 percent of workers had employer-provided pension coverage. The Survey of Consumer Finances shows that IRAs extend coverage to an additional 13 percent of households. That is, less than half of the 28 percent of households with IRAs do not have pensions. Adding this 13 percent to the 49 percent with employer-provided pension coverage brings the total to 62 percent with some form of coverage, leaving roughly 40 percent with no pension coverage.

Table 7-4. *IRA Participation and Pension Coverage, 1995*[a]

Income	Percent of households with IRA	Median amount (dollars)	Percent of IRA households with pension coverage
Less than 10,000	4.0	20,000	31.1
10,000–24,999	14.6	11,000	17.8
25,000–49,999	26.6	12,000	44.7
50,000–99,999	42.8	20,000	65.6
100,000 or more	65.2	70,000	61.9
All	28.1	20,000	52.3

Source: Authors' calculations based on the Federal Reserve's 1995 Survey of Consumer Finances.
a. In 1998 dollars.

those households with incomes under $100,000, the median amounts in these IRA accounts were relatively small—$11,000 to $20,000.

As a result of this pattern of usage, Congress substantially tightened IRA provisions in the Tax Reform Act of 1986. Specifically, contributions to IRAs were fully tax deferred only for persons who were not active participants in an employer-sponsored pension plan or whose adjusted gross income fell below certain thresholds ($40,000 for a couple and $25,000 for an individual). Individuals ineligible for tax-deferred treatment on their contribution could make taxable contributions to an IRA and still enjoy tax-deferred earnings. These restrictions were eased for low- and moderate-income workers in 1997.[10]

It is not surprising that IRAs cannot solve the problem of limited pension coverage. After all, low and moderate earners have many pressing needs for current income, and left to their own devices, they are unlikely to save adequately for retirement. Tax relief is also unlikely to affect their decisions because many low and moderate earners face low marginal tax rates. Since expanded options for tax-favored individual savings do not reach these intended beneficiaries, it makes sense to put stricter limits on contributions to IRAs than on those to employer-sponsored plans.

10. The original ERISA legislation allowed employees without an employer-provided plan to contribute up to $1,500 a year. In 1976 the limit was increased to $1,750 for an employee with a nonworking spouse. When the Economic Recovery Tax Act of 1981 extended IRA benefits to all employees, it also raised the contribution limit to $2,000. The Taxpayer Relief Act of 1997 gradually increased the income limits for fully deductible IRAs to $80,000 for a couple and $50,000 for an individual by 2007. It also introduced spousal IRAs, which permit a full $2,000 for a spouse not covered by a pension plan for couples with adjusted gross income up to $150,000. Finally, the legislation introduced the Roth IRA, which permits nondeductible contributions of $2,000 each for couples with incomes up to $150,000 and individuals with incomes up to $95,000. Qualified distributions from the Roth IRA are tax-free.

Table 7-5. *Workers without Pension Coverage, by Employer Sponsorship, 1993*

Type of employer	Number of workers (thousands)	As a percentage of uncovered workers	As a percentage of total workforce
Firms sponsoring plans	15,736	28.9	14.7
Firms not sponsoring plans	38,859	71.1	36.2
Total	54,595	100.0	50.9

Source: Calculations based on U.S. Department of Labor and others (1994, tables B1, B3).

The major issues facing the private pension system today can be divided into two broad categories: concerns over participation and the protection of benefits for those who work for employers that offer a pension plan; and concerns relating to the large number of employers that do not maintain plans at all. This last category is quite important to bear in mind. As shown in table 7-5, just 29 percent of workers without pension coverage are employed by firms sponsoring pension plans, while 71 percent work for employers without plans. We discuss these issues in turn in the next two sections.[11]

Improving Participation and Protecting Retirement Income in Existing Plans

The goal of pension policy is to encourage employers to establish retirement programs that, together with Social Security, enable career employees to maintain their pre-retirement standard of living once they stop working. For this to occur the employee must participate in the plan and earn benefits, and the benefit level must be adequate. If these conditions are not satisfied, the existence of the employer plan may not provide adequate retirement protection.

A key problem facing would-be reformers of the current system is that private pensions are a voluntary arrangement, and the more pressure put on employers, the less likely that they will maintain pension plans at all. The struggle over the rules applicable to qualified plans and much of the ensuing complexity comes from an attempt to push hard—but not *too* hard—for greater pension coverage and benefits.

Expanding Participation within Pension Plans

Within existing pension plans, the lever for gaining maximum participation is the nondiscrimination test, that is, the set of rules stipulating that benefits for highly compensated employees be given favorable tax treatment only if a high proportion of rank-and-file employees are also covered by the plan. Yet existing

11. For an earlier discussion of these issues, see Halperin (1993).

Table 7-6. *Reasons for Noncoverage of Wage and Salary Workers Employed by Firms Sponsoring Pension Plans*[a]

Reason	Number of workers (thousands)	Percent of total
Do not meet age or service requirements	4,789	30
Do not work enough hours, weeks, or months a year	4,105	26
Choose not to contribute	4,105	26
Type of job not covered under plan	1,368	9
Other reason or don't know	3,421	22
Total uncovered workers in firms sponsoring plans	15,736	11

Source: Calculations based on U.S. Department of Labor and others (1994, table B3).

a. Figures do not sum because some workers identified multiple reasons for lack of coverage.

rules allow employers a variety of means for not covering all employees, including minimum service conditions for eligibility or vesting, the exclusion of certain employees by classification (for example, part-time or hourly workers), and the option for low- or moderately paid employees to choose between deferred and current compensation. Table 7-6 indicates the reasons why the 15 million workers employed by firms sponsoring pension plans are not covered.

These rules that allow employers to delay or avoid offering pension coverage to certain groups of workers could be amended in various ways. Under current law pension participation can be conditioned on completing one year of service and attaining age twenty-one. In addition, benefits may be forfeited for failure to complete five years of service. Administrative concerns support the continuation of the eligibility requirement of one year of service, and pension coverage for those under twenty-one is not essential. Five-year vesting, however, seems much longer than necessary. The difficulty with a lengthy vesting period is that participants have no sensible way to respond to the risk of forfeiture. On one side, if people assume that vesting will happen, they will end up saving too little when it does not; on the other side, if people assume they will not become vested, they then end up having saved too much when they do. Earlier vesting would allow individuals to plan their saving better and ensure more benefits to workers already covered by a plan.

Current law also does not require uniform pension coverage of all employees. A year of service requires at least 1,000 hours of work during a twelve-month period (approximately twenty hours a week), which means that most part-time and seasonal workers will never clear the hurdle, even if they remain with a single employer for a long time. Second, individuals classified as independent contractors or considered to work for a third-party service provider will never be eligible, even if they perform substantial services for the same company over a long period of time. Third, employees in a collective bargaining unit need not be eligible for pensions as long as pensions are a subject of good-faith bargaining.

Finally, the highly technical and complex Treasury regulations require only that the classification for participation be "reasonable" and that the level of participation from the highly compensated group be not "too much" greater than the level of participation from the remainder of the work force.[12] Specific requirements arise only when participation of the non-highly compensated is less than 70 percent of that of the highly compensated; in that case, under a rule enacted in 1986, the employer must establish that, taking account of all employer plans, the average benefit for the non-highly compensated as a percentage of pay is at least 70 percent of that for the highly compensated as a percentage of pay. Thus, the nondiscrimination requirement actually permits a substantial disparity between the benefits for different groups. A fairer and simpler rule would require an employer to provide uniform coverage for all employees, or at least for all employees working in a given line of business.[13] Under such a rule, no one earning less than any other participant could be excluded because of the nature of the job.

This approach does not preclude the possibility that employers will continue to exclude employees from pension coverage based on part-time status, membership in a collective bargaining unit, or lack of employee status (either as independent contractor or third-party service provider). On the last two of these points, we have little to say. The treatment of the collective-bargaining and employee-status issues are too thorny to tackle here and require more knowledge of the collective-bargaining process than we possess. We believe, however, that there is no justification for excluding part-time workers from the plan if they average ten hours a week for a year. Part-time workers as a group may be less likely to value saving for retirement than the typical employee, but not all part-time workers are the same. As discussed below, we suggest providing for low-wage workers through a government-sponsored plan, which would allow exclusion of many part-time workers from the employer's plan.

Encouraging Employees to Choose Pension Coverage

About 30 percent of pension participants are covered only under section 401(k) and other defined contribution arrangements, many of which allow employees

---

12. A safe harbor permits the percentage of highly compensated employees participating to be between two and five times higher than the participation rate for the rank and file, with the factor increasing as the proportion of the work force made up of non-highly compensated employees increases. A "facts and circumstances" test would allow a greater disparity at each point.

13. Plans may differ by industry, and a company might well be placed at a competitive disadvantage if forced to have a better or worse plan than its competitors, merely because it was operating in another line of business with a different norm. Current law allows an employer to satisfy some aspects of the nondiscrimination test solely by reference to employees of a line of business. The challenge would be to find a simpler way than current law to define a separate line of business while not permitting abuse, such as attaching supervisory employees solely to the line of business with the more generous plan.

Table 7-7. *Participants in Private and Public Pension Plans, by Type of Plan, 1993*
Percent

Sponsor	Defined benefit	Defined contribution	Both	Total
Private	33.9	25.5	13.6	73.0
Public	17.8	5.0	4.2	27.0
Total	51.7	30.5	17.8	100.0

Source: Calculations based on U.S. Department of Labor and others (1994, tables A2, B1).

individually to choose between current and deferred compensation (table 7-7). These plans do not ensure that pension coverage will reach as large a share of the work force as do the traditional plans under which contributions are made on behalf of some employees who would not elect to defer compensation if presented with the choice.[14] Although 401(k) plans are here to stay, concern about their impact on lower-paid employees makes it important to maintain existing incentives both to supplement 401(k) plans with traditional plans and to encourage lower-income employees to participate in 401(k) plans.

Current law maintains an incentive to establish traditional plans by providing a significantly higher limit on contributions to such plans than on elective contributions to 401(k) plans; for 2001 the annual limit on contributions to traditional defined contribution plans is $35,000, whereas the annual limit on elective contributions to a 401(k) plan is $10,500. We oppose increasing the 401(k) plan limit because it would encourage a further shift toward 401(k) plans, which is likely to harm the pension coverage of low- and moderate-income workers.

Moreover, the rules about including rank-and-file workers in 401(k) plans have evolved in recent years in ways that seem likely to result in lower rates of pension coverage for such workers. Under the original 401(k) law, the permitted level of contributions by the highly compensated depended upon the average contribution by the workers who were not highly compensated. With this rule

14. The extent to which 401(k)-type plans have added to the total level of pension coverage or, alternatively, have merely substituted for traditional defined benefit plans, remains unclear. Studies by Gustman and Steinmeier (1992), Kruse (1995), and Papke, Petersen, and Poterba (1996) find that growth in defined contribution plans like 401(k) plans has not primarily constituted an outright termination and displacement of defined benefit plans. Instead, Gustman and Steinmeier argue that much of the trend is attributable to a shift in the employment mix toward firms that have not historically offered extensive defined benefit arrangements. A recent study by Papke (1999), however, arrives at a different conclusion. She compares pension plan offerings by sponsors of defined benefit plans in 1985 with their offerings in 1992 and discovers that 401(k)-type plans have substantially substituted for terminated defined benefit plans. For more discussion of these issues, see the chapter by Gale, Papke, and VanDerhei in this volume.

in place, the employer had an incentive to educate moderate and low earners about the virtues of saving for retirement, or if that failed, the employer could make contributions to their 401(k) on its own. The law was later amended to create a "safe harbor" provision, namely, if the employer offers to match employee contributions at a certain rate, the pension plan qualifies for favorable tax treatment even if no non-highly compensated employees take up the offer. Clearly, this provision alters the incentives for employers considerably. Namely, the employer has nothing to gain from educating reluctant savers and encouraging them to participate, since the employer's costs increase when employees choose to participate. One could argue that the safe harbor provision might cause some employers to sponsor pension plans that they might not have otherwise. Encouraging employers to sponsor a plan but then giving them perverse incentives not to include the rank and file is not a sensible policy mix. Requirements that employers notify employees and encourage participation can mitigate these perverse incentives but cannot overcome them.

In our view, the rules for elective plans should require a substantial contribution for all potential participants—with that contribution coming from employers if necessary. This approach would make the law consistent with the general framework of pension policy, in which favorable tax treatment is offered in exchange for pension coverage for the rank and file.[15]

Achieving Adequate Benefit Levels

The ideal pension plan would combine with Social Security to allow low- and moderate-income employees to maintain their pre-retirement standard of living. Because no employer is required to have a pension plan in the first place, it is not sensible to require existing plans to provide a given level of benefits. The only rational requirements are to mandate that pension benefits for lower-paid employees be proportional in some sense to the benefits provided to the higher paid and that promised benefits actually be delivered. But for various reasons even this milder goal may not be achieved under existing law. One difficulty involves the way pension plan benefits are integrated with Social Security.

As shown in table 7-1, Social Security replaces a higher level of pre-retirement earnings for a low-wage worker than for a high earner. The "integration rules" in pension law allow employers to compensate for this difference by taking account of Social Security benefits in determining whether the plan discriminates. One rationale is that in the absence of integration, plans designed to achieve full replacement for high-income workers may provide low-income workers with retirement income in excess of full replacement—and excessive

15. Under current law a minimum contribution is required only if the plan is "top heavy." It would be far superior to require such a minimum contribution in all 401(k)s rather than loosening the top-heavy protection as many advocate.

pension benefits would unnecessarily reduce pre-retirement earnings for this already struggling group.

With integration, many low and moderate earners end up with pension income that is well below the recommended 80 percent or so of pre-retirement income. This outcome is not consistent with the goals of pension policy. Hence, we think that tax-favored plans generally should be required to provide benefits or contributions that are equal in proportion to income without regard to Social Security. The only exception would be those instances where the plan provides replacement rates for full career employees that, in combination with Social Security, equal or exceed the recommended 80 percent. If the firm can show that the combined expected benefits from Social Security and the private plan would replace more than 80 percent of pre-retirement income, the sponsor would then be permitted to reduce pension benefits by the lesser of the excess or the expected government payment.

Preserving the Value of Termination Benefits for Mobile Workers

For workers who remain with one employer throughout their work lives, defined benefit plans have the advantage of offering a predictable benefit, usually expressed as a percent of final pay for each year of service. Problems arise, however, in the case of mobile employees. One difficulty is that firms have vesting requirements, which require a worker to stay with a firm for a specific period of time before being eligible for any pension at all. Even if vesting were immediate, however, mobile employees in a defined benefit pension plan would receive significantly lower benefits as a result of changing jobs than they would have received from continuous coverage under a single plan. This difference arises because final earnings levels usually determine pension benefits in defined benefit plans. Workers who remain with a plan receive benefits related to earnings just before retirement, but employees who switch jobs, say, every ten years would find that their pensions were based on a combination of earnings at ages thirty-five, forty-five, fifty-five, and sixty-five. It is straightforward to construct numerical examples in which mobile workers in a world of defined benefit pension systems find that their eventual pension is one-third or more lower than that of workers with identical earnings profiles who stayed at one job for an entire career. Thus, mobile employees face a serious loss of benefits under a defined benefit plan, and this loss of benefits takes on greater importance as job mobility increases.

The loss of benefits under a defined benefit plan can occur because employers are allowed to "back-load" their contributions; that is, to put aside more in the pension plan for older and higher-paid workers than for younger and lower-paid ones. Back-loading is possible because an employer can use one of two tests to establish that a plan does not discriminate against the rank and file. Under so-called contributions testing, a plan is not discriminatory if the employer can show that contributions as a percentage of pay are no higher for highly compensated employees than for the rank and file. Alternatively, if the percentage of contributions is greater for older employees, who are more likely to be higher paid, the plan is not considered discriminatory if the employer can show that the benefits promised by the plan are no higher as a percentage of pay for the highly compensated employees than for the non-highly compensated—benefits testing. In other words, although the contributions are larger for older employees, the ultimate benefit as a percentage of pay would be equal, because the funds would be invested for a shorter period of time.

There is an immediate temptation to argue that sponsors of pension plans should not be allowed to back-load their contributions. We would certainly take that position with respect to small businesses. But before giving in to that temptation totally, it is important to realize that back-loading of contributions is particularly helpful for defined benefit plans, which have many advantages over defined contribution plans. Defined benefit plans promise a benefit equal to a certain percentage of final pay, and they are likely to meet their target replacement rate. The employer assumes the investment risk, the risk of unexpected increases in salary, and perhaps the risk of life expectancy as well. In addition, the value of the benefit can be adjusted in the case of early or late retirement. The employer is required to provide adequate funding, and in the event of employer default, the PBGC guarantees the bulk of benefits.[16] A specific benefit promise in terms of a percentage of final pay allows the employee time to provide additional savings if the benefit might be insufficient to maintain pre-retirement living standards. In contrast, it is nearly impossible to hit a target rate of replacement under a defined contribution plan. A sponsor of a defined contribution plan may have such a target and set contributions to reach the target by making an assumption as to when employees will begin participation, retire, and die and by estimating the rates of investment return and salary growth. The target will be achieved, however, only if the employer makes the promised contributions and the employee follows the assumed salary path, achieves the predicted investment performance, conforms to both the beginning and retirement ages, and either purchases an annuity or lives to the expected average age of death. Little wonder that workers covered by a defined contribution plan appear to have very little idea of the annual income stream that can be provided by a given level of accumulation.

16. Under current law the employer is sometimes responsible for payment of benefits before they would be required to be funded, and to some extent this obligation is backed up by the PBGC. It seems much more sensible to limit the promise to the funding obligation, which would mean that the employer and the PBGC would be liable only if the employer defaults on its obligation to fund or there is actuarial error, most importantly in the assumption as to the return on investment. This change in law would require either faster funding or, preferably, a slower phase-in of the guarantee of promised benefits.

The allocation of risks concerning future retirement income seems much more sensible under a defined benefit plan than a defined contribution plan. Employers have much greater capacity than employees to absorb the risks associated with investment performance, salary growth, retirement age, and mortality. The employer can average out investment results among cohorts of retirees, so it need not worry about a temporary market downturn. Similarly, since the employer need only predict a salary scale for the work force as a whole, not for each employee, it is better able to assume the risk of deviations from projected growth. The employer would also be more likely to have access to a fairly priced annuity at a group rate.

Furthermore, higher contributions for older employees may make up, to some extent, for the lack of coverage earlier in life. Specifically, back-loading enables employers to provide past service benefits for employees who are in mid-career when the plan is adopted. In addition, some would suggest that back-loading contributions closer to retirement age is consistent with a sensible pattern of saving. Younger people have the expenses of purchasing a home, raising children, and paying for their education. Only when workers reach their late forties or fifties can they begin to save substantial amounts for retirement. Even if the offset between pension accruals and wages is not dollar for dollar, it may still make sense to target pensions more toward older workers, who place more value on retirement savings. Some will argue, however, that back-loaded accruals make it too expensive to hire older employees and awkward to discharge younger employees, who will suffer a large loss in expected benefits.

Is it possible to retain many of the attractive features of defined benefit plans just described, yet mitigate some of the loss of benefits experienced by mobile employees? The problem of mobile workers could be solved very easily, in a mechanical sense, by having each employer provide the terminating employee a lump sum that reflected the value of benefits based on projected earnings at age sixty-five, rather than earnings at the time of termination, so that the mobile employee would suffer no loss in benefits. Increasing benefits for terminated employees would increase employer cost, however, and mean either lower benefits for remaining employees or lower wages for all employees. Furthermore, firms may want to provide lower benefits to mobile employees, since after all, one of the motivations for establishing pension plans in the first place is to reduce turnover and retain skilled workers. A milder option along these lines that might be more acceptable to employers would be to pay a lump sum to a terminated employee that reflected current salary indexed only for expected inflation.

An alternative approach that imposes the risk of unexpected salary growth on the employee but protects the mobile employee as long as the new employer has a similar plan is a defined benefit plan with benefits based on career average pay rather than final average pay. In this case, the pension benefit accrued in a given year is a specified percentage of the earnings for the year, which can be thought of as a life annuity beginning at normal retirement. Since the benefit is not affected by future salary increases, an employee who moves to an employer with an identical plan is not harmed by a job change, as that employee would be in a traditional defined benefit plan. The overall level of expected retirement benefits earned in a career average plan can be set equal to that of a final average pay plan, although the pattern of payments into the pension system would differ between the two approaches.

Both the inflation indexing and the career average approaches call for back-loading contributions and therefore require retaining benefits testing to ensure nondiscrimination. As long as benefits testing is an option, however, employees who change jobs will be vulnerable if a new employer tests on the basis of contributions. In addition, employees whose employers switch plans midway through their careers would also risk being covered by a plan subject to benefits testing when they were young and one subject to contribution testing when they are older. In such cases, contributions on their behalf when they were young would be inadequate to hit the desired target, and just as they were about to receive disproportionately large contributions, the test would change to require equal contributions for all participants. Thus, such employees would do less well than if they had been covered by the same type of plan for a full career. This pattern explains much of the outcry from mid-career employees whose employers have switched the form of their defined benefit plan from final pay to cash balance. To avoid this inequity, our view is that when employers change plans, they should be required to protect the expectations of any employee with a significant period of service, either by continuing accruals under the old plan or giving the employee the benefit of the new plan retroactive to the date of hire.

If the transition were handled in an equitable fashion, cash balance plans would have some obvious advantages—particularly for mobile employees. They can shift the investment risk to the employer without back-loading contributions. Under these plans the promised benefit is the amount that could be provided from the cash balance that would accumulate if the employer made contributions equal to a certain percentage of pay and the plan earned a specified rate of return, such as the rate on Treasury bonds. (In such a plan, the goal may be to guarantee the employee a constant real rate of return.) In practice, however, the employer does not invest in Treasury bonds, but in higher yielding instruments, such as equities. Because employers anticipate earning higher returns, they can contribute less than the stated percentage. The plans, however, are defined benefit plans, and so employees are not put at risk if the investment performance turns out poorly; they are entitled to the promised benefit, backed up by the PBGC. The advantage for mobile employees is that contributions are not related to final pay, and therefore the employees' benefits would not be affected by a job change if they moved to an identical plan. Since a cash balance plan is a form of a defined benefit plan, a business could subsidize early retirement if it desired to do so.

The question remains whether benefits testing is ever appropriate in a plan in which the employer has no responsibility for the ultimate benefit. Some defined contribution plans determine the contribution as the amount necessary to replace the same percentage of current pay for each participant. These so-called age-weighted profit-sharing plans are similar to the career average defined benefit plans described earlier, except that annual contributions are not mandatory and the employee assumes the risk of the investment return on the contributions. Because the discrimination test assumes that benefits will be received, it is hard to justify when benefits are so uncertain. At the very least, the law should require that the employer make annual contributions as a condition of benefits testing. In effect, this would convert the profit-sharing defined contribution plan into what is called a "money purchase" plan. A further step would require that the employer assume the investment risk.

Limiting Distributions before Retirement

Existing law discourages pre-retirement distributions from pension plans by imposing an excise tax on most distributions made before the recipient reaches age fifty-nine and one-half and, in some situations, prohibiting distributions outright. The law does not, however, prohibit distributions upon separation from service or termination of the plan. Furthermore, the excise tax does not apply to certain distributions used to cover high medical expenses, to purchase a residence, to pay college tuition, or to cover the costs of health insurance premiums in the event of long-term unemployment. (The last three exceptions apply to withdrawals from an IRA only.) Some attempt is made to encourage employers to make distributions from the plan directly into an IRA by withholding 20 percent for personal income taxes on distributions not directed toward IRAs. The possible threat to retirement income security created by cashing out money received in a lump sum when an employee leaves a job was one of the issues left uncovered in the ERISA debates of the early 1970s.

The availability of lump-sum distributions from both defined benefit and defined contribution plans has increased substantially over time. According to data from the 1983 and 1993 employee benefits supplements to the Current Population Survey, less than half (47.8 percent) of pension plan participants had the option of a lump-sum distribution in 1983, compared with 71.5 percent ten years later. The dollar amount of lump-sum distributions amounted to $81.6 billion in 1990.[17]

17. For the information based on CPS data, see Scott and Shoven (1996, p. 4). For the estimate of lump-sum distributions in 1990, see Yakoboski (1997, p. 4). Defined benefit plans cannot provide lump-sum payments without the consent of participants unless the present value of benefits at termination is $5,000 or less.

Several surveys have confirmed that lump-sum distributions are often cashed out. The Employee Benefit Research Institute (EBRI) conducted a survey of lump-sum payments from large pension plans and found that most distributions are not rolled over; among job changers, a full 60 percent of distributions were cashed out and only 40 percent were rolled over into other qualified retirement plans in 1996.[18] The 1996 Retirement Confidence Survey found similar results.[19] It queried workers on the receipt of lump-sum payouts in the three years before the survey. Of workers who reported receiving a distribution, 46 percent reported rolling at least some of the money into either an IRA or the new employer's plan, and 27 percent reported saving at least some of the money in another vehicle. By comparison, 50 percent reported spending some or all of the distribution.

It is true that large lump-sum distributions are much more likely to be rolled over than small ones. In 1996, for example, 95 percent of distributions greater than $100,000 were rolled over, compared with only 20 percent of distributions under $3,500. As a result, more than 75 percent of total dollars distributed were rolled over. It is also true that the 40 percent rollover rate found by the EBRI survey in 1996 was higher than the 35 percent rollover rate that the survey had found in 1993.

Nonetheless, the surveys imply that roughly $20 billion a year leaks out of the private pension system. Moreover, small distributions currently being cashed out in large numbers could ultimately translate into a large loss of retirement income. Considering that the average work force entrant today will hold more than eight jobs before reaching retirement, several small distributions over the working life could become the norm. Thus the cashing out of lump-sum distributions is a serious issue.

Ideally all payments from pension plans should take the form of annuity payments beginning at normal retirement age. This rule could be stretched to allow a fixed number of installment payments after retirement, to alleviate objections by those who do not expect to live long enough to benefit from receiving all benefits in the form of a life annuity. If it is not feasible to require an annuity for some employees, then imposing an increased tax on other forms of distribution could be a backdoor method of encouraging this form of payment. At the very least, the law should require that all pre-retirement or lump-sum distributions be made to an IRA. Although a beneficiary can make withdrawals from an IRA, the necessity for an affirmative action might discourage spending. Further restrictions should be considered if substantial dissipation of pension funds before retirement continues.

18. Yakoboski (1997).
19. Yakoboski (1997).

A competing consideration should be taken into account: if retirement assets become less available, employees who fear they may need savings for other purposes might become less willing to participate in a pension plan in the first place. This reaction would directly reduce savings in the case of a 401(k) and would in all cases make it more difficult for an employer to maintain a plan. To alleviate these concerns, distributions could be permitted without penalty in more circumstances, but establishing these conditions could prove administratively difficult.

Preserving the Real Value of Pension Benefits against Inflation

Inflation can erode pension benefits after retirement, but private sector defined benefit pension plans generally do not provide postretirement cost-of-living adjustments. Consequently, even moderate rates of inflation can noticeably erode the purchasing power of benefits fixed in nominal terms. The lack of postretirement inflation adjustment has not received much attention lately because the inflation rate has been so low. But even at 3 percent inflation, the real value of a $100 benefit declines to $63 after fifteen years, $54 after twenty years, and $47 after twenty-five years. Given that life expectancy at age sixty-five is about twenty years, this erosion remains an important problem.

Although Congress discussed the issue of protecting the value of pensions against inflation during deliberations on ERISA, the legislation did not contain any guidelines about postretirement cost-of-living increases. Some employers have offered ad hoc cost-of-living increases in their pensions, but these adjustments tend to offset no more than one-third of inflation's erosive impact. Furthermore, very few employer-sponsored plans guarantee cost-of-living adjustments, and those that do—primarily plans sponsored by state and local governments—usually have annual caps of 2–3 percent. Consequently, even beneficiaries who do receive annual adjustments experience a considerable reduction in the purchasing power of their benefits.

Now, however, better inflation protection may be possible. One reason that private pension plan sponsors have not provided a guaranteed inflation adjustment is that they have not had access to a financial asset that could offer them full protection against a resurgence of inflation. This roadblock was eliminated in 1997 when the U.S. Treasury began to issue inflation-indexed securities, which fully protect investors against the deterioration of principal and interest due to inflation. With these indexed bonds, pension plan sponsors should be able to provide inflation-adjusted annuities, if the pension sponsors and recipients so desire. It would now be practicable to require that defined benefit plans offer employees the option of an annuity that adjusts with inflation.

In a defined contribution pension plan, the likelihood of protection against inflation depends on the form of the distribution. If the account balance is converted to a fixed annuity on retirement, it will suffer from the same lack of inflation protection as a typical defined benefit plan. If assets continue to be invested in the market, however, then the real value of the pension benefit can be at least partially protected.

Indeed, at least one defined contribution pension plan is offering some protection against inflation. The nation's major defined contribution pension plan, Teachers Insurance and Annuity Association (TIAA) and College Retirement Equities Fund (CREF), has designed annuities that pattern benefits to reflect expected inflation. For example, TIAA offers a graded benefit payment, under which benefits are significantly lower to start but then increase each year in relation to the amount by which actual investment experience exceeds the nominal interest rate. CREF offers a variable annuity under which benefits are adjusted each year to reflect the performance of the fund's stock portfolio, thus also serving as a loose adjustment for lower rates of inflation. Neither of these options, however, would provide complete protection against unexpectedly high rates of inflation.

Increasing the Number of Employers Who Offer Pension Plans

With respect to employers who have not established qualified plans, particularly small business owners, it would seem that the existing combination of tax benefits and regulations are not sufficient to lead to plan adoption. Can the pie be sweetened for this group without providing a costly and undesirable windfall to those who already maintain plans? Alternatively, it may be possible to identify barriers to the establishment of retirement plans by small businesses (such as high administrative cost per employee) that could be mitigated in some manner. We consider three possible means of increasing the incentive to establish plans: providing more benefits to the higher paid, in total or in relation to the benefits for the rank and file; making it easier for employers to exclude reluctant savers from the plan; and reducing or mitigating administrative costs.

Providing More Benefits to the Highly Paid

Increasing the proportion of the tax benefits from favorable treatment of pension plans that flow to the highly compensated might make companies more willing to offer such plans. This might be done in one of two ways: increasing the maximum allowable contributions (or benefits) or raising the compensation limits.

Maximum allowable contributions or benefits are defined differently for defined benefit and defined contribution plans. The Internal Revenue Code limits contributions to defined contribution plans to the lesser of 25 percent of compensation or a fixed ceiling that rises with inflation each year (the ceiling was $35,000 in 2001). For the purpose of this calculation, compensation cannot exceed a specified limit, $170,000 in 2001. The tax code places no limit on the amount of accumulation or the total benefits that can be provided.

The maximum benefit from defined benefit plans is 100 percent of final pay averaged over three years or an indexed amount that was $140,000 for 2001.[20] Contributions are allowed as necessary to fund these benefits in accordance with certain allowable actuarial methods. Excess contributions are not deductible for tax purposes and subject the employer to an often prohibitive excise tax. If investment results are below expectations, additional contributions may be made to the extent necessary to fund the promised benefits.

Two implications of these rules are worth particular notice. First, larger contributions can be made to defined contribution plans for younger workers,[21] whereas contributions to defined benefit plans can be larger for older workers.[22] Second, because defined contribution plans have no limit on benefits, the accumulation of assets can be much greater than would be permitted in a defined benefit plan.

It has been noted that pension plans that qualify for favorable tax treatment provide the equivalent of consumption tax treatment, because they result in the exemption of investment income. For this reason, supporters of a consumption tax may favor increases in the limits or their elimination altogether as a way of moving toward similar treatment for all savings. The premise of existing law, however, is that qualified plan treatment is an exception to the norm and is warranted only to the extent necessary to provide "adequate" retirement income for the rank and file. In this spirit, the tax subsidy should help finance only a limited amount of retirement income; above that amount each household should be on its own.

It is difficult to say what limited amount of retirement income should be considered adequate or appropriate for favorable tax treatment, but the annual annuity of $140,000 available under a defined benefit plan and the far greater amount that could be financed with a defined contribution plan (or a combination of a defined benefit and a defined contribution plan) seem more than adequate. Thus, the case for a higher limit has to be that it is essential to encourage employers to establish plans that will lead to retirement protection for low- and moderate-income groups. That being the case, any increase in the limits should apply only to plans that can establish that they truly provide for the rank and

---

20. These limitations, which were first introduced by ERISA in 1974, are substantially lower in real terms than the limits first put into effect.

21. For younger employees, the $35,000 allowable contribution would be larger than necessary to fund the maximum benefit payment currently allowed, and the law does not allow inflation adjustments to the $140,000 limit to be anticipated. We view this as unfortunate.

22. For older workers, the cost of the allowable benefit could be much larger than $35,000. The amount of back-loading in defined contribution plans would be limited by the contribution limits, an approach that is consistent with our belief that benefits testing is generally inappropriate in defined contribution plans.

file in the sense that a significant portion of contributions are on behalf of a wide range of such employees.

A second broad method of increasing pension-related tax benefits to the highly compensated is to alter the maximum earnings provisions. As noted earlier, the maximum earnings that could be taken into account for determining the percentage contribution or benefit for the highly paid was $170,000 in 2001. This rule was intended to prevent the maximum limit on contributions and benefits from producing very low contributions for lower earners. For example, if the owner were earning $700,000, the maximum contribution to a defined contribution plan of $35,000 would be 5 percent of pay. Limiting earnings to $170,000 means that a $35,000 contribution is 20.6 percent of pay. If discrimination is tested on the basis of percentage of income contributed, then this level of contributions must be made for other participants as well.

Again, it is difficult to say what the optimal level of includable compensation should be, but it should be related in a sensible fashion to the maximum level of contributions or benefits. The maximum benefit from a defined benefit plan of $140,000 is 82.35 percent of the $170,000 compensation limit, which would be a rich plan—slightly above the goal of replacing 80 percent of income even near the very top of the income distribution—but perhaps not too far out of line with an ideal target.

In contrast, a maximum contribution of $35,000 and includable compensation of $170,000 suggests a contribution rate of 20.6 percent. If this is viewed as too high, as it seems to be, judging from what appears to be the typical contribution rates in pension plans, then either the maximum contribution should be reduced or the includable compensation increased to bring the numbers in line with a sensible level of contribution. Since it appears that under reasonable assumptions a $35,000 annual contribution could produce a benefit well in excess of $140,000 annually (even as indexed for inflation), a reduction in the contribution limit seems appropriate in the context of the present system.

In summary, the maximum allowable contributions and included compensation are already at quite high levels, and we see no rationale for increasing them.

Excluding Reluctant Savers

A second approach sometimes proposed for encouraging more companies to offer pension plans is to make it easier for such firms to exclude reluctant savers. The philosophy here is that fairness should require only that companies offer a matching plan; whether employees want to use that plan should be up to them. A number of proposals have been made along these lines. Generally, it seems counterproductive to us to consider weakening the requirements for including rank-and-file workers in order to encourage more plans. Because we think that employer pension plans should offer something closer to universal coverage, not further away from it, we would not endorse a policy that enabled the employer to narrow coverage further.

Thus the movement discussed earlier to design safe harbors for 401(k) plans that require no particular participation by the non-highly compensated group also seems ill advised. Most troublesome is the rule now applicable to salary reduction plans for employees of tax-exempt institutions under 403(b) of the tax code (essentially a 401(k) plan for tax-exempt institutions). This rule requires only that employees have the opportunity to participate; the employer need not make any special effort to encourage participation through a match or educational efforts. Again, we think the movement should be in the opposite direction so that employers would have to make further efforts to encourage participation by rank-and-file employees. To that end we favor the rules passed in 1986 that require the benefit levels as a percentage of pay for the non-highly compensated to be at least 70 percent of the benefits percentage for the highly compensated and would oppose eliminating this requirement.

The only case for which it makes some sense to facilitate exclusion of certain employees would be for those with very low incomes, near the poverty level, for whom saving is simply not feasible. For this group the only real option is expansion of Social Security or the introduction of a government-subsidized retirement savings account, since any change that cuts their pre-retirement income would be unwise.

Reducing or Mitigating Administrative Costs

Qualified employer pension plans involve administrative costs that do not apply to other forms of savings, like personal savings. Although some of these costs vary with the number of employees, the fixed costs are substantial. For an employer with many workers, the tax benefits derived from the use of a qualified plan make it sensible to absorb these costs. But if the work force is small or if the need to subsidize the earnings of reluctant savers absorbs the bulk of the tax benefits, the administrative costs may be prohibitive. This might suggest subsidizing such costs for small plans that provide a high proportion of benefits to low- and moderate-income employees. In this way, mitigating administrative costs for small employers might hold promise as a means of increasing the number of plans. Marginal changes, however, in the existing system are unlikely to correct significantly for the lack of coverage and inadequate benefits.

Fundamental Reform of America's Pension System

The discussion to this point has mentioned several potential reforms to the existing system of employer-provided pensions. We have expressed support for some and opposition to others, along with a number of qualifications. But regardless of the merits of particular proposals, we do not believe that piecemeal changes will solve the problem. Rather, we think it is time to acknowledge that today's voluntary employer-sponsored pension system is not capable of providing coverage for most of those individuals who end up in the lowest two quintiles of the retirement income distribution. In any event, employer-sponsored retirement provisions inevitably involve some reduction in current wages for deferred pension benefits, which is not desirable for low-income workers who are already struggling to make ends meet. Comprehensive reform of America's private pension system is needed both to increase the lifetime income of low-income workers and to ensure them adequate income in retirement. Reform is also needed to improve coverage and benefit adequacy for the rank and file.

The reform proposal described below has two components. First, it provides for low-income workers directly, through a program similar to the Clinton administration's 1999 Universal Savings Accounts (USA) proposal, which has a government-financed payment plus matching credits for individual contributions.[23] Because employers are relieved of providing for their low-paid workers, some of the favorable tax treatment now accorded pensions would be removed through the imposition of a 5 percent tax on the investment earnings of pension funds. The second part of our proposal is aimed at increasing coverage for the rank and file through enhanced incentives, namely, increasing contribution and benefit limits for employers who cover all workers in their organization. These two changes should have the net effect of producing a much more adequate pattern of retirement income in a much more efficient manner.

Trading Less Coverage for Low-Income Workers for Slightly Fewer Tax Benefits

If the goal is for low-income workers to have more retirement income without a cut in their wages during their working years, the government needs to increase their lifetime income in the form of deferred retirement benefits. Only by financing such an increase through general revenues is it possible to avoid the incentive for employers to reduce cash wages.

In 1999 the Clinton administration proposed a two-step program to address the problem. First, the government would make an automatic contribution in the form of a refundable tax credit deposited directly to individual Universal Savings Accounts. Second, individuals could contribute to their USAs, and the government would match their contributions dollar-for-dollar for low- and moderate-income individuals, phasing down to a 50 percent match for higher income levels. This approach would effectively substitute a tax credit for the deduction usually associated with contributions to a tax-subsidized retirement plan. A

---

23. In 2000 the Clinton administration proposed Retirement Savings Accounts, which had matching credits but no government-financed payments.

dollar-for-dollar match is equivalent to a 50 percent tax credit, since the contributor must put up only fifty cents for every dollar that ends up in the account.[24]

Because we believe that increased savings by low-income individuals may not be possible or desirable, the program should be structured so that the automatic grant alone, when combined with Social Security, is sufficient to provide full replacement for individuals earning $20,000 or less.[25] The automatic grant could be phased out as income increases above that point. The matching program should be directed at individuals at somewhat higher income levels, who have the capacity to save. A 50 percent credit is a substantially enhanced subsidy over current law, where contributors in the 15 percent bracket have to put up eighty-five cents for each dollar that ends up in their account. Although a question exists about the amount of increased savings that this enhanced subsidy would generate, it is worth trying as a supplement to the existing IRA program.

To ensure that workers would not shift contributions from private 401(k)-type plans to USAs, the government would pay the matching contribution for payments to either USAs or 401(k)s.[26] Individuals would be able to invest their accounts in a universal retirement plan similar to the Federal Thrift Savings Plan (TSP) now available to federal employees, or with private fund managers. Withdrawals from a USA would be prohibited before age sixty-five unless the account holder dies, and after withdrawals commence, no additional contributions could be made to the account. (A similar prohibition on withdrawals would be ideal for all tax-favored retirement savings.)

Under our proposal, once low-earning workers are covered by a government-financed supplementary retirement system, employers would no longer be required to include these individuals in their plans. Furthermore, USA automatic credits for workers earning more than $20,000 would reduce the amount that employer pension plans would have to provide for these workers to achieve full replacement of pre-retirement earnings. Both of these changes should make it more attractive to employers to offer such plans to their workers. No longer would employers have to bribe lower-paid workers who have little interest in retirement saving to participate by increasing their total compensation. That in

24. If the matched contribution is also deductible, as proposed in 2000, the equivalent credit is somewhat higher.

25. As proposed by the Clinton administration in 1999, the government contribution for workers and their spouses in low- or moderate-income households is $300 a year. This automatic credit is phased out between $40,000 and $80,000 of adjusted gross income for a couple filing jointly; $20,000–$40,000 for singles; and $30,000–$50,000 for single heads of households.

26. Because contributions to a 401(k)-type plan are excludable from taxable income while USA contributions are not, joint filers with adjusted gross income of more than $50,000 ($25,000 for single filers; $37,500 for head-of-household filers) who receive government matches would be required to include in taxable income 80 percent of the portion of the 401(k) contribution that is matched.

turn would increase the potential gain to the higher paid from the favorable tax treatment of qualified plans.

In our view this diminished responsibility on the part of employers for providing pension coverage to low-income workers, together with the probable gain to the remaining workers, justifies some reduction in the pension-related tax benefits to offset in part the cost of USAs. Probably the most practical way to limit the tax benefits for qualified plans is to tax pension earnings. The current treatment of pension plans, as discussed earlier, is equivalent to exempting from taxation the earnings on the money that would have been invested after tax, assuming the employee remains in the same tax bracket; taxing pension earnings at the employee's rate eliminates this exemption. In theory, earnings in pension funds could either be taxed by imputing a certain amount of income to individuals and then taxing the individuals or by taxing the funds directly. The practical difficulties with allocating contributions and pension fund earnings to individuals are substantial. First, these amounts would fluctuate widely from one year to the next, depending on the performance of the stock market, introducing substantial volatility into the individual employee's annual tax payments. Second, unless contributions and earnings were attributed only to those whose pensions were vested, some individuals might be taxed on benefits that they might never collect. Third, some individuals would have difficulty finding the funds to pay tax on income they have not yet received. With these concerns in mind, our view is that taxing pension funds is better done at the fund level. Thus, the proposal is to retain the deductibility of contributions and the taxation of benefits after retirement, but to tax a portion of pension earnings at the fund level.

The appropriate level of a tax on pension earnings would be about 5 percent. To put that number in perspective, a 5 percent levy should eliminate about 18 percent of the tax benefit (assuming the average pension beneficiary is in the 28 percent bracket). If the current revenue loss from the favorable tax treatment of pensions is about $80 billion, as suggested earlier, then reducing the tax expenditure by 18 percent would save about $15 billion annually. Back-of-the-envelope calculations based on the Federal Reserve's Flow of Funds suggest a higher number: for the period 1991 to 1999 the earnings averaged $295 billion for private pension funds and $217 billion for state and local funds.[27] Subjecting these amounts to a 5 percent levy would have produced average annual revenues of $26 billion altogether.

Taxing pension earnings may also slightly reduce pension benefits, but any losses in this direction are likely to be more than offset by the overall boost to pensions as a result of eliminating the need to bribe low-wage workers to participate. Thus, the first part of the reform proposal trades less coverage for low-income workers through employer-sponsored plans for fewer tax benefits, leaving

27. Board of Governors (1999, pp. 23, 68).

low-income workers better off under a government program and remaining private pension participants probably unaffected. The money gained by the 5 percent tax could be used to help fund USA-type accounts.

Trading More Coverage for the Rank and File for Higher Limits

The second part of the reform proposal is aimed at improving the coverage and benefits for the rank and file. Because improvements in coverage and benefits would require the pension system to do more than it does currently, this part of the proposal offers sweeteners, namely, higher contribution and benefit limits solely for plans that cover all workers.

The centerpiece of improving coverage for the rank and file requires jettisoning the complicated Treasury regulations regarding participation of the highly compensated versus the non-highly compensated and replacing them with the simple requirement that a qualified pension plan must provide benefits for all employees (in a given line of business). The only exception would be employees earning less than $20,000 (indexed for annual wage growth), who would be covered under the public USA plan. Unlike current law, the new provisions would not tolerate any disparity between the benefits for the higher and lower paid. No longer would it be acceptable for the participation by the highly compensated to be not "too much" greater than the level of participation by the remainder of the work force and for the average benefit as a percentage of pay for the non-highly compensated to be 70 percent of that for the highly compensated. Nondiscrimination would mean that all employees are covered by the same participation and benefit provisions. If the plan failed this simple test, none of the participants would be eligible for favorable tax treatment.

Three additional changes would be required to maximize the effectiveness of this form of comprehensive pension coverage. First, the vesting provisions would be changed to require full vesting after no more than one year. Second, the definition of a year of service would be revised so that part-time employees working at least ten hours a week would be covered by the plan. Third, the guidelines for integrating pension benefits with Social Security would be revised so that tax-favored plans would have to provide benefits or contributions at the same proportion of income at all income levels, without regard to Social Security, until the benefit is sufficient to provide full replacement for workers whose entire earnings are covered by Social Security.

The expansion in coverage would also be accompanied by three provisions to preserve the value of vested benefits. First, all lump-sum payments would be required to be rolled over to an IRA. Yes, funds could be withdrawn from an IRA, but the expectation behind this rule is that the need for affirmative action to access these payments will significantly reduce the likelihood that they will be spent. Second, all plans must offer the option of an inflation-indexed annuity.

The third change is aimed at reducing the erosion in value of termination benefits for the mobile employee. Our judgment is that it would be desirable from a national perspective, for any level of pension resources, to reallocate pension contributions from career employees to mobile employees. No solution is perfect here, but the most feasible would be to ensure that projected benefits are based on a projection of current salary that includes an inflation adjustment for what that salary would be just before retirement. This adjustment would compensate for expected inflation but would make no provision for real salary growth.

While it would be convenient to mandate the changes suggested above, the private pension system is a voluntary arrangement, and the more pressure put on employers, the less likely that they will maintain plans. Thus, some incentives are needed to induce employers to adopt these reforms voluntarily. The proposal is to make a dramatic adjustment in the maximum contribution and benefit constraints. Ideally, the proposed adjustment should be no greater than is necessary to cause employers to sponsor plans with the proposed changes. It is impossible, however, to know what that amount would be, and in any event it would vary from company to company.

One possibility is to restore the limits for maximum benefits originally introduced in ERISA. That legislation set the maximum for annual benefits payable under a defined benefit plan at $75,000. If that amount had been allowed to grow with inflation, instead of being reduced by subsequent legislation, the limit would now be about $270,000. Of course, there is nothing magical about the limit set in 1974. Before then the tax code placed no constraint on benefits from a qualified plan, and it was very difficult to get any constraint included in ERISA. Thus the initial levels adopted in 1974 were set so that they did not affect existing benefits significantly. Splitting the difference between the current maximum benefit of $140,000 and the ERISA limit as indexed would put the maximum for benefits at approximately $200,000. The original limit on contributions to a defined contribution plan was one-third of the benefit limit, or $25,000. Over the years the contribution limit was reduced to 25 percent of the benefit limit. As discussed earlier, even this ratio appears to be too high. Reducing the ratio to 20 percent would produce a contribution limit of $40,000.

To maintain a sensible relationship between the benefit and contribution constraint and the compensation that can be taken into account, these new limits would require an increase in includable compensation for those plans that take advantage of the increase. If the current relationship, which suggests a benefit equal to about 82 percent of compensation, were retained, the compensation limit would be set at about $245,000 for a plan with a maximum benefit of $200,000. Perhaps a more reasonable limit would be $265,000, which would assume a benefit of approximately 75 percent of pay and a contribution of approximately 15 percent of pay.

Such a dramatic increase in limits does not mean that current limits are in any way inadequate in terms of producing reasonable levels of tax-subsidized retirement income for the highly compensated. The proposed increase is offered purely and simply to induce employers to sign on to a new comprehensive definition of coverage that would greatly enhance the well-being of the rank and file and significantly simplify the tax code. Because the goal is increased private pension coverage, no rationale exists for simultaneously increasing the limits on IRAs.

Furthermore, since the goal is increased coverage for the rank and file, it is sensible to deny the increased limits to any pension plans that are primarily for owners and other very highly compensated individuals. Such a provision currently applies to the exclusion from taxes on gross income for corporate amounts expended for child care, whereby such an exclusion is not applicable if more than 25 percent of the benefits go to 5 percent shareholders. We suggest that a similar test be applied to our proposal to increase the limits of pension plans.

In short, the second part of the comprehensive reform proposal is to trade comprehensive coverage and extensive benefit protection through an increase in termination benefits, mandatory rollovers to IRAs, and full postretirement cost-of-living protection in exchange for a dramatic increase in subsidized benefits for the highly paid. This proposition should be viewed as an all-or-nothing proposal: without a significant improvement in pension protection for rank-and-file employees, our view is that no increase is warranted in either the contribution or benefit limits.

Conclusion

In this paper we have considered how to reform the pension system to give greater assurance of adequate retirement income both for those covered by employer-sponsored plans and for those currently excluded. Our proposals were driven in part by some of the frustrations that Groom and Shoven expressed in their paper in this volume. The current system is excessively complex and overly regulated, yet it does not provide the retirement income needed by many middle-income employees and fails low-income workers altogether. Although we observe the same history and problems as Groom and Shoven do, we have presented diametrically opposed proposals. They favor lifting regulations and relying on consumer sovereignty; we favor establishing a structure that will ensure better outcomes.

We start from the perspective that the tax treatment of pensions is special; it is more favorable than the treatment of other types of saving. In some sense it does not matter whether pension treatment is correct and nonpension treatment is too harsh, or whether nonpension treatment is correct and pension treatment favorable. This is not a paper about optimal tax policy. The point is that pension saving is treated better under the tax code than nonpension saving. Both the congressional and executive branches publish estimates of how much this favorable treatment reduces tax revenues. And the legislative history makes it clear that the current goal of these favorable tax provisions has been to encourage tax-qualified pension and profit-sharing plans to ensure greater retirement security for all employees, not just highly paid executives.

After nearly sixty years, it is obvious that this strategy has failed totally for the bottom 40 percent of the income distribution. The lack of pension income for low-wage workers would not be a source of concern if Social Security provided enough income for them to maintain their pre-retirement standard of living, but along with Groom and Shoven, we conclude that Social Security alone is inadequate when viewed either in terms of replacement rates or relative to poverty thresholds. We would like to see Social Security enhanced for this group by counting unemployment insurance payments and the Earned Income Credit as earnings, among other changes, but a major expansion of Social Security is unlikely at this time given the need to eliminate its long-run deficit.

With the bottom 40 percent of the income distribution having little chance of receiving more from Social Security, we believe that sweeping reform is needed so that the welfare of this group does not depend on the existing employer-sponsored system. The system is currently providing very little to the bottom 40 percent and is unlikely to do a significantly better job in the future. Moreover, we go a step further and argue that people with a lifetime of low wages are not in a position to sacrifice additional current consumption for additional retirement income. These people are struggling to make ends meet during their working years and cannot afford a cut in current wages in exchange for income after retirement.

Our first major proposal, therefore, is that the people at the low end of the wage distribution ($20,000 or under, indexed for wage growth) should receive their retirement income directly from the government and should be excludable from the employer-sponsored pension system, if the employer so desires. This program could be financed by general revenues, but it seems reasonable to place more of the burden on those now enjoying tax-subsidized savings. Moreover, relieving employers of the responsibility for covering these unwilling savers justifies some reduction in the tax preference. Our proposal is to introduce a 5 percent levy on pension fund earnings or an equivalent tax on pension fund assets, the proceeds of which can be used to finance USA-type accounts with a particular focus on improving the lifetime income of the near poor.

The USA-type arrangement also effectively creates a national 401(k) plan by providing a government match for individual contributions. The enhanced nature of the match, which replaces the current deduction (where contributors in the 15 percent bracket have to put up eighty-five cents for each dollar that ends up in their account) with a 50 percent credit that requires them to put up only fifty cents, is likely to increase individual saving by moderate earners.

While USA-type accounts provide some protection for middle- and high-wage workers, the private pension system remains the appropriate mechanism to provide the bulk of supplementary retirement income. This system is in place, well understood, and based, at least to some extent, on the employer's interest in deferring a portion of compensation. But the current system fails to provide meaningful benefits to many middle-income employees.

Here Groom and Shoven suggest the answer is to eliminate the discrimination provisions and to raise the caps on contributions and benefits. We oppose elimination of discrimination testing as Groom and Shoven advocate. With all its difficulties, the current system of better tax treatment for employer-sponsored plans that do not discriminate "too much" in favor of the highly paid contributes importantly to retirement savings for moderate-income people who would not save as much if saving was purely an individual choice. Elimination of discrimination testing would move the country further away from adequate protection for rank-and-file workers, even if it somehow increased overall savings. Sure, the discrimination test is much too complicated, but that occurs mainly as a result of accommodating employer desire to discriminate between segments of the work force.

We also oppose raising contribution and benefit limits, unless accompanied by the proposed reforms to improve coverage and benefit security. The Bureau of Labor Statistics reports that full-time workers at the ninetieth percentile of the wage distribution were earning $66,924 in 2000. It is not credible that people in the bottom 90 percent or even the bottom 95 percent of the income distribution are in any way constrained in their retirement saving by today's contribution and benefit limits. If Groom and Shoven want to subsidize the saving of the top 5 percent or 1 percent of the population, they should be clear that they are focusing on an elite minority.

Our proposal for improving the pension system involves changes to ensure uniform coverage and meaningful benefits. We would require that all of an employer's employees in a given line of business be included in the plan after one year of service, and that all benefits be immediately vested and generally uniform without regard to integration with Social Security. To be meaningful, benefits must be protected in the case of termination, not cashed out when received as a lump sum and not eroded by inflation after retirement.

We recognize the danger that simply mandating these changes might significantly reduce the number of plans. Hence, we propose offering a major increase in the benefit and contribution limits to those employers who sign on to the new system and can establish that a substantial portion of benefits goes to those other than business owners and others who are very highly paid. We adamantly oppose any increase in tax benefits for retirement savings that does not buy increased retirement security for low and moderate earners.

In short, we believe that the societal goal should be to foster a greater level of income replacement than Social Security now provides. We think that the changes we have proposed would accomplish this goal. In contrast, Groom and Shoven advocate "an equal opportunity and access to pensions." This is a nice slogan, but it will not achieve adequate retirement income.

References

Board of Governors, Federal Reserve System. 1999. "Flow of Funds Accounts of the United States, 1991–1999." Washington (June 9).

Gottschalk, Peter. 1997. "Inequality, Income Growth, and Mobility: The Basic Facts." *Journal of Economic Perspectives* 11 (Spring): 21–40.

Grad, Susan. 1990. "Earnings Replacement Rates of Newly Retired Workers." *Social Security Bulletin* 53 (October): 2–19.

Gunderson, Morley, Douglas Hyatt, and James E. Pesando. 1992. "Wage-Pension Trade-Offs in Collective Agreements." *Industrial and Labor Relations Review* 46 (October): 146–60.

Gustman, Alan L., and Thomas L. Steinmeier. 1992. "The Stampede toward Defined Contribution Pension Plans: Fact or Fiction?" *Industrial Relations* 31 (Spring): 361–69.

Halperin, Daniel I. 1993. "Special Tax Treatment for Employer-Based Retirement Programs: Is It 'Still' Viable as a Means of Increasing Retirement Income?" *Tax Law Review* 49 (Fall): 1–51.

Kruse, Douglas L. 1995. "Pension Substitution in the 1980s: Why the Shift toward Defined Contribution?" *Industrial Relations* 34 (April): 218–41.

Montgomery, Edward, Kathryn Shaw, and Mary Ellen Benedict. 1992. "Pensions and Wages: An Hedonic Price Theory Approach." *International Economic Review* 33 (February): 111–28.

Papke, Leslie E. 1999. "Are 401(k) Plans Replacing Other Employer-Provided Pensions? Evidence from Panel Data." *Journal of Human Resources* 34 (Spring): 346–68.

Papke, Leslie E., Mitchell Petersen, and James M. Poterba. 1996. "Do 401(k) Plans Replace Other Employer Provided Pensions?" In *Advances in the Economics of Aging*, edited by David A. Wise, 219–39. University of Chicago Press.

Sass, Steven A. 1997. *The Promise of Private Pensions: The First Hundred Years*. Harvard University Press.

Schiller, Bradley R., and Randall D. Weiss. 1980. "Pensions and Wages: A Test for Equalizing Differences." *Review of Economics and Statistics* 62 (November): 529–38.

Scott, Jason S., and John B. Shoven. 1996. "Lump-Sum Distributions: Fulfilling the Portability Promise or Eroding Retirement Security?" EBRI Issue Brief 178. Washington: Employment Benefit Research Institute.

Smith, Robert S., and Ronald G. Ehrenberg. 1983. "Estimating Wage-Fringe Tradeoffs: Some Data Problems." In *The Measurement of Labor Cost*, edited by Jack E. Triplett, 347–69. University of Chicago Press.

Social Security Administration. 2000a. *Annual Statistical Supplement*. GPO.

———. 2000b. *Fast Facts & Figures about Social Security*. GPO.

———. 2000c. *Income of the Aged Chartbook, 1998*. Washington.

U.S. Department of Labor, Bureau of Labor Statistics. 2000. "Usual Weekly Earnings of Wage and Salary Workers: Third Quarter 2000." Washington.

U.S. Department of Labor and others. 1994. "Pension and Health Benefits of American Workers: New Findings from the April 1993 Current Population Survey." GPO.

U.S. Office of Management and Budget. 2000. "Budget of the United States Government, Fiscal Year 2000, Analytical Perspectives." GPO.

Woods, John R. 1994. "Pension Coverage among the Baby Boomers: Initial Findings from a 1993 Survey." *Social Security Bulletin* 57 (Fall): 12–25.

Yakoboski, Paul. 1997. "Large Plan Lump-Sums: Rollovers and Cashouts." EBRI Issue Brief 188. Washington: Employment Benefit Research Institute.

8

From Fiduciary to Facilitator: Employers and Defined Contribution Plans

PAMELA PERUN AND C. EUGENE STEUERLE

Although it represents a striking success in some ways, the private pension system suffers from at least two major flaws: it is too complicated and it covers too few workers. A vigorous debate on whether the best approach to fixing these problems is to expand or contract the role of the government in the pension system is exemplified by the papers in this volume by Groom and Shoven and by Halperin and Munnell.

We take a different—and complementary—approach to pension reform. Specifically, we focus on proposals that would alter the role of the *employer* in the provision of pensions. In the current pension system, employers are expected or required to perform many roles, from the simplest facilitation of saving—through payroll deductions and wiring the funds to an account, for example—to extremely complicated regulatory tests involving funding rules, contribution limits, nondiscrimination standards, and the maintenance of fiduciary standards. There appears to be no logical reason why employers should be saddled with so many responsibilities, especially when it comes to defined contribution plans, since similar products offered by the financial services industry are free of such rules. In addition, the burdens placed on employers, particularly fiduciary standards, are inconsistent across types of plans.

Our approach would be to encourage firms to do more by requiring them to do less. In particular, we would maintain and emphasize the role of the employer in facilitating saving behavior by workers. This role includes providing

191

payroll deductions and simplified enrollment, making or matching contributions, and serving as an intermediary between employees and the financial services industry. But we would also move the defined contribution system more toward a system of individual accounts held, managed, and administered by the financial services industry. Under this approach, tax law would continue to encourage employers to offer plans and make contributions, while the financial services industry would provide those other services (such as providing investment alternatives and education, along with tax reporting and participant record-keeping and communication) that represent its comparative advantage. Overall, this approach would provide the pension system with an allocation of functions and responsibilities more appropriate for defined contribution plans than that now found in the Employee Retirement Income Security Act (ERISA) of 1974. Along the way, we believe that the simplification could be done in a way that would only increase the incentives to save, partly by reducing administrative costs and risks to employers.

Employers' Responsibilities before ERISA

Pension regulations were modest in scope before ERISA.[1] The central requirement was that pension plans had to satisfy legal rules to qualify for special tax treatment. Most of the rules governing contributions aimed to ensure that some of the tax benefits flowed to rank-and-file employees. Other provisions described when and how distributions of benefits would be taxed. Few rules described how contributions were to be invested because state—not federal—law then set the standards for plan investments. Assets had to be held in trust apart from the plan sponsor's other assets and for the "exclusive benefit of employees and their beneficiaries" until all liabilities were satisfied, but there were no explicit standards for the investment of assets and the regulations gave trustees wide discretion. The rules were more explicit on how trust assets should *not* be invested, creating special rules for employer securities and prohibitions on conflicts of interest or self-dealing.

Penalties were largely tax-related and imposed on the plan. When violations occurred, the plan was immediately disqualified, the trust lost its tax-exempt status, and participants were taxed on their vested benefits. It seems extraordinary today, but participants had no effective legal means to protect their assets from harmful actions by plan officials or to obtain redress from those responsible for injuring the plan, even though they alone bore the consequences of plan disqualification.[2]

1. Employers' responsibilities were set out in Internal Revenue Code sections 401(a)(1)–(7) and supporting regulations in effect before ERISA.
2. Before enactment of ERISA, participants had no private right of action to contest a plan disqualification and even today they have only such rights as are available through ERISA. Internal Rev-

Employers' Responsibilities under ERISA

The passage of ERISA in 1974 was inspired in part by the bankruptcy in 1963 of the Studebaker Company, whose pension plan also failed. The purpose of ERISA was to secure the pension promise by adding new protections for participants and by ensuring that plans had assets sufficient to pay promised benefits. In aiming to meet these goals, ERISA fundamentally altered the organization and administration of pension plans and created a comprehensive legal and regulatory structure.

New provisions considerably strengthened tax rules for coverage, participation, funding, and benefit accrual. Participants have legal rights to information about the plan, and plan officials who do not provide such information face civil and criminal penalties.

Of particular interest for this paper, ERISA imposed stringent fiduciary standards on plan investments and fiduciary duties on those who performed them. In the usual contractual relationship, each party makes a series of promises to the other and is liable for the monetary value of a promise it breaches. In a fiduciary relationship, however, one party assumes responsibility for the affairs of others and must act on their behalf and in their best interest. Fiduciaries must conduct themselves with the utmost good faith and fidelity and are personally liable if they breach their duties. Liability is measured by how much it would cost to make the beneficiaries "whole," that is, to place them in the position they would otherwise have been in if no breach had occurred. A fiduciary breach often results in much greater financial liability than a contractual breach.

The standards incorporated into ERISA require fiduciaries to act prudently as investors from both a procedural and a substantive point of view.[3] Fiduciaries are judged not so much on the outcome of a particular investment decision but on whether they initially used appropriate methods to evaluate its merits.[4] ERISA also imposes an "exclusive benefit" standard, requiring plan fiduciaries to

---

enue Code section 7476 permits a plan participant, in certain cases, to ask the Tax Court to intervene when the continuing qualification of a plan has become the subject of an actual controversy with the Internal Revenue Service. As might be expected, few participants avail themselves of this right.

3. ERISA, section 404(a)(1)(B) requires a fiduciary to act "with the care, skill, prudence, and diligence under the circumstances then prevailing that a prudent man, acting in a like capacity and familiar with such matters would use in the conduct of a enterprise of a like character and with like aims."

4. The regulations under ERISA, section 404(a) require a fiduciary to determine that a particular investment decision, as part of the portfolio, is "reasonably designed . . . to further the purposes of the plan by taking into consideration the risk of loss and the opportunity for gain associated with the investment" choice. A fiduciary, in making an investment decision, must consider the following factors: the composition of the portfolio with regard to diversification, the liquidity and current return of the portfolio relative to the anticipated cash flow requirements of the plan, and the projected return of the portfolio relative to the funding objectives of the plan. See DOL Regulation, section 2550.404a-1(b)(2).

consider only the interests of participants when making investment decisions. As one court has expressed it, this standard requires fiduciaries to act with "an eye single" to the interests of participants when dealing with plan assets.[5] Fiduciaries must also diversify plan investments to minimize the risk of large losses and avoid specified prohibited transactions that involve conflicts of interest and self-dealing.

In the normal case, the plan trustee is the primary investment fiduciary because ERISA assigns plan trustees the "exclusive authority and discretion to manage and control the assets of the plan." There are three permissible exceptions. First, a named fiduciary can retain investment authority, in which case the trustees are merely conduit or "directed" trustees, with no fiduciary responsibility.[6] Second, a named fiduciary can appoint an investment manager, in which case the trustee is no longer a fiduciary with respect to those assets. The named fiduciary, however, retains responsibility for all such appointments and must monitor the performance of the investment manager carefully. Third, there is a special exception for self-directed plans—commonly known as 404(c) plans after the authorizing section of the legal code—where participants choose their own investments. The exception states that "if a participant . . . exercises control over the assets in his account (as determined under regulations of the Secretary)—(A) such participant . . . shall not be deemed to be a fiduciary by reason of such exercise, and (B) no person who is otherwise a fiduciary shall be liable . . . for any loss, or by reason of any breach, which results from such participant's . . . exercise of control."

In a 404(c) plan, then, plan participants, not plan fiduciaries, are responsible for the outcome of their own investment decisions. Even in a 404(c) plan, though, a named fiduciary is ultimately responsible for the menu of investment choices available to participants. Fiduciaries are answerable to plan participants, the Department of Labor, and the courts for plan investment performance and face personal liability and financial penalties for misconduct. Being an ERISA fiduciary, particularly of plan assets, is very serious business. In most cases, fiduciary responsibility comes to rest ultimately on the company sponsoring the plan.

The Role of the 404(c) Regulations

The new fiduciary duties imposed by ERISA did not result in significant litigation by disgruntled parties, for any of several reasons. Defined contribution plans were then mostly supplemental plans and represented a small share of the

---

5. *Donovan* v. *Bierwirth*, 680 F.2d 263 (2d Cir.), cert. denied, 459 U.S. 1069 (1982).

6. Trustees, however, may only follow directions that are "proper," made in accordance with the terms of the plan, and not contrary to ERISA. So trustees must perform at least some minimal form of review on the merits of the directions they receive if they wish to avoid the fiduciary label.

pension universe. The relatively few plans that were self-directed offered small numbers of investment options and permitted investment changes infrequently—some only annually. Many employers hired investment advisers to create unique investment pools for their plans that did not routinely provide information about their assets or value. So employees had little information about their investments and could not track investment performance easily.

In addition, while ERISA gave participants the right to sue, it included some features almost guaranteeing that litigation would be a last resort, if it were resorted to at all. For example, the typical ERISA claim—a claim for individual benefits involving only a small amount of money—is not attractive. A participant can win at most the benefit to which he or she is entitled.[7] ERISA does not permit punitive damages or damages for pain and suffering and effectively preempts state laws that do.[8] Attorneys' fees are rarely awarded, so a participant either pays for litigation out of pocket or through any recovery. As a result, few plan participants exercised their newly granted rights to challenge how their plans were managed.

Since then the landscape for self-directed plans has changed considerably. Defined contribution plans have expanded rapidly. Participants are more knowledgeable about their benefits. Employees have assumed a higher share of the responsibility for funding their own pensions through 401(k) and 401(k)-type plans. And increasingly participants have assumed responsibility for the investment performance of their plan accounts. The last fact is attributable largely to the issuance of final regulations for 404(c) plans in 1992.

As noted above, a 404(c) plan that permits participants to exercise investment control over their accounts relieves fiduciaries of some of their usual investment responsibilities. A fiduciary sued for a breach of duty can use this section of ERISA to argue that participants are alone responsible for any bad investment outcomes in their accounts. Before 1992 the status of self-directed plans as 404(c) plans was unclear. Once the regulations were issued, however, fiduciaries of self-directed plans could finally take some concrete steps to obtain 404(c) protection.

The regulations themselves seem straightforward. They contain three broad requirements.[9] Each plan seeking 404(c) status must provide

—*A broad range of investment alternatives.* A 404(c) plan must have at least three different investment alternatives that permit diversification of accounts to minimize the risk of large losses and afford participants a reasonable opportunity to materially affect the potential return and degree of risk in their portfolios.

---

7. ERISA, section 502(a)(1).

8. ERISA, section 514(a) provides that the provisions of ERISA "shall supersede any and all State laws insofar as they may now or hereafter relate to any employee benefit plan," except those state laws that regulate insurance, banking, or securities.

9. These regulations can be found at DOL Regulation, section 2550.404(c)-1.

—Appropriate frequency of investment instructions. Participants must be able to change their investment choices frequently enough to be appropriate for the volatility of each investment alternative and no less than once every three months.

—Sufficient investment information. A 404(c) plan must provide participants with sufficient information to make informed investment decisions, an explanation that plan fiduciaries are not responsible for participants' investment losses in a 404(c) plan, information about the objectives and risk/return characteristics of each alternative, procedures for choosing and changing investment choices, and descriptions of transaction fees or expenses charged to participants' accounts.

If a plan complies perfectly with the 404(c) regulations, then plan fiduciaries have effectively relieved themselves of liability for participants' investment choices and their outcomes. But plan fiduciaries remain subject to the general ERISA fiduciary requirements of prudent behavior and the exclusive benefit rule. In addition, the Department of Labor has warned that in a 404(c) plan "the plan fiduciary has a fiduciary obligation to prudently select . . . [the investment] vehicles as well as a residual fiduciary obligation to periodically evaluate the performance of such vehicles to determine, based on that evaluation whether the vehicles should continue to be available as participant investment options."[10]

Few investment professionals will assume liability associated with selecting a 404(c) plan's investment options. Those who do charge a premium. Even with investment professionals, a plan fiduciary—generally the plan sponsor—retains a duty to monitor their performance. So, inevitably, it is the plan sponsor—usually the employer—who bears ultimate responsibility for the investment options in a 404(c) plan, no matter who selects them.

The 404(c) regulations are significant not so much because they changed the law—they did not—but for the effect they had on plan design. The regulations are sensible, practical, and consistent with ERISA's fiduciary scheme. But their issuance sparked a rush by plan sponsors to add self-directed investment options to their defined contribution plans. By 1997 almost one-half of all profit-sharing plans and almost one-third of all money purchase plans—the most common defined contribution plans among corporate employers—described themselves as participant-directed plans.[11] Moreover, 404(c) plans account for 65 percent of

10. See the Preamble to DOL Regulation, section 2550.404(c)-1.
11. These numbers are based on calculations of data provided by Judy Diamond Associates, Washington. These data include the Form 5500 filings of about 800,000 pension benefit plans for the 1997 plan year. These data do not include data from governmental plans and have minimal information on plans offered by nonprofit organizations. But the fiduciary rules of ERISA usually do not apply to these plans in any event. The figures provided were based upon a subset of profit-sharing and money purchase plans that had not terminated during the 1997 plan year. The term "active participants" means those participants who are currently employed or are terminated but still entitled to service credit under the plan if they are rehired.

the assets of profit-sharing plans and almost 70 percent of all active participants. Among money purchase plans, the comparable figures are about 40 percent and 30 percent, respectively.

Plan sponsors transferred investment control to plan participants largely in the expectation that the transfer would reduce their fiduciary exposure. Even though there was no obvious threat of large-scale litigation over plan investments, plan sponsors felt they had nothing to lose—and perhaps a lot to gain—by conforming their plans to the 404(c) regulations. They also found that, prompted by the popularity of 401(k) and 401(k)-type plans, participants expressed more interest in the performance of their accounts and more willingness to accept investment control. Participants in these plans typically feel strongly that their contributions are their funds, and they should be permitted to decide how these should be invested.

The mutual fund industry—for whom the 404(c) regulations were almost tailor made—was also influential in persuading employers to shift responsibility for investment choice to employees. The industry already had the product—a vast array of investment funds—necessary to satisfy the broad range of alternatives requirement of the 404(c) regulations. It already had the technology—daily transfers, voice (and now Internet) initiated transactions—necessary to satisfy the frequency of investment instructions requirement. And it already had the disclosure material—prospectuses prepared under Securities and Exchange Commission (SEC) requirements—necessary to satisfy the sufficient investment information requirement. It also had a bundled product of investment options, record-keeping services, and prototype plans to offer just as employers were beginning to lessen their administrative burden through outsourcing. Most important, it held a very important trump card over its competitors: banks offering common and collective trust funds, and insurance companies offering separate accounts as investment options. The mutual fund industry alone had been granted a total exemption from the fiduciary liability provisions of ERISA when it was enacted.[12] Although mutual funds are subject to fiduciary standards under the securities laws, the same standards apply whether an investor is a private individual or a plan participant. The industry could therefore heavily promote the 404(c) regulations to expand its defined contribution business without assuming additional fiduciary liabilities. It took several years for banks and insurance companies to convert their traditional investment products into the technical legal form of a mutual fund and become competitive on this front.

---

12. Mutual funds are technically known as investment companies, registered under the Investment Company Act of 1940. They are regulated by the Securities and Exchange Commission and their exemption from ERISA's fiduciary responsibility rules was apparently based on the theory that there was no need for duplicate federal regulation through the Department of Labor. See ERISA, sections 3(21)(B) and 401(b)(1), and the plan assets regulations under DOL Regulation, section 2510.3-101.

The mutual fund industry utilized the 404(c) regulations as a marketing tool to employers, and they responded. Since the regulations were issued, the mutual fund industry has rapidly increased its market share and the amount of assets under management. In 1992, for example, mutual funds held an 18 percent share in the defined contribution plan market, with about $184 billion in assets; by 2002, the comparable figures were a 45 percent share and $1 trillion in assets. In 1992 they held a 15 percent share of the 401(k) asset market, with about $82 billion in assets; by 2002 that market had grown to $1.5 trillion in assets, and the share held by mutual funds had tripled to 45 percent, or about $686 billion in assets.[13]

The irony is that as employers turned to the 404(c) regulations as insurance against litigation over plan investment performance—litigation that was not even on the horizon—they may have inadvertently created what they sought to avoid. The 404(c) regulations provide both the substance and the means for fiduciary litigation on a large scale. Class-action lawyers have recently discovered 404(c) plans as a source of potentially lucrative litigation, and 404(c) plans have all the ingredients they need: large numbers of similarly situated plaintiffs, identical causes of action, huge amounts of potential damages, and possible generous awards of attorneys' fees.

Even before the recent stock market crash, class-action lawyers sued several large employers for fiduciary violations related to the investment options offered in their plans, alleging that the options had been improperly chosen or supervised and seeking to have the accounts of thousands of plan participants made whole.[14] Cases arising from the stock market crash and the promotion of employee investment in company stock by companies such as Enron are now working their way through the judicial system. The ultimate legal disposition of these cases is still uncertain, and it is not clear how the law will develop. But they will provide a good test of the value of a 404(c) defense to fiduciary violations for employers. At the very least, 404(c) plans will likely result in the creation of something that ERISA has always lacked: a plaintiffs' bar. Courts will scrutinize the conduct of 404(c) plan fiduciaries where they are most vulnerable: the performance of the available investment alternatives, the size of the investments fees charged, the adequacy of the investment information provided, and the failure of fiduciaries to put the interest of plan participants first when selecting plan investments. The most predictable consequence of the 404(c)

13. Investment Company Institute (2000; 2003, pp. 5, 11–15). The data include both non-ERISA and ERISA plans.

14. First Union Bank, for example, recently agreed to pay $28 million to settle two well-publicized cases involving its fiduciary duties to select and monitor investment options in its 401(k) plans. Although these cases do not make new law, the settlement will certainly bring these types of issues to the attention of both employers and class-action lawyers (who will receive $8 million from the settlement). A good discussion of the implications of the First Union cases can be found in Reish, Ashton, and Faucher (2001).

regulations is litigation. Sooner or later some plaintiffs will win a big case and some employer will pay large damages. When that happens, employers will recognize that a 404(c) plan is not a liability-free form of plan sponsorship. Their financial exposure may be so great they will rethink their alternatives but find very few. The trend to self-directed plans seems irreversible. Making investment decisions for participants will not be practicable and would just give plan sponsors more, not less, fiduciary exposure. Many will question whether they really want and can afford to be the involuntary insurer of their employees' investment choices. And many plan sponsors—particularly small employers—will probably decide they do not.

Rethinking the Role of the Employer

This prospect alone is sufficient to motivate a reexamination of the role of the employer in providing pension plans, as opposed to merely contributing to or collecting employee deposits to retirement plans. Several additional factors also suggest that the role of employers in today's pension system is based on outdated and unproductive notions. In this section, we outline five factors that seem central to designing a better pension system.

1. *Employers play very significant and special roles in today's defined contribution plans.* For a variety of reasons, employers seem to be crucial to "saving" by employees. Many of the routine services they provide encourage saving by making it easy and convenient: payroll deductions, simplified enrollment, periodic reports, and investment education. There is much evidence that employees contribute much more when employers are involved than when similar tax incentives are offered merely at the individual level, as with Individual Retirement Accounts (IRAs). Employers may also add their own financial incentives to save through matching contributions. They also serve as an important intermediary between their employees and the financial services industry and thus simplify the investment process for their employees. These roles are important and often critical determinants of employee saving, but in performing them employers act more as facilitators than as fiduciaries.

2. *ERISA's fiduciary scheme suits defined benefit—but not defined contribution—plans.* Under a defined benefit plan, employers promise today to pay benefits many years in the future. If the plan has insufficient assets as the promised benefits mature, the obligation to make good any shortfall lies with the employer and ultimately, after ERISA, with the government-run insurance program.[15] It was logical to require the defined benefit plan sponsor to be the ultimate fiduciary under ERISA in order to compel it to keep the plan solvent and to keep its other promises. To protect taxpayer resources, it was also rational to

---

15. See ERISA, sections 4001–4402, which govern the Pension Benefit Guaranty Corporation and its program of plan termination insurance.

impose personal liability on plan officials and investment professionals and hold them accountable for mismanagement of these large pools of assets. The fiduciary structure created by ERISA has served defined benefit plan participants well.

But defined contribution plans are fundamentally different. The employer promises only to make a contribution from time to time. There is still a risk that employees will reach retirement and find no pension, but not because the employer has defaulted on a promise to contribute. The employer fulfills that contractual promise, or both tax code and ERISA enforcement systems soon compel it to do so. The pension risk in defined contribution plans is that not enough dollars will be saved or that the dollars saved will be poorly invested. In today's defined contribution world, that risk has largely been transferred from the employer to the employee anyway.

3. *Defined contribution plans today are like other financial services industry products. But employers remain responsible under ERISA.* Many employers today do not operate or manage their own defined contribution plans. The typical 404(c) plan is actually a bundle of services provided by an investment provider or through a strategic alliance of consulting firms and mutual fund families. The employer's unique contribution is to decide whether to make a contribution in a given year and to deduct employees' contributions from wages. The employer's primary role—and it is an extraordinarily important one—is to collect contributions (most economists would consider even employer contributions to be close to a mandated contribution from employees because employees generally pay for their cost by reduced wages) out of total compensation, and then to serve as the conduit of contributions (its own and participants') to the investment provider. In addition to investment services, the provider in turn performs most other plan functions: accounting, record keeping, discrimination testing, compliance, tax reporting, and disclosure. It also provides a "check-the-box" prototype plan. Participants communicate directly with the provider when they wish to choose or change their investment options.

Today, the employer remains liable even though third parties actually perform almost all plan functions. Standard legal documents usually provide that plan officials "direct" the activities of service providers (so they are not ERISA fiduciaries), who assume liability only for "gross" negligence. Many plan sponsors routinely sign such documents without knowing not only that they have not reduced their own fiduciary liability, but that they have also assumed liability for the actions of third parties over whom they have no control. As a result, while the employer's operational significance has decreased in today's defined contribution plan, its ERISA responsibilities have actually grown.

4. *The private pension system has no consistent rule about fiduciary liability for employers in self-directed plans.* If the true purpose for imposing fiduciary liability is to protect participants, it would seem logical to apply these standards to employers in a more consistent fashion. Simplified Employee Plans (SEPs), an

IRA-based defined contribution plan, are employer sponsored and funded and are subject to ERISA, but participants' accounts are actually their own IRAs, and the participants bear investment responsibility for their own accounts. ERISA completely exempts from fiduciary liability governmental employers who sponsor similar types of self-directed plans. Employees of charitable and educational institutions contribute to tax-sheltered annuities that are also exempt from ERISA's fiduciary liability rules under the theory that the annuities are really not employer sponsored or funded. But by that standard, some 401(k) plans are not truly employer funded either because they only permit contributions by employees; nonetheless, employers are subject to ERISA fiduciary standards. Largely for historical reasons, for-profit employers consequently bear the greatest burden of fiduciary liability.

5. *Self-directed plans are evolving toward offering multiple funds and fund families in place of a fixed investment menu.* Few 404(c) plans today restrict themselves to the minimum three investment options required by the regulations. The financial services industry continues to create new funds and products, and employers continue to expand their plan menus. In 2001, 69.8 percent of plans offered ten or more fund options, compared with 61.5 percent of companies in 2000 and 51.2 percent in 1999.[16] Moreover, some plan sponsors are moving to a completely open-ended option. This format allows participants to buy and sell virtually any asset—any mutual fund or individual security—available through a stockbroker. The technology to service such accounts already exists, and the financial services industry is promoting them heavily. The advantage of an open-ended structure is that it represents one possible end run around the 404(c) fiduciary dilemma. It easily satisfies the basic requirements for the 404(c) regulations and provides enhanced protection for employers. In addition, it holds class-action lawyers at bay. Because every participant has a unique portfolio and free choice of investments, claims for fiduciary breaches should be fewer in number, individual in nature, and smaller in size.

A Model of Pension Reform

Based on the analysis above, we propose to simplify pension law to fit the defined contribution plan of today and tomorrow. This would involve the following key features.

—*Create separate individual accounts out of today's employer plan.* Like an IRA and most 403(b) tax-deferred annuities, defined contribution plans could be disaggregated into individual accounts—the equivalent of each participant's

16. These figures come from a synopsis of the 45th Annual Survey of Profit-Sharing and 401(k) Plans conducted by Profit Sharing/401k Council of America (www.psca.org/data/45th.html [August 2003]).

individual account in today's employer plan—to receive all contributions and hold all investment options in which those contributions are invested. This approach would relieve employers from liability for the day-to-day responsibility for their employees' retirement assets, assets that are effectively held and managed by third-party administrators and investment professionals.

Dodging for the moment the different tax rules on contributions and withdrawals for different types of defined contribution plans, these accounts could be established by individuals, independent of their employment status, at participating financial institutions. Of course, employers might also serve as an intermediary and arrange for financial institutions to offer such plans to their employees, much like the arrangement today in most of the 403(b) world. Employers might also choose a single financial institution for an initial deposit of their own and their employees' contributions, with employees having the right, as is true today under a SEP, to transfer those contributions to their provider of choice. Any number of different arrangements—to suit both employers who wish to assist their employees in their investment choices and those who do not—would be feasible. Of course, one result would be an increased ability for individuals to combine together multiple accounts, as opposed to the situation today, where an individual might have IRA accounts in one place, profit-sharing and money purchase accounts in another, and a 403(b) account in yet another place. Thus, for instance, employers could also facilitate employee deposits to what are now individual IRAs. (Note that this requires simplification and unification, especially of penalty and withdrawal rules, an issue we do not address further here.)

—Have regulated financial institutions hold the accounts. The legal significance of this requirement is that the accounts—rather than an umbrella employer plan—are the legal owner of each employee's retirement savings. This would relieve the employer from fiduciary responsibility for employees' retirement savings. Today's voluminous plan document would be replaced by a simple document spelling out the legal relationship between the employee and the financial provider holding those funds, as is true of an IRA today. To ensure that such accounts were held by responsible entities, it would be preferable to permit only regulated financial institutions to offer them.[17] Tax law would set guidelines for eligible financial institutions, again as is true with IRAs today.

Today's trust document would also disappear as the accounts would be custodial in nature, as is true today for most IRAs, and governed by contract law without an overlay of trust and fiduciary law. Breaches by custodians could be subject to contractual remedies that might include punitive damages, not available

17. Almost anyone, including private individuals, can serve as a plan trustee, unless barred by ERISA, section 411 from acting in any capacity on behalf of a plan. But, under Internal Revenue Code, section 408(a)(2), IRAs may only be held by a bank or by any other entity or individual that has received specific approval from the Treasury Department to act in such a capacity.

today. This arrangement, of course, would apply only to defined contribution plans. ERISA in its current form would continue to apply to defined benefit plans. The treatment of hybrid plans would depend on which type of plan—defined contribution or defined benefit—they most closely resembled. Cash balance plans, for example, could easily be accommodated within the proposed new account structure as employers could contribute contributions and interest credits directly to them.

—*Use tax law to promote employer participation and to structure the accounts.* In this model the employer's primary function is merely to serve as a conduit of contributions to its employees' accounts. It deducts employee contributions from their pay, adds its own contributions, if any, and wires those funds directly to the appropriate provider for transfer to each employee's plan. In many ways, this would be no more complicated than the direct deposit of payroll checks or the direct transfer of 401(k) contributions to the investment provider that most employers now do routinely.

But the employer would continue to play its unique and very valuable role as a contributor to its employees' accounts. How much it contributes and to whom would be governed by tax law, and many of today's rules could continue to apply. Tax law would still attempt to encourage employer participation by providing special tax benefits for contributions while discouraging contributions that disproportionately favor highly compensated employees. So employer contributions would still be subject to rules on participation, coverage, and nondiscrimination. There would still be per-employee limits on the annual contributions any account could receive and any employer could make. And this scheme could easily accommodate any movement toward a mandated employer contribution, which is what many Social Security reform plans contemplate when they envision individual accounts. Today's automatic 401(k) contribution certainly looks and acts a lot like a mandatory employee contribution. Perhaps someday there might be a parallel provision for employees or employers, either as part of the nondiscrimination rules or in place of them, or as part of a Social Security reform plan. (Such Social Security accounts might be integrated with other defined contribution arrangements, but that is the subject for a future paper.)

Tax law would continue to have rules for how much employees could contribute to their plans every year. After all, it is Congress' job to decide how tax benefits should be allocated. It would also determine when employees could or must take distributions, just as it does today. For example, these accounts could offer loans and hardship distributions much like an employer plan does today. Tax law would also include rules that the account would have to satisfy to remain tax qualified and impose penalties for violations of those rules, much like it does today for pension plans and IRAs.

—*Use labor and tax law to protect employees' rights to contributions.* Employees would continue to look to labor law as well as tax law to protect their rights to an employer contribution. Any promised contribution would become a legal part of each employee's contract of employment and be enforceable by employees and the Department of Labor. An employer who failed to make a promised contribution would be subject to contractual damages and equitable relief as well as enforcement penalties imposed by the Department of Labor.

—*Encourage employers to promote saving and serve as intermediaries for their employees.* In this model it is not so much that employers' roles would diminish as that they would be concentrated on what they do best: bargain on behalf of the employee (especially in larger firms) for better service providers, create viable pension and insurance options (especially in larger firms), and provide direct deposit, payroll deduction, and tax services for employer and employee contributions to pensions. Many still will engage in low-cost paternalistic efforts to encourage their employees to save enough so they can retire when their skills decline. And, whether or not there are 404(c) regulations to compel them, they may wish to perform some sort of oversight function over where and how their employees save.

—*Use securities laws to regulate the investment industry and create new products for retirement saving.* The federal securities laws are the primary regulators of the financial services industry as well as of its investment products, investment providers, and investment advisers. Eliminating the fiduciary role of employers in defined contribution plans does not mean that these accounts would be completely deregulated. Instead, their investment function would be supervised and protected by the primary regulator of the financial markets—the SEC. The SEC already oversees most investment markets and the securities they offer, as well as the behavior of investment professionals who provide custodial, management, and advisory services.

It is important to recognize, however, that federal securities laws today do not provide retirement plan investors special treatment or protections. Whether they should do so is certainly open to argument. It is unlikely that the industry would agree to assume additional fiduciary responsibility toward retirement plan investors. But the industry has shown itself to be adept at creating special products and services for niche investors in the past. Perhaps that ingenuity could be turned to the service of retirement plan investors. Many feel that 404(c) plans impose too much investment risk on participants who are unprepared or incapable of assuming investment control over their accounts. The investment industry might well take the lead on designing new investment products to minimize risk or simplify investing for participants. It might be possible, for example, to create a special family of government-approved "retirement" mutual funds with appropriate diversification strategies and low fee structures. This would provide retirement plan investors with simple, low cost, and suitable investment alternatives as default options. Other products that protect retirement plan investors against some of the risks inherent in the markets and educate them about investing are certainly feasible and desirable.

Conclusion

Our proposal recognizes that each participant's account in today's defined contribution plan is really a separate plan with a unique contribution pattern and investment portfolio. The proposal strips away the superstructure of the increasingly obsolete employer plan. What is left is a personal defined contribution account for individuals. Eventually many employees could even create a centralized account for all their retirement funds. Employees would largely control how their own funds are invested and where they are held, so portability and rollovers would be vastly simplified. Employers would be free to focus on the function we want most to encourage: making contributions for or on behalf of employees. Employers need only send contributions to their employees' individual accounts, with no other plan management responsibilities, liabilities, or costs.

But employers would still play the critical role of being facilitators for their employees' retirement savings. Many would choose to retain oversight and act as intermediaries in a variety of ways from encouraging saving to providing investment education and retirement planning services. Moreover, many would wish to designate a preferred provider for their employees or to review the quality and limit the number of providers they make available to employees. The financial services industry would likely respond by creating new types of investments and innovating new services, products, and providers. These accounts, for example, could be run as easily by a TIAA-CREF or a Federal Thrift Board as by a brokerage house or mutual fund family that offers access to almost any mutual fund or individual security. And employers would play an important role in helping their employees make a successful transition through those new products and services to appropriate providers.

This model is not particularly revolutionary. In fact, it is prerevolutionary. It looks a lot like the classic TIAA-CREF account that has been available for years. The model thus borrows features and systems available elsewhere and applies them to ERISA plans. Its primary contribution is to recognize that the regulatory structure in ERISA was created for defined benefit plans, never fit defined contribution plans well, and has become increasingly outdated. In particular, the full burden of liability placed on the employer is no longer justifiable, given the dominant role played by the financial services industries.

Rethinking the role of the employers in defined contribution plans is just one of many reforms needed in the pension system today. But changing pension law to fit today's defined contribution world—and today's employer—is crucial. Facilitating expanded involvement of employers in pensions is just one way of increasing the probability that employees reach retirement with adequate wealth.

References

Investment Company Institute. 2000. *Fundamentals: Mutual Funds and the Retirement Market*, 9 (2, May).
———. 2003. *Fundamentals: Mutual Funds and the Retirement Market*, 12 (1, June).
Reish, Fred, Bruce Ashton, and Joe Faucher. 2001 "The Settlement of the First Union Cases." ASPA 01-10. Arlington, Va.: American Society of Pension Actuaries (April 4).

Glossary

To help readers without extensive background in pensions to understand some of the technical terms mentioned in the papers published in this volume, we have reproduced, with permission and with slight modifications, a number of pension terms from *Employee Benefit Plans: A Glossary of Terms,* 10th edition, 2000, edited by Judith A. Sankey and published by the International Foundation of Employee Benefit Plans, Brookfield, Wisconsin.

Accrual of Benefits In the case of a defined benefit pension plan, the process of accumulating pension credits for years of credited service, expressed in the form of an annual benefit to begin payment at normal retirement age. In the case of a defined contribution plan, the process of accumulating funds in the individual employee's pension account.

Accrued Benefits For any retirement plan that is not a defined benefit pension plan, a participant's accrued benefit is the balance in his or her plan account, whether vested or not. In the case of a defined benefit pension plan, a participant's accrued benefit is his or her benefit as determined under the terms of the plan expressed in the form of an annual benefit commencing at normal retirement age. Under ERISA, three alternative methods of benefit accrual are allowed. See *Back-Loading.*

Reprinted with permission from *Employee Benefit Plans: A Glossary of Terms,* 10th edition, published by the International Foundation of Employee Benefit Plans, Brookfield, Wisconsin.

Actual Contribution Percentage (ACP)   In a qualified retirement plan, the average of the ratios of aggregate contributions (matching contributions and after-tax employee contributions) to compensation. It is figured for two groups: highly compensated employees and non-highly compensated employees. The ratio for each employee is calculated, and then it is averaged for the group. See also *Aggregate Limit; Alternative Limitation.*

Actual Deferral Percentage (ADP)   In a qualified retirement plan such as a 401(k) plan, the average of the ratios of elective contributions to compensation is figured for two groups: highly compensated employees and non-highly compensated employees. The ratio first is figured for each employee, and then averaged for each group. See also *Aggregate Limit; Alternative Limitation.*

Actuarial Accrued Liability   (1) The actuarial accrued liability of a pension plan at any time is the excess of the present value, as of the date of valuation, of total prospective benefits of the plan (plus administrative expenses if included in the normal cost) over the present value of future normal cost accruals, determined by the actuarial cost method in use. (2) That portion, as determined by a particular actuarial cost method, of the actuarial present value of pension plan benefits and expenses that is not provided for by future normal costs. The presentation of an actuarial accrued liability should be accompanied by reference to the actuarial cost method used.

Actuarial Assumptions   Factors used by the actuary in forecasting uncertain future events affecting pension cost. They involve such things as interest and investment earnings, inflation, unemployment, mortality rates, and retirement patterns.

Actuarial Soundness   (1) An actuarial concept relating to the degree of assurance (existing under an employer's program for funding pension cost) that the funds set aside under a pension plan will be sufficient to meet the pension payments provided for in the plan. Actuaries have not defined objective standards for determining actuarial soundness. (2) The statement that the money set aside under a pension plan will be sufficient to meet the pension payments as calculated.

Actuarial Valuation   (1) An examination of a pension plan to determine whether contributions are being accumulated at a rate sufficient to provide the funds out of which the promised pensions can be paid when due. The valuation shows the actuarial liabilities of the plan and the applicable assets. (2) The determination, as of a valuation date, of the normal cost, actuarial accrued liability, actuarial value of assets, and related actuarial present values for a pension plan.

Age Discrimination in Employment Act (ADEA)   Protects workers over age 40 from compulsory retirement at any age so long as they are capable of performing their jobs adequately. It also protects them from adverse job actions based on age (for example, refusal to hire; discriminatory layoff) and against benefits discrimination. Employers are subject to ADEA if they engage in an industry affecting interstate commerce and had 20 or more employees in each working day of 20 or more weeks in the current or preceding calendar year.

Aggregate Limit In nondiscrimination testing, this is used to determine inequalities in the deferral or contribution rates of highly versus non-highly compensated employees when at least one highly compensated employee is eligible to participate in a 401(k) plan. The aggregate limit is a combination of the ADP and ACP of the non-highly compensated employees: 125 percent of the higher percentage and the lower percentage plus 2 points (the higher percentage can be up to 200 percent of the lower percentage). The sum of ADP and ACP of the highly compensated cannot exceed the aggregate limit. See also *Alternative Limitation.*

Alternative Limitation An alternative nondiscrimination test. The ACP and ADP percentage of highly compensated employees cannot be more than double the ACP and ADP of non-highly compensated employees. In addition, the difference cannot exceed 2 percentage points. See also *Aggregate Limit.*

Annuity (1) A contract that provides an income for a specified period of time, such as a number of years or for life. (2) The periodic payments provided under an annuity contract. (3) The specified monthly or annual payment to a pensioner. Often used synonymously with *pension.*

Asset Reversion Following the termination of a pension plan, the recovery by the sponsoring employer of any pension fund assets in excess of those required to pay accrued benefits. The recovered assets are subject to regular corporate income tax as well as an excise tax of either 20 percent or 50 percent, depending on subsequent retirement arrangements made for employees.

Back-Loading The practice of providing a faster rate of benefit accrual after an employee has attained a specified age or has completed a specified number of years of service. For example, back-loading occurs in a plan that provides a benefit of 1.5 percent of compensation for each year of service before age 50 and 2 percent a year thereafter. The practice is limited under ERISA. See also *Accrued Benefits.*

Cash Balance Plan A defined benefit plan that simulates a defined contribution plan. Benefits are definitely determinable, but account balances are credited with a fixed rate of return and converted to a monthly pension benefit at retirement.

Compulsory Retirement When the employee must retire when he or she reaches a given age. Now prohibited under ADEA if based solely on age, except for certain executives or where public safety outweighs individual protection (such as airline pilots). Also known as *automatic* or *mandatory retirement.*

Contribution The transfer of funds or property by either an employer or an employee to an employee benefit plan.

Contribution Limit The maximum dollar limit on annual additions (employer contributions, certain employee contributions, and forfeitures) for an employee under defined contribution plans of an employer.

Current Liability   Money owed and payable by a company, usually within one year.

Defined Benefit Plan   Both ERISA and the Internal Revenue Code define a defined benefit plan as any plan that is not an individual account plan. Under a defined benefit plan, there is a definite formula by which the employee's benefits will be measured. This formula may provide that benefits be a particular percentage of the employee's average compensation over his or her entire service or over a particular number of years; it may provide for a flat monthly payment; or it may provide a definite amount for each year of service, expressed either as a percentage of his or her compensation for each year of service or as a flat dollar amount for each year of service. In plans of this type, the employer's contributions are determined actuarially. No individual accounts are maintained as is done in the defined contribution plans. (Defined benefit plans are subject to regulation by the Pension Benefit Guaranty Corporation and are "pension plans" under the Internal Revenue Code. That is, they are designed primarily for retirement.)

Defined Contribution Plan   A defined contribution or individual account plan is defined by the Internal Revenue Code and ERISA as a plan that provides for an individual account for each participant and for benefits based solely on (1) the amount contributed to the participant's account plus (2) any income, expenses, gains and losses, and forfeitures of accounts of other participants that may be allocated to the participant's account. 401(k), 403(b) and 457 plans are defined contribution plans.

Early Retirement   A termination of employment involving the payment of a retirement allowance before a participant is eligible for normal retirement. The retirement allowance payable in the event of early retirement is often lower than the accrued portion of the normal retirement allowance.

Employee Retirement Income Security Act of 1974 (ERISA)   Federal statute that requires persons engaged in the administration, supervision, and management of pension monies to have a fiduciary responsibility to ensure that all investment-related decisions are made (1) with the care, skill, prudence, and diligence that a prudent man familiar with such matters would use and (2) by diversifying the investments so as to minimize risk. This wording mandates two significant changes in traditional investment practice: the age-old "prudent man" rule has been replaced by the notion of a prudent "expert"; and the notion of a prudent investment has been replaced by the concept of a prudent portfolio.

ERISA also established the Pension Benefit Guaranty Corporation (PBGC), an insurance program designed to guarantee workers receipt of pension benefits if their defined benefit pension plans should terminate. ERISA includes requirements for funding, bonding, trusts, claims procedures, reporting and disclosure, and prohibited transactions. It regulates the majority of private pension and welfare group benefit plans in the United States.

Employee Stock Ownership Plan (ESOP)   A qualified stock bonus plan or a qualified stock bonus and money purchase plan. Like a stock bonus plan, the contributions need not be dependent on profits, and benefits are distributable in the stock of the employer corporation. Typically, the ESOP is used as a financing vehicle for the employer corporation: The plan borrows money from the employer, or uses the employer's credit, and purchases employer stock. The borrowed money is paid to the employer for its stock. The loan is repaid with annual employer contributions.

Enrolled Actuary (EA)   A person who performs actuarial service for a plan and who is enrolled with the federal Joint Board for the Enrollment of Actuaries.

Entry Age Actuarial Cost Method   Also called *entry age normal actuarial cost method*. A method under which the actuarial present value of the projected benefits of each individual included in an actuarial valuation is allocated on a level basis over the earnings or service of the individual between entry age and assumed exit age(s). The portion of this actuarial present value allocated to a valuation year is called the *normal cost*. The portion of this actuarial present value not provided for a valuation date by the actuarial present value of future normal costs is called the *actuarial accrued liability*. Under this method, the actuarial gains (losses) are reflected as they occur in a decrease (increase) in the unfunded actuarial accrued liability.

Excise Taxes   An employer that contributes to a qualified plan will be subject to an excise tax liability for failing to contribute the amount determined to be an accumulated funding deficiency (excess of total charges over total credits in funding the standard account). The tax initially is to be 5 percent of the accumulated funding deficiency at the end of the plan year.

Fiduciary   (1) Indicates the relationship of trust and confidence where one person (the fiduciary) holds or controls property for the benefit of another person; for example, the relationship between a trustee and the beneficiaries of the trust. (2) Under ERISA any person who (a) exercises any discretionary authority or control over the management of a plan or the management or disposition of its assets, (b) renders investment advice for a fee or other compensation with respect to the funds or property of a plan, or has the authority to do so, or (c) has any discretionary authority or responsibility in the administration of a plan. (3) One who acts in a capacity of trust and who is therefore accountable for whatever actions may be constructed by the courts as breaching that trust. Under ERISA, fiduciaries must discharge their duties solely in the interest of the participants and beneficiaries of an employee benefit plan. In addition, a fiduciary must act exclusively for the purpose of providing benefits to participants and beneficiaries in defraying reasonable expenses of the plan.

Final Pay Plan (Final Pay Formula)   A benefit formula that bases benefits on the employee's compensation over a specified number of years near the end of the employee's service period or on the employee's highest compensation periods. For example, a plan might provide annual pension benefits equal to 1 percent of the employee's average salary for the last five years (or the highest consecutive five years) for each year of service. A final pay plan is a plan with such a formula.

Flexible Benefit Plan   A benefit program under section 125 of the Internal Revenue Code that offers employees a choice between permissible taxable benefits, including cash, and nontaxable health and welfare benefits such as life and health insurance, vacation pay, retirement plans, and child care. Although a common core of benefits may be required, the employee can determine how his or her remaining benefit dollars are to be allocated for each type of benefit from the total amount promised by the employer. Sometimes employee contributions may be made for additional coverage.

Form 5500   A joint agency financial form developed by the IRS, Department of Labor, and PBGC that may be used to satisfy the annual reporting requirements of the IRC and titles I and IV of ERISA.

401(h) Plan   A provision of a pension or annuity plan that provides for the payment of benefits for sickness, accident, hospitalization, and medical expenses of retired employees, their spouses, and their dependents, subject to certain requirements.

401(k) Plan   A plan under which employees can elect to defer income by making pretax contributions. The plan also may allow for employer matching contributions. A section 401(k) plan is a defined contribution plan.

403(b) Annuity   An annuity that provides retirement income for employees of certain tax-exempt organizations or public schools. Also known as a *tax-sheltered annuity.*

457 Plan   An elective contribution tax-deferred arrangement available to states, political subdivisions of a state, or any agency or instrumentality of a state under Code section 457.

Frozen Plan   A qualified retirement plan that has stopped employer contributions and benefit accrual by participants. The plan sponsor continues to distribute plan assets and maintain the trust.

Fully Funded   (1) A specific element of pension cost (for example, past service cost) is said to have been fully funded if the amount of the cost has been paid in full to a funding agency. A pension plan is said by some to be fully funded if regular payments are being made under the plan to a funding agency to cover the normal cost and reasonably rapid amortization of the past service cost. (2) If a specific part, or benefit, is fully paid for (such as the past service cost), then this item is fully funded. The total plan is considered fully funded if there are sufficient assets to make all payments due at particular times. This can apply either to level funding or to entry age calculations, provided that both are the normal costs and the conservative amount of amortization costs for the past services have been paid.

Funded Ratio   Ratio of the assets of a pension plan to its liabilities.

Funding Method   Any of the several techniques actuaries use in determining the amounts of employer contributions to provide for pension costs. An actuarial cost method.

Funding Policy   The program regarding the amounts and timing of contributions by the employer(s), participants, and any other sources (for example, state subsidies or federal grants) to provide the benefits a pension plan specifies.

Hardship Withdrawal   A withdrawal of an employee's contributions to a 401(k) plan prior to retirement at age 55 or attainment of age 59. A hardship withdrawal may be made only in cases of financial emergency provided there are no other sources available to meet the need; the withdrawal is taxable as an early distribution and subject to a 10 percent excise tax.

Highly Compensated Employee (HCE)   Either a 5 percent owner or a person who earned more than $80,000 during the current or preceding year. Discrimination in favor of this group is prohibited.

Individual Retirement Account (IRA)   Individuals, whether they are covered by a pension or not, are now permitted to save money on a tax-deferred basis in a qualified IRA plan. Although money can be withdrawn, a 10 percent penalty has been placed on those assets withdrawn prior to the individual turning 59, in addition to the normal taxes, which must be paid upon withdrawal. An individual can set up his or her own plan with a bank, insurance company, brokerage house, or mutual fund. A company can also deduct an agreed-upon amount from employees' paychecks and send it to a designated agent or set up its own plan, where managers are selected to manage the assets.

Integration with Social Security   (1) A plan wherein benefits are integrated with the Social Security benefit. Under regular corporate plans, the regulations define the percentages applicable to the various benefits. Under a self-employed program, the only offset permissible is the amount of Social Security tax paid for the employee. If more than one plan is instituted for the same company, only one program may be integrated. (2) The basic concept of integration is that the benefits of the employer's plan must be dovetailed with Social Security benefits in such a manner that employees earning more than the taxable wage base will not receive combined benefits under the two programs that are proportionately greater than the benefits for employees earning less than the taxable wage base.

Keogh Plan   A qualified retirement plan for self-employed persons and their employees to which yearly tax-deductible contributions up to a specified limit can be made, if the plan meets certain requirements of the Internal Revenue Code. Keogh plans, also known as HR 10 plans, include defined benefit and defined contribution plans.

Lump-Sum Distribution   A distribution that qualifies for forward averaging or rollover treatment. The requirements include that the distribution include the entire balance to the credit of the employee, and that it be made on account of the employee's death, attainment of age 59, separation from service (except for the self-employed), or disability (self-employed persons only).

Maximum Benefit   The highest annual or lifetime benefit that can be paid by a qualified defined benefit plan.

Minimum Participation Standards   In general, the maximum amount of time a qualified retirement plan can require an employee to work before becoming eligible to participate is one year of service, and the highest age a plan may require a participant to have attained before being admitted is 21. There are exceptions made for plans maintained by tax-exempt educational institutions and for plans that feature immediate vesting upon participation.

Multiemployer Plan   Under ERISA a multiemployer plan is one that requires contributions from more than one employer and is maintained pursuant to a collective bargaining agreement. They are also known as jointly administered or Taft-Hartley plans. The Multiemployer Pension Plan Amendments Act of 1980 (MPPAA) made substantial changes to ERISA and the Internal Revenue Code that had the effect of enhancing the funding requirements for multiemployer pension plans, providing new rules for multiemployer plans, and revising the termination insurance provisions applicable to these plans.

Nondiscrimination Rules   The requirements in section 105(h) of the Internal Revenue Code that self-funded employee benefit plans not provide significantly greater benefits to higher paid employees and owners than to lower-paid employees. Although some disparity is permitted, there are limits which, if crossed, result in the benefits being deemed taxable income to the beneficiaries. Similar rules apply to 401(k) plans, flexible benefit plans, and pension plans.

Nonqualified Deferred Compensation Plan   An agreement whereby one person (or legal entity) promises to compensate another for services rendered currently with actual payment for those services delayed until sometime in the future. Such agreements are almost invariably reduced to writing and are mutually supported by the employer's promise to pay deferred benefits and the employee's promise to render services in exchange. Such plans do not receive tax advantages.

Normal Retirement   A termination of employment involving the payment of a regular formula retirement allowance, without reduction because of age or service and with special qualifications such as disability.

Pension Benefit Guaranty Corporation (PBGC)   The federal agency, established as a nonprofit corporation, charged with administering the plan termination provisions of ERISA title IV and the Multiemployer Pension Plan Amendments Act of 1980. Employers pay a premium to the PBGC, which guarantees benefits up to a specific maximum for participants and beneficiaries when defined benefit plans terminate.

Portability (1) Any provision for retaining pension rights and credits when changing from one employer to another. Vested rights are nonforfeitable. The retention of nonvested (contingent) rights depends upon remaining within the scope of a multiemployer plan or its reciprocating plan under a reciprocal agreement. (2) The ability of the consumer to take health insurance from job to job. (3) The right of an employee to take with him or her, upon separation from the employer, the total accumulation of monies carried in his or her account.

Projected Benefits Those pension plan benefit amounts that are expected to be paid at various times under a particular set of actuarial assumptions, taking into account such items as the effect of advancement in age and past and anticipated future compensation and service credits. That portion of an individual's projected benefit allocation attributable to service to date, determined in accordance with the terms of a pension plan and based on future compensation as projected to retirement, is called the *credited projected benefit*.

Qualification Requirement The rules and regulations issued in order to determine whether a proposed pension or profit-sharing plan will be fully deductible for tax purposes.

Replacement Ratio The portion of pre-retirement earnings under any retirement plan that is replaced by benefits following retirement.

Required Distributions (1) Payments that must be made once a participant reaches age 70 or retires (whichever is later); they are calculated to span his or her life expectancy. (2) When a participant dies, the payments that must be made to the participant's beneficiary.

Service Employment taken into consideration under a pension plan. Years of employment before the inception of a plan constitute an employee's past service; years thereafter are classified in relation to the particular actuarial valuation being made or discussed. Years of employment (including past service) prior to the date of a particular valuation constitute prior service; years of employment following the date of the valuation constitute future service; a year of employment adjacent to the date of valuation, or in which such date falls, constitutes current service (included in future service).

Simplified Employee Pension Plan (SEP) A SEP is a simplified alternative to a profit-sharing or 401(k) plan. A SEP is a pension plan to which contributions are made by the employer to an individual retirement account or annuity established by an employee (subject to special rules on contributions and eligibility).

Surviving Spouse Benefit Payments to the spouse of a deceased participant.

Thrift Plan A defined contribution plan to which employees make contributions on an after-tax basis, usually as a percentage of salary. Incentive matching or partially matching contributions are also made on behalf of the participating employees by the employer.

Top-Heavy Plan   A qualified plan in which the share of benefits allocable to key employees is more than 60 percent. The plan may be subject to special accelerated vesting provisions and minimum contribution rates.

Unit Credit Actuarial Cost Method   (1) A method of computing pension benefits based on certain units, such as percentage of salary and years of service. (2) An acceptable actuarial cost method under which the plan's normal cost for a year is the present value of the benefit credited to all participants for service in that year and the accrued liability is the present value at the plan's inception of the units of benefits credited to participants for service before the plan's inception. This method is also known as the *accrued benefit cost method.*

Vested Benefits   Accrued benefits of a participant that have become nonforfeitable under the vesting schedule adopted by the plan.

Vesting Schedules   Under the Tax Reform Act of 1986 there are two minimum schedules: 100 percent vesting after five years of service; and graduated vesting beginning after three years, with 100 percent vesting after seven years. The ten-year cliff, 5–15 year rule, rule of 45, and class-year vesting are no longer permitted. If a plan has immediate 100 percent vesting, the eligibility period may be two years of service.

Contributors

Robert L. Clark
North Carolina State University

Theodore R. Groom
Groom Law Group

Daniel I. Halperin
Harvard Law School

Alicia H. Munnell
Boston College Carroll School
of Management

Leslie E. Papke
Michigan State University

Pamela Perun
Urban Institute

Joseph F. Quinn
Boston College

Sylvester J. Schieber
Watson Wyatt Worldwide

John B. Shoven
Stanford University

C. Eugene Steuerle
Urban Institute

Jack VanDerhei
Temple University

Mark J. Warshawsky
TIAA-CREF Institute

Index

Accounting: actuarial accrued liability, 39–40, 41; entry age normal cost method, 36; pensions and, 135; projected unit credit actuarial cost method, 36

Accrued benefit security ratios, 27

Achenbaum, Andrew, 16

Aetna Inc., 23

Age Discrimination Act Amendments (*1986*), 79

Aging and issues of the elderly: financial status, 104; older workers, 16, 17, 20, 21, 22

American Express, 12

American Savings Education Council, 61

Anderson, Patricia M., 93–94

Annuities: adequate retirement income and, 177; appreciation of, 72; cash balance plans, 54; characteristics of, 2; contributions and, 143; defined benefit plans and, 52, 67, 68, 130, 171–72, 175; defined contribution plans and, 53, 66, 68, 105, 170, 171, 175–76; ERISA and, 24, 25, 201; inflation adjustment and, 175, 183; PBGC and, 149; pension payouts and, 150, 174; Studebaker and, 23; tax-deferred and -sheltered annuities,

143, 201; tax factors, 35; terminated plans and, 8, 34–35, 149; value of, 20

Attanasio, Orazio P., 109, 113, 114

Auerbach, Alan J., 117

Avery, Robert B., 110

Baby boom and baby bust: bridge jobs and, 97; cash balance plans and, 47; effects of, 129–31; funding of retirement benefits, 36, 41–42; pensions and, 129–30; retirement security of, 4, 47–48

Back-loading. *See* Benefits

Baltimore & Ohio (B&O) Railroad, 12–13

BankAmerica, 57

Banks and banking issues, 13–14, 197

Benefits: accrual of, 69–73, 79–82, 87, 89, 93, 114, 133, 138; back-loading, 52, 53, 54, 64, 69–70, 80, 169–70, 171; beneficiaries of, 138–39; benefits testing, 170, 172–73, 177n22; calculation of, 81; cash outs, 67, 68; effects on employment and retirement choices, 80, 87–95; inflation and, 175–76; limits on, 141, 142, 184–85; rolling over, 53, 55, 67n36, 82, 105, 173–75; Social Security and, 88, 89; vesting and, 52, 80, 88–89, 90.

See also Employee Retirement Income
Security Act; Policymaking and policies
Retirement: comparisons of retirement patterns, 88–92, 95–97; cost and standard
of living in, 125, 126, 157, 164; early or
delayed retirement, 88–95; effects of
pensions on, 5, 6, 79, 81, 86–95; income
during, 1, 66, 104, 125, 157, 164, 169,
177–78; limiting distributions before
retirement, 173–75; lower-income workers and, 158, 180–83; mandatory retirement, 92; older workers and, 16, 17, 20,
21, 22; preparation and funding for, 2–3,
17, 115–16, 125; provision and support
for, 1, 115; retirement decisions and pensions, 86–95
Retirement Confidence Survey (*1993*), 174
Retirement Equity Act (REACT; *1984*), 32
Retirement History Study (*1970s*), 86, 95
Retirement plans: accounting rules for,
35–36; accrued benefit security ratios,
27; benefits of, 17, 19, 26–27, 30–31,
36, 38; contributions and funding, 26,
27, 37–43; costs of, 25; coverage and
participation, 22, 27–28, 32; design of,
19, 160; early retirement plans, 88–89,
92; economics of retirement finance,
43–48, 157; elective plans, 166–68;
employee direction of investments,
52–53; ERISA and, 25–27; goals of,
12–14, 23; liabilities of, 39–41, 69; low-
income workers, 180–83; offset plans,
33; problems of, 22–23; proposals for
changes to, 141–52; rationale for, 16–17;
risks of, 53; self-directed plans, 194, 195;
service requirements, 32–33; supplemental plans, 26–27, 58, 59; targeted plans,
31; tax expenditures for, 29, 31, 32;
TEFRA and, 31; termination of, 25,
34–35; trends and their causes, 55–73;
during World War II, 22. *See also* Government-sponsored individual accounts;
Pensions; Personal security accounts;
Regulation and regulations; Social Security; *individual plans by name or type*
Research and research methods: analysis of
savings, 6; bridge jobs, 95; compensating
wage differentials, 82–83; cross-sectional
analysis, 106–08; defined benefit plans,
110; microeconomic studies of pension
replacement and substitution, 59–62;
pensions and firm productivity, 83–84;

pensions and retirement decisions,
86–95; pensions and turnover, 84–86;
retirement income, 65–66; retirement
plans, saving, and private wealth, 104,
106–16; shifts in the composition of
pensions, 62–65
Revenue Acts (*1921, 1926, 1938, 1942*), 14,
15, 16, 21, 123
Rohwedder, Susann, 109, 113, 114
Roosevelt (Franklin D.) administration, 17
Ruhm, Christopher J., 95

Samwick, Andrew A., 92–93
Sass, Steven A., 14, 16
Sauvigne, Donald, 61
Savings and wealth: back-loading and, 171;
benefits of, 141, 149; consumption and,
17; defined benefit plans and, 109–14;
defined contribution plans and, 105–08;
economic factors, 6, 7–8, 17, 103–18,
138; employer pensions and, 78,
178–79, 191–92, 204; *401*(k) plans and,
60; life-cycle savings, 6; low and moderate earners and, 163, 180–81; new
wealth, 109; pension wealth, 79–80,
112; pensions and, 6, 115–18, 125, 138,
143, 159; precautionary savings, 6; reasons for saving, 6; role of employers in,
199; saving rates, 140–41; vesting and,
165. *See also* Investment issues
SCF. *See* Survey of Consumer Finances
Schieber, Sylvester J., 3, 4, 11–49, 126–27,
129–30
Scholz, John Karl, 106, 108, 114
SEC. *See* Securities and Exchange
Commission
Sectors. *See* Economic issues
Securities Act (*1933*), 147
Securities and Exchange Commission
(SEC), 135, 197
Self-directed accounts, 68, 195–96, 200–201
Senate Committee on Labor and Public
Welfare, 23
Senate Finance Committee, 23
SEPs. *See* Simplified Employee Plans
Shoven, John B., 1–9, 19, 46, 123–53, 185,
186, 187, 188, 191
SIMPLEs, 139
Simplified Employee Plans (SEPs), 139,
200–201, 202
SIPP. *See* Survey of Income and Program
Participation